TACITUS
ANNALS XIV

TACITUS
ANNALS XIV

Edited with Introduction,
Commentary and Vocabulary by
E.C. WOODCOCK

Bristol Classical Press

First published in 1939 in Methuen's Classical Texts
Published by Bradda Books Ltd, 1980
Published by Basil Blackwell Ltd, 1984

This edition published in 1992 by
Bristol Classical Press
an imprint of
Gerald Duckworth & Co. Ltd
61 Frith Street
London W1D 3JL
e-mail: inquiries@duckworth-publishers.co.uk
Website: www.ducknet.co.uk

Reprinted 1995, 1996, 1997, 2001

A catalogue record for this book is available
from the British Library

ISBN 1-85399-315-8

PREFACE

THE editor of Tacitus is fortunate in having at his disposal Rostagno's excellent photographic reproductions of the two Medicean manuscripts. *Annals* XIV is contained in the second Medicean. Where this needs emendation, a choice has been exercised between readings suggested by previous authorities. Accordingly, in passages where a reading different from the Oxford Text has been adopted, it has been thought advisable to print the reading of the latter in a footnote. Reasons for the choice of reading are usually given in the notes. Koestermann's more sensible numbering of the sub-sections has been adopted.

In preparing the commentary, I have tried to keep in view the needs of less advanced students and to make sure that the construction of all difficult sentences shall be understood. At the same time it is hoped that many of the notes on syntactic usage are sufficiently advanced to make the edition useful to university students. In conformity with the object of the series, a vocabulary is included. It should be pointed out, however, that a boy who pursues the study of Latin to the stage of reading Tacitus can scarcely dispense with the use of a dictionary, if he is to derive full benefit from his studies. As the vocabulary contains many references to the notes, it may serve as a Latin index.

It is difficult to make specific acknowledgements to previous editions, since a good deal of my debt is probably unconscious, but the following are the chief editions which have been consulted from time to time: Jacob Gronovius (with notes of Rhenanus, Muretus, Lipsius, J. F. Gronovius, etc.) 1721; Ernesti, rev. by Oberlinus, 1825; Orelli, 1859; Frost, 1872; E. Jacob, 1896; Nipperdey, rev. by

Andresen, 1908; Furneaux, rev. by Fisher, 1907; Goelzer, 1925. The following works have also been found useful: Kühner-Stegmann, *Ausführliche lateinische Grammatik*, 1912; Leumann-Hofmann, *Lateinische Syntax und Stilistik*, 1928; Löfstedt, *Syntactica* I, 1928, II, 1933; Eriksson, *Studien zu den Annalen des Tacitus*, 1934; Sörbom, *Variatio Sermonis Tacitei*, 1935; Gerber und Greef, *Lexicon Taciteum*.

My greatest thanks are due not only to Dr. A. W. Pickard-Cambridge, the general editor of the series, but also to Professors W. H. Semple and T. B. L. Webster, of Manchester, for many helpful criticisms and suggestions; also to Professor D. Atkinson, who read through the historical chapters of the Introduction, and to Dr. L. R. Palmer, who read through chapter III. For any errors or improbable views that remain, I must take full responsibility.

E. C. W.

Manchester,
June, 1939

CONTENTS

ILLUSTRATIONS

INTRODUCTION

I

OF the life of P. Cornelius Tacitus little is known except what can be inferred from his own works and scattered references in the letters of Pliny the Younger. As Tacitus calls himself *iuuenis admodum* at the dramatic date of the *Dialogus de Oratoribus* (A.D. 75), we gather that he must have been born near the beginning of Nero's reign (A.D. 54). His father may have been the C. Tacitus whom the Elder Pliny mentions as an *eques Romanus* and procurator of Belgic Gaul. If Tacitus spent part of his boyhood in Belgic Gaul, that might account for his interest in the tribes of Germany. Also the following story told of him by Pliny in *Ep.* IX, 23, 2, suggests that he may have spoken with a non-Roman accent. At the Circus one day Tacitus got into conversation with a man who asked him, ' Are you an Italian or a provincial? ' To which Tacitus replied, ' You know me well enough, and from my literary work.' ' Are you Tacitus or Pliny? ' asked the other. We learn from the *Dialogus* that Tacitus applied himself with great zeal to the study of rhetoric, receiving instruction in their own homes from Marcus Aper and Julius Secundus, two great advocates of the time, who figure in the dialogue. Who his official teachers were, we do not know. One of them may even have been the great Quintilian himself, but the Ciceronian style of the *Dialogus* is no evidence for that. It is clear from Pliny, VII, 20, 4 that Tacitus had already in early manhood won fame as an orator. In

A.D. 77, when he cannot have been more than twenty-five, he was betrothed to the daughter of the distinguished Cn. Julius Agricola, who had served under Suetonius Paulinus in Britain during Boudicca's rebellion, and had since risen by successive stages to the command of the 20th legion, to the governorship of Aquitania in A.D. 74, to the consulship in A.D. 77, and returned to Britain as governor in the same or the following year.

It was probably to this alliance that Tacitus owed the start of his official career, which he describes in *Hist.* I, 1 as ' having been begun by Vespasian, advanced by Titus, and further advanced by Domitian '. We learn from *Ann.* XI, 11 that the last step refers to the praetorship, which he held in A.D. 88. The two previous offices were presumably the quaestorship, held probably in 80–1, and then either the office of *tribunus plebis* or the aedileship, which at this period were alternative approaches to an official career. From A.D. 90 to 93 Tacitus and his wife were absent from Rome for four years, probably in an imperial province to which he had been assigned as *legatus propraetore*. While they were away, Domitian had grown cool towards Agricola, who died under suspicious circumstances in A.D. 93.

We know nothing of Tacitus during the years 93–7. Domitian's cruel hostility to the senatorial order was then at its height, and possibly Tacitus, as a relative of Agricola, was in danger of his life. At any rate, like many others, he was afraid to take an active part in public life or to publish anything, and refers to this as the period when all the liberal arts were driven into banishment. When he began to write again, his tone was bitter. Of other men of letters, Quintilian, Martial, and Statius lived long enough to see Domitian at his worst. Juvenal had not yet begun his satires, the Younger Pliny published nothing during these years, and Tacitus, so far as we know, had not produced anything besides the *Dialogus de Oratoribus*.

Towards the end of A.D. 96 Domitian was murdered and Nerva became emperor. In the following year Tacitus was appointed *consul suffectus*, in which capacity he pronounced the funeral oration over his deceased predecessor, Verginius Rufus, the conqueror of Vindex. Pliny pays a tribute to his eloquence on this occasion. The last public appearance of Tacitus of which we hear was when he was appointed along with Pliny as counsel for the prosecution of Marius Priscus on a charge of misgovernment in Africa. But his public career was not yet over, for an inscription discovered in Caria names Publius Cornelius Tacitus as proconsul of Asia, a post which he probably held *c.* A.D. 112. The date of his death is not known, but he must have lived to the end of Trajan's reign (A.D. 117).

The following are the extant works of Tacitus :—

(1) *Dialogus de Oratoribus*, a dialogue on the causes of the decline of oratory under the Empire. The dramatic date of the dialogue is *c.* A.D. 75. It is now generally agreed that this is the earliest of Tacitus' works and that it was published before Domitian's reign of terror had imposed silence on literature. We may assume that it was published about A.D. 80. The style is neo-Ciceronian, like that of Quintilian. This, however, is not conclusive evidence for an early date, since in an imitative age the style of Cicero was the obvious model for a rhetorical treatise, just as Sallust was the model for the writing of historical monographs and history.

(2) *De uita et moribus Iulii Agricolae*, published in A.D. 98. Probably the *Germania* was published in the same year. In these two monographs Tacitus has abandoned smooth Ciceronian periods and adopted the more concise and pointed style of Sallust. Already it is possible to recognize the peculiar and original style of the Histories and the Annals in the making, but Tacitus has not yet reached the severe compression of his later style. In both these minor works are to be found those biting Tacitean epigrams that abound in the Histories and Annals.

(3) *Germania*, or *De origine, situ, moribus ac populis Germanorum*. This short work is our best source of information about the ancient Germans.

(4) *Historiae.* We learn from the letters of Pliny that the Histories were written between the years A.D. 104 and 109. They comprised the history of the years from the fall of Nero to the fall of Domitian (A.D. 68–96), and were thus chiefly concerned with the Flavian dynasty. They were probably in fourteen books (possibly twelve), of which the first four and part of the fifth are extant. In the Histories Tacitus' individual style is fully developed.

(5) *Ab excessu diui Augusti (Annales).* It was probably on his return from his proconsulship of Asia that Tacitus began to write the history of the period preceding that treated in the Histories. The Annals began with the death of Augustus in A.D. 14 and ended with the death of Nero in A.D. 68, which was the end of the Julio-Claudian house. If the Histories were in fourteen books, the Annals were in sixteen, since we know that the two together comprised thirty books. There are extant Books I–IV, parts of V and VI, and Books XI–XVI, though the last section is mutilated at the beginning and end. We know that Book II was written between A.D. 115 and 117, but when all were published is not known. Tacitus' eccentricity of style reaches its peak in *Ann.* I–VI; in *Ann.* XIII–XVI there is a return to greater normality, at any rate in matters of vocabulary,[1] which suggests that there may have been long intervals in composition.

II

TACITUS AS AN HISTORIAN

In estimating the value of any ancient historian it is necessary to take into account the fact that the ancients' views of a historian's duties differed much from the modern view. They held, of course, that a historian, unlike a poet or writer of fiction, was bound to tell the truth. He must not dare to invent; there is no truth which he must not dare to reveal; he must not be biased by partiality or

[1] See Nils Eriksson, *Studien zu den Annalen des Tacitus,* Intro.

hostility.[1] They also knew that it was not enough to give a bare record of the facts, that no history is readable or valuable which does not try to trace causes and effects. Unfortunately they fell short of the moderns by not realizing that the historian has other duties besides honesty and intelligent exposition. They were apt to take their facts for granted and to trust previous authorities too much. They rarely used scientific methods of research, and when their authorities differed, they would not often take the trouble to search out some objective evidence with which to check a statement.[2] Livy, for instance, would follow the account of a previous annalist for long stretches, only adapting it to his own literary style. If he found a different account in another author, he either gave both versions, or chose the one which seemed to him more probable.

It will be seen at once that such careless methods make all professions of honesty and impartiality almost worthless. If our historian is honest, how do we know that his authorities were? Moreover, no history readable or worth reading has yet been written by an author with no mind of his own. A historian with a mind will have conclusions to urge. If his criticism of his material is only subjective, he will believe the true version to be that which fits his own views. Therefore, in estimating an ancient historian, we must find out whether his views were such as to lead him astray in his criticism of his material, and we must find out how he compares with others in his diligence in collecting it. If he was connected in any way with the events which he relates, we must take into account his own experience when we estimate his impartiality.

Tacitus was well aware that the lasting value of a historical work depended on its truth and impartiality: *Hist.* I, 1, ' When, after the battle of Actium, the interests of peace demanded the conferment of all power on one man, there were no more great historians such as those

---

[1] Cic. *de Or.* II, 62.
[2] That they did sometimes can be seen from Suet. *Gaius*, c. 8;' cf. Livy IV, 20.

(of the Republic) ; at the same time historical veracity was impaired in a number of ways, first through the writers' ignorance of statecraft as being another's business, and secondly through the passion for flattery or the opposite passion of hatred against those in power . . . but the historian who professes incorruptible honesty must not write of anyone in a spirit of partiality or of anger ' *Ann.* I, 1, ' It is my design to deal briefly with the end of Augustus' reign, and then to treat the principate of Tiberius and the rest *without anger and without bias*, from motives to which, at this distance, I am immune '. After such earnest professions we cannot help believing that Tacitus will tell us the truth so far as he knows it.

But he had a particular view of the purpose of history, and confesses to a moral purpose in writing it: *Ann.* III, 65, ' I think the chief task of the historian is to rescue virtuous behaviour from oblivion and to threaten bad words and deeds with the fear of being branded with infamy by posterity '. Holding the view that history is useful, he must also have believed in his heart that there is some principle underlying the course of historical events, even if Chance plays a part in determining particular incidents, though occasionally his belief seems to waver.[1] The chief passage in which he definitely states that a useful purpose is served by the study of history is *Hist.* I, 4 : ' Before I proceed with my design, I think I ought to recall what was the state of the city, the temper of the armies, the condition of the provinces, what points of strength and weakness existed in the world at large, in order that not only the incidents and issues of events, which are very often fortuitous, but their underlying principles and causes may be known '. Such an attitude is almost modern, and shows that Tacitus is a historian of grasp comparable even with Thucydides. Social tendencies and economic causes come within his view.

What effect his own political views and experience had on his credulity and credibility is difficult to decide. We

---

[1] See *Ann.* IV, 20; VI, 22; also commentary on XIV, 12, 2.

have seen that he lived through Domitian's reign of terror, which might influence him to believe, and try to make his readers believe, the worst of previous emperors. Some maintain that the effect of his experience was to make him an ardent republican; others (*e.g.*, Sir Samuel Dill) that he had no sympathy with the republican Opposition.[1] But he always speaks in a tone of great admiration for the few men, such as Thrasea Paetus and Helvidius Priscus, who refused to cower before tyranny. Depreciatory remarks put in the mouths of their most despicable enemies are not evidence for Tacitus' own views. Nevertheless there is a hint of a sneer at Thrasea in *Ann.* XIV, 49: '(Thrasea did not retreat from his opinion) through his usual firmness of mind *and in order not to lose his reputation* '. But cannot we allow Tacitus the human weakness of being a little jealous of a courage he had not shown himself? Shame and indignation breathe through his work in passages such as the following: *Agr.* 45, ' Presently our hands led Helvidius to prison; us the sight of Mauricus and Rusticus put to shame, us Senecio stained with his innocent blood '; *Ann.* I, 7, ' but in Rome consuls, senate, and knights rushed to proclaim their serfdom. The more illustrious they were, the greater their hypocrisy and haste . . .'; *Ann.* XIV, 14, (Nero has persuaded with money descendants of noble houses to appear on the stage) ' they are now dead, and I consider it a tribute due to their ancestors to conceal their names '; *Ann.* XV, 71, ' One having had his son put to death, another a brother, relative, or friend, gave thanks to God, decked his house with laurel, grovelled at the emperor's knees and wore out his hand with kisses '. Such being Tacitus' opinion of the senatorial order, it is impossible to credit him with desiring the restoration of republican government under senatorial control. In *Ann.* VI, 42, he definitely states that oligarchy is akin to monarchical tyranny. In *Ann.* IV, 33, he implies that the ideal mixture of popular government, aristocracy, and benevolent autocracy is

[1] Dill, *Roman Society from Nero to M. Aurelius*, p.24.

impossible of attainment. On the whole, he pessimistically accepts autocracy, with all its dangers, as the lesser of evils; see *Hist.* I, 1 (above); *Hist.* IV, 8, *bonos imperatores uoto expetere, qualescumque tolerare ; Hist.* I, 16 (Galba speaks : the best hope is to abolish the hereditary principle of succession) : *loco libertatis erit quod eligi coepimus et . . . optimum quemque adoptio inueniet.*

It must be admitted that, holding such views as these, Tacitus might be tempted to exercise unfair selection in gathering his material. He was in danger of painting villainy too black and virtue too white. His desire to hold up examples of right or wrong motives might lead him to over-emphasize the importance of human character in determining the course of history. On this point *Ann.* IV, 32, is an important passage: ' I am well aware that much of what I have related and shall relate may seem petty and trifling. . . . My task is restricted in scope and inglorious, for peace was hardly disturbed, affairs in the city were disheartening, and the emperor had no care to extend the bounds of the empire. Yet it will not be without use to examine those seeming trifles, out of which the setting in motion of great events often takes its rise.' In other words, the prosperity of the empire now depended on the emperor; therefore petty doings of court circles are important, if they throw light on the emperor's character and on intrigues which influenced his policy.

This is a perfectly reasonable attitude to take towards the history of the early Roman Empire, and need not have prevented Tacitus from being a great historian in the modern sense. Unfortunately the words ' had no care to extend the bounds of the empire ' reveal a serious defect in his equipment. Although he had experience of the functioning of government and understood the difficulties of administration, he did not appreciate the broader principles of statesmanship which must guide the head of the State. He implies that Germanicus was recalled by Tiberius from Germany, Suetonius Paulinus by Nero from Britain, and Agricola from the same province by

Domitian through motives of fear and jealousy. The alternative possibility is obvious to us, but Tacitus does not suggest it.

This brings us to the question of Tacitus' honesty in the handling of facts. It must be said at once that rarely has he been convicted by archaeological or other evidence of falsifying facts. Moreover, the very fact that his own narrative can often bear a different interpretation from the one he desires to suggest, shows that he has told the truth so far as he knew it. In collecting his material he was more careful and industrious than other Roman historians are known to have been. We learn from Pliny's Letters that he did not rely solely upon previous written histories, but gathered material at first hand, whenever he could.[1] He consulted official records, such as the *Acta Senatus* (the Roman ' Hansard '), against the falsification of which he was on his guard,[2] and did not disdain even the *Acta Vrbis* (the official ' Daily Gazette ').[3] Nevertheless, he mentions previous authors so often, not always by name, that we are justified in concluding that they were his chief source of information. The only two whom he quotes in *Ann.* XIV are Cluuius Rufus and Fabius Rusticus (see c. 2). The former was born about the beginning of the Christian era, took part in the civil war of A.D. 68–70, and wrote a history the limits of which are not known, but which probably extended from the death of Augustus to the accession of Vespasian. His tone towards Gaius and Nero was probably moderate. Less is known of Fabius Rusticus, who was a protégé of Seneca and probably upheld the latter's character at the expense of Nero's (cf. the version quoted from him in c. 2). Among authors mentioned in other books is C. Plinius Secundus (the Elder Pliny), a most valuable authority, who wrote a history of the German wars and also continued the history of Aufidius Bassus at least up to the end

---

[1] Pliny, *Ep.* VI, 16; VI, 20.
[2] *Ann.* V, 4; XV, 74.
[3] *Ann.* XII, 24; XIII, 31; etc.; Pliny, *Ep.* VII, 33.

of Nero's reign. Though moderate in judgment, he called Nero *faex generis humani et hostis*. Besides regular histories, there was a multitude of pamphlets, biographies, monographs, and memoirs which Tacitus may have been industrious enough to collect and some of which he is known to have consulted. Among the latter are the memoirs of Agrippina, mother of Nero (see *Ann.* IV, 53). This source was necessarily tainted, being adverse to Tiberius and favourable to any one connected with the house of Germanicus, especially to her son. Cn. Domitius Corbulo composed memoirs of his own campaigns, which Tacitus seems to be quoting in *Ann.* XV, 16. This must have been a very valuable first-hand source, as also the memoirs of Suetonius Paulinus, which Tacitus may have consulted, though he does not say so.

Tacitus' diligence in dealing with such a mass of material is attested by the admiration of Pliny,[1] and we can feel sure that he was superior to other ancient historians in this respect. His essential honesty may also be assumed, in spite of attacks that have been made on it. There remains the question of his historical ability and the value of his resulting narrative. All that can be said is that his moral purpose in writing may have led him to stress aspects of history different from those which a modern historian might have stressed. Although his narrative is the most valuable record that has come down to us of any part of Roman antiquity, it is as a literary artist rather than as a scientific historian that he has a claim to fame. He believed that by branding bad characters with infamy he might bring about a general improvement in morals and bring back a sense of responsibility to the autocratic rulers whom Rome had now to accept. He brings to his task an uncanny understanding of human weakness, a power to penetrate motives and delineate character, and a mastery of language that will make his works live for ever as great literature.

[1] *Ep.* VII, 33.

III

STYLE AND SYNTAX

Tacitus is one of the most difficult of Latin prose-authors, not because he invents a syntax of his own, but because he makes full use of all the syntactical resources which the literary language of his time offered him. Style consists in the reasoned choice of available methods of expression, and the originality of Tacitus' style lies in the way in which he exercised this choice. Perhaps some day research may discover the reasons and motives which guided him in developing his peculiar style, but here all that can be done is to indicate its leading characteristics.

Perhaps what strikes the reader first and most forcibly is the almost crazy avoidance of the same method of expression in parallel clauses or phrases.   If, for instance, a bare case is used in one member, a prepositional phrase must be used in another, as 1, 1, *crebris criminationibus, aliquando per facetias ;* 38, 3, *aduersa prauitati ipsius, prospera ad fortunam referebat ;* if the abl. of respect is used with one epithet, the gen. must be used with another, 19, 1, *ut par ingenio, ita morum diuersus*; in 49, 3, of four different causes assigned for an action two are expressed by *ne*-clauses, one by a nom. adj. agreeing with the subject, and one by a causal abl., . . . *pars ne principem obiecisse inuidiae uiderentur, plures numero tuti, Thrasea sueta firmitudine animi et ne gloria intercideret*; similarly a causal abl. of a noun is often joined with a causal clause, as 47, 2, *quiete defensus et quia . . . ;* the alternation of abl. phrases, whether of quality or of other types, and adjs. agreeing with the noun is common, as 1, 1, *Nero . . . coalita audacia et flagrantior . . . ;* 23, 2, *dux Romanus diuersis artibus, misericordia . . . celeritate . . . immitis . . . ;* 36, 3, *uetus miles et multa proeliorum experientia.* The craze for variety which is found in the parts of the sentence is found also in the structure of the sentence as a whole. Tacitus has moved a long way from the balanced, rhythmical, and well-organized unity

of the Ciceronian or Livian period. When he writes a
sentence of any length, it is organized indeed, but to produce
a\ studied effect of lack of organization. Instead of the
subordinate ideas being grouped in subordinate clauses
around a main clause containing the main idea, very often
the most important idea will be contained in a subordinate clause, or even in a loosely attached participial
phrase. When we start to read a period in Cicero or Livy,
we know how the construction must end and what the
subject of the main verb will be. Tacitus loves to give an
unexpected twist to the construction, which often ends in
sheer anacoluthon (cf. notes on cc. 4, 3; 23, 2).

Another striking feature of Tacitus' style is its brevity.
His most impressive thoughts are conveyed in a syntax
that is stripped to the bone, so that not a word in the
sentence could be made to do more work than it does.
Often there is an ellipse of the verb, or one that is there
has to do double duty; often an important point which
would seem to require a new sentence is contained in a
mere parenthesis, and is all the more impressive for that.
Naturally this striving after brevity and conciseness of
expression is seen most clearly in those epigrammatic
remarks which partake of the nature of the ' sententiae '
common in Silver Latin prose, e.g. :—

> 6, 2, *testamentum Acerroniae requiri bonaque obsignari iubet, id
> tantum non per simulationem.*
>
> 10, 2, *non, ut hominum uultus, ita locorum facies mutantur.*
>
> 15, 3, *accesserat cohors militum . . . et maerens Burrus ac
> laudans.*
>
> 40, 3, *Marcellum memoria maiorum et preces Caesaris poenae
> magis quam infamiae exemere.*
>
> 46, 2, *Trebellium dum uterque dedignatur supra tulere.*
>
> 50, 2, *libros exuri iussit, conquisitos lectitatosque donec cum
> periculo parabantur: mox licentia habendi obliuionem attulit.*
>
> 56, 3, *Seneca, qui finis omnium cum dominante sermonum, grates
> agit.*
>
> 62, 2, *quia malorum facinorum ministri ·quasi exprobrantes
> aspiciuntur.*

In some of these extracts notice the poetic, imaginative, and almost English way of putting things. 'Memory' and 'Entreaties' are made the subjects of the sentence; 'Retribution' is deprived of her victim; 'Licence to possess consigns to oblivion,' &c.

The fondness for 'sententiae' (epigrammatic remarks, clever phrases, 'bons mots', 'points') Tacitus shared with other writers of the Silver Age, as also his striving after variety of expression, his avoidance of the rounded period, and his use of personification and abstractness of expression which is normally only found in the poetry of the Golden Age. The style of Tacitus is unique for all that. Variety assumes a form in him which is not found elsewhere, at least in the same degree. His 'sententiae' are not laboured and do not sacrifice truth to ingenuity. The narrative in between them does not fall flat by contrast, but the elevation of style is maintained. The common impression given by Silver Latin literature is one of artificiality and affectation. Cleverness in juggling with words is a substitute for real thought and feeling. This is a sign of decadence, which was partly due to changed political conditions, partly to the Roman system of education, and partly to the influence of Virgil. The restriction of free speech in political life and the stereotyped subjects set for declamation in the rhetorical schools caused men to exhaust their ingenuity in trying to say old things in a new way, and led to extravagance, obscurity, and shallowness of thought in literature. The attention of the listener or reader is now captured not by an appeal to the reason set out in a well-organized and sonorous period, itself symbolic of pondered judgement, but by a flash of wit in a concise sentence. For such expressions the paratactic style invented by Virgil for poetry was a more suitable vehicle than the periodic structure of Cicero or Livy. Virgil had an enormous influence on the Roman world, and his style affected subsequent prose as well as verse. The new style of rhetorical prose adopts both the more imaginative expression of poetry and the more concise and disconnected structure. In Tacitus even verbal reminiscences of Virgil abound.

But although Tacitus shares common features with his contemporaries, the differences are greater. He is the master of rhetoric, not its slave. In him there is no labouring of points, and he does not give the impression of artificiality. This cannot be entirely due to artistic genius. His respect for courage and moral integrity and his bitter resentment of the vice and tyranny of the new regime, to which he attributed the degeneration of his time, must have been real. To aid him in giving expression to this bitterness he had a mastery of the Latin language and an artistic genius never surpassed. He considered variety of expression necessary to relieve the monotony of a tale of continued vice and injustice. The times were out of joint, the Roman State was under the control of emperors who were mentally unbalanced, and the style in which he tells the story and points the moral must be unbalanced too.

The following account of syntactical usage in Tacitus is drawn up with special reference to *Ann.* XIV, but, even so, it does not pretend to be complete. Other minor differences from Ciceronian usage will be pointed out in the commentary. Very few of the usages dealt with are peculiar to Tacitus, but all are characteristic of him :—

I. ACCUSATIVE

(i) The accusative of the ' Goal of Motion ' is confined in classical prose to the names of towns, small islands, *domum* and *rus*. The poets, however, are much freer in the omission of prepositions, e.g. Virg. *Italiam . . . Lauinaque uenit litora.* It is probably under their influence that Tacitus occasionally uses the bare acc., as *Ann.* II, 59, *Aegyptum proficiscitur*; *Ann.* XII, 51, *Hiberos . . . peruadit.* Similar is the omission after compound verbs, where classical Latin would repeat the preposition or use the dat., e.g., *Ann.* XIV, 35, 1, *ut quamque nationem accesserat*; XIV, 15, *scaenam incedit.*

(ii) In poetry intr. verbs expressing emotion, such as *flere, pauescere,* are used in a trans. sense with the acc. So Tacitus, *Ann.* XIV, 30, 2, *ne muliebre et fanaticum agmen pauescerent.*

(iii) Another poetic device sometimes used by Tacitus is an acc. phrase ' in apposition to the sentence '. Such accusatives, describing or amplifying the action, or indicating a result produced, are really ' internal ' or ' inner-object ' accusatives. Cf. Virg. *Aen.* VI, 222, *pars ingenti subiere feretro, triste ministerium,* ' Some took up the mighty bier, a sad service '. So *Ann.* XIV, 53, 3, *quibus claritudo uenit, . . . grande huius rei pretium.* This would more naturally be expressed by a *quod*-clause in prose. This usage is found in prose first in Sallust, then in Livy, but is most frequent in Tacitus. (See Kühner-Stegmann, Vol. I, p. 247.)

2. GENITIVE

Though none of Tacitus' uses of the genitive are completely without precedent in previous authors, some of them are very bold and difficult to explain. In trying to explain any given usage, it must be borne in mind that the gen. in Latin performs a ' labelling ' function, i.e. it is usually adjectival to a noun. But it is also used to qualify or limit the action of certain verbs and the application of certain adjectives (e.g., *capitis damnare, taedet uitae, plenus uini,* &c.). It cannot be shown that these *adverbial* uses are in any way derived from the *adjectival* ones, indeed they may be older, but perhaps the connexion between them will be easier to comprehend if we suppose that a gen. with a verb is really qualifying the verbal noun (substantival idea) implied by the verb, whether such a noun is in actual use or not, e.g. ' to condemn ' = ' to inflict a *loss* or *doom* or *penalty* on ', and the verb *damnare* is found construed with all the types of gen. which could qualify the noun *damnum.* Hence *capitis damnare* = ' to inflict on someone the loss of his head (i.e., life or citizenship) '; *iniuriarum damnare* = ' to inflict the penalty of wrong-doing '; *repetundarum damnare* = ' to inflict the penalty of, or connected with the recovery of moneys'. Similarly *piget me laboris* = 'the irksomeness of work is active upon me'.

(i) *Genitive of Reference with Adjectives*

The chief types of adj. which may be qualified by a gen. in classical prose are the following: (*a*) Adjectives with an active sense, which seem logically to demand an objective gen., e.g. *auidus potentiae* (Sall.); *sapientiae studiosus* (Cic.). (*b*) Adjectives denoting 'knowledge of' and the reverse, e.g., *conscius, inscius, memor, immemor.* (*c*) Adjectives denoting 'partition', which will naturally be followed by a partitive gen., e.g. *particeps, expers,* &c. (*d*) Adjectives denoting 'fullness' and the reverse, e.g. *plenus, inanis,* &c. All these classes of adjectives were gradually extended by later writers by including other adjectives into which a similar idea could be read, until at last it is difficult to decide to what particular type the gen. belongs, since it seems merely to denote that 'in respect of which' the adj. is applied. Tacitus is the boldest author of all in using the gen. in this way, e.g. *Ann.* XIV, 7, 1, *uindictae properam,* 'hasty in respect of' or 'eager for vengeance'; 19, *morum diuersus,* 'different in respect of character'; 33, 2, *aliorum segnes,* 'slothful with regard to other things'; 40, 2, *morum spernendus,* &c.

(ii) '*Legal*' *Genitive*

The gen. of the 'charge', 'punishment', or 'matter involved', which is used in classical Latin after verbs of 'accusing' and 'condemning' and certain adjectives, e.g. *reus,* connected with them, is widely extended by Tacitus and the writers of his age, e.g. *Ann.* XIV, 29, 1, *ambitionis manifestus* 'clearly guilty of . . .'; 46, 1, *repetundarum . . . interrogantibus*; 48, 1, *maiestatis delatus.* It will be clear from the general remarks on the gen. above that it is not necessary to suppose the ellipse of *crimine* or any other abl. word in order to explain the construction. If *de* with the abl. or *crimine* is sometimes found, that is only an alternative, and not the sole construction.

(iii) ' *Appositional* ' or ' *Defining* ' *Genitive*

Tacitus sometimes uses this gen. where classical Latin would put the defining word in the same case in apposition (*urbs Roma*), e.g. *Hist.* IV, 18, *castra quibus Veterum nomen est*, where classical Latin would say *Vetera* (or *Veteribus*) ; *Ann.* XIV, 50,1, *quibus nomen Codicillorum dederat*, where see note.

(iv) *Partitive Genitive*

The use of the partitive gen. after neut. sing. pronouns or adjectives, in nom. or acc., expressing quantity, or after comparative or superlative adjectives, needs no comment, since it is classical: e.g. *aliquid boni, multum alicuius rei, fortissimus Graecorum.* In these instances the pronoun or adj. itself implies ' a quantity of ' or ' partition '. What is rare in classical Latin is (*a*) the use after neut. adjectives or pronouns in an oblique case or depending on a preposition, e.g. *Ann.* XIV, 2, 1 *medio diei* (found also in Sallust) ; (*b*) after neut. adjectives other than those mentioned above, e.g. *Ann.* XIV, 56, 1 *lubricum adulescentiae nostrae*; (*c*) after neut. plural adjectives, e.g. *Ann.* XIV, 60, 1, *cuncta scelerum*; (*d*) after positive adj., e.g. *Ann.* XIV, 8, 2, *obuios seruorum*.

(v) *Genitive of Gerund and Gerundive*

Tacitus often uses the gen. of the gerund or gerundive in such a way that it is difficult to decide what particular type of relationship between two substantives the gen. denotes, and in a manner hard to parallel in earlier authors. In an example like *Ann.* XIV, 2, 1, *ardore retinendae potentiae*, ' in her passionate desire for retaining power ', there is no difficulty, since the gen. is a perfectly classical objective gen., denoting the object of the verbal idea of ' desiring ' contained in *ardore*. But in c. 44, 1, *creditisne seruum interficiendi domini animum sumpsisse*, ' do you think a slave raised the courage to kill his master . . .? ' and c. 59, 1, *constantiam opperiendae mortis . . . suasisse*, ' urged firmness in awaiting death ', the objective idea is not so clear. In the former there is an idea of purpose, which, in classical Latin, would seem to require *ad interficiendum dominum*. In the latter, the gen. more vaguely defines the ' sphere within which' the firmness is shown, which would be more naturally expressed by *in opperienda morte* (cf. the gen. of reference above). But in considering the origin of these usages it should be borne in mind that the objective gen. enjoyed a wide extension even in classical Latin; e.g. besides representing the direct object after a verbal noun from a transitive verb, it can also represent an internal object (see note on c. 13, 2), and even the indirect object after a noun derived from an intransitive verb. Thus, although ' to encourage to face danger ' is *incitare ad pericula*, Cicero can still say (*pro Arch.* 23) *periculorum incitamentum* for ' encouragement to face danger '. In the light of this, *animus interficiendi domini*, ' courage ' or ' intention to kill one's master ' does not seem so bold. Precedent for it is even to be found in Caesar, e.g. *B.G.* 7, 76, 2, *consensio libertatis uindicandae*, ' unanimity for *or* in *or* about the assertion of liberty ' (cf. *constantiam opperiendae mortis*).

Sometimes the gen. is nothing but a ' defining ' one, as e.g. *Ann.* IV, 2, *neque senatorio ambitu abstinebat clientes suos honoribus ornandi*, ' he did not refrain from senatorial intrigues *consisting in* the advancing of his followers to office '. But perhaps the greater number are to be likened to that type of gen. of quality which denotes what is entailed, e.g. Livy, 38, 4, 1, *consuli magni operis oppugnatio uisa est*, ' to the consul an attack seemed to involve great labour '. So one might say *res magni laboris*, ' an affair involving great toil '. It is only necessary to substitute a gerundive adj. for the epithet in these expressions in order to denote that a thing is connected with some action, e.g. *res euitandi laboris*, ' a thing connected with the avoiding of labour ', ' a device for avoiding labour ' (purpose), but the precise nature of the connexion may depend on the context. Precedents are to be found in Sallust and Livy, and even as early as Terence, e.g. Sall. *Or. Phil. fr.* 1, 77, 11, (*arma*) *quae ille . . . cepit . . . legum ac libertatis subuortundae*; Livy, 4, 30, 10, *piacula pacis deum exposcendae*.

In some examples in Tacitus, the substantive which the

gen. qualifies is not expressed, but is left to be understood out of the verb; i.e. the gen. seems to be in apposition to the sentence, e.g. *Ann.* II, 59, *Germanicus Aegyptum proficiscitur cognoscendae antiquitatis*, ' . . . set out to view the antiquities '. Here the gen. possibly qualifies the notion of *iter* contained in *proficiscitur*, ' he set out on a *sight-seeing tour* ', though the influence of the Greek use of the gen. of the article with the infin. in expressions like Thuc. 1, 4 τὸ λῃστικὸν καθῄρει, τοῦ τὰς προσόδους μᾶλλον ἰέναι αὐτῷ, cannot be ruled out. It should be pointed out, however, that in many of the examples often quoted the termination may equally well be dat., in which case the dat. is one of purpose, on which see below.

3. DATIVE

The dative is above all the case which denotes the *person* interested, whether as the receiver of something concrete, as after verbs of ' giving ', or as the receiver of a more abstract benefit. But by the popular logic which develops expressions in pairs of opposites, the dat. also indicates the person to whose ' disadvantage ' something is done. Therefore, beside *dare aliquid alicui* one says *adimere aliquid alicui*, instead of using the more logical abl. of separation. The notion of advantage and disadvantage is, of course, extended to things, whether concrete or abstract, so that the dat. can also indicate ' that for which ' an action is performed. The notion of ' benefit ' can still be seen in the predicative dat., and in the dat. denoting purpose or result; for, in the case of a thing the benefit may consist in its being brought about. Hence *hoc laudi est*, ' this is *for* praise ' = ' results in praise being given ', ' is creditable '. Also the dat. in the phrase *morti, leto dare* was retained when *mittere* was used (*morti, leto mittere*), and from this single phrase developed the occasional use by poets and later prose-writers of the dat. to denote the goal of motion, a function which really belongs to the acc.[1] It must be insisted,

[1] Greek influence undoubtedly helped this development, though see Leumann - Hofmann, *Lateinische Grammatik*, p. 419, §45.

however, that this is not the fundamental notion contained in the dat. The English preposition 'for' gives a better idea of its sense than the preposition 'to'. It is clear that classical writers felt this distinction, for Cicero and Caesar, although they say *terrorem inicere alicui*, 'to cast fear into someone', where the notion is that of the indirect object affected, say *se in medios hostes inicere*, 'to cast oneself into the midst of the enemy', where real motion is implied. The poets, for whom the simple case-ending was often handier than a prepositional phrase, do not observe this distinction. Neither do Livy and Tacitus.

The following usages, though not necessarily peculiar to Tacitus, are particularly characteristic of him:—

(i) *Dative with Verbs of Depriving*

The use of the dat. of disadvantage with some verbs of 'depriving', even when they are compounded with prepositions requiring the abl., e.g. *eripere, detrahere*, has been mentioned above. From Livy on, this dat. is often extended to other verbs, and even applied to the 'thing' from which separation takes place, e.g. *Ann.* XIV, 40, 3, *Marcellum . . . preces Caesaris poenae magis quam infamiae exemere*; 64, 1, *vitae exempta*; and often.

(ii) *Dative of the Agent*

In classical Latin this is confined to use with the gerund and gerundive, and sometimes with past participles. It is only in the poets and in post-Augustan prose that it is obviously used as an alternative to *ab* with the abl. In origin it is the dat. of the 'person interested', e.g. *mihi currendum est* = 'for me there is running to do'; *mihi consilium captum est* = 'as far as I am concerned, the decision is taken'. Cicero may be responsible for the extension of the usage to finite forms of verbs, though he never uses it as a complete equivalent to the abl. of the agent: e.g. *Verr.* II, 5, 118, *cui . . . certa merces comparabatur* = 'for him a sure reward was being stored up', rather than '. . . was being acquired *by* him'. In *De Sen.* 38, *in his studiis uiuenti non intelligitur quando obrepat senectus*, the dat. is rather that of ' the person judging ', and is parallel to the dat. with *uidetur*, or else it depends on *obrepat*. In the poets and in Livy and Tacitus examples are more numerous, and the dat. seems to be regarded as an alternative to the abl. with *ab*, e.g. *Ann*. XIV, 32, 1, *ut Britannis ad spem ita ueteranis ad metum trahebantur*; 58, 1, *pluribus salus eius curabatur*.

(iii) *Dative denoting Direction*

How the dat. may have come to usurp the function of the acc. in denoting ' direction towards ' has been indicated in the general remarks above. Instances in *Ann*. XIV are c. 5, 3, *uillae suae infertur*; 61, 4, *imperatorio fastigio induci*.

(iv) *Dative of Purpose or Result*

The dat. denoting what a thing is ' for ', i.e. the predicative dat., dat. of purpose, dat. of result, is, of course, a classical construction, but as the dat. is an adverbial case, it is normally used only with certain verbs, and its use is much restricted. Besides its use with *esse* (*exemplo est*), the construction is extended to verbs meaning ' to consider ', ' to interpret ' (*uitio uertere*), and to verbs of motion (*auxilio uenire, mittere*), but to few others, though we find in Caesar expressions like *locum deligere casιris*, ' to choose a spot *for* a camp ', and *petere diem indutiis*, ' to ask for a date for a truce '. Apart from the military phrase *receptui signum*, ' signal for retreat ', the use of this dat. attached directly to a noun appears to be colloquial and poetic, e.g. Cato, *R. R.* 5, 8, *pabulum ouibus*, ' food for sheep '; Plaut., *Curc.* 578, *linteum extersui*, ' a towel for rubbing down '. In poetry this method of expression, being warmer and more intimate than the more formal qualifying gen., is very common indeed.

Post-Augustan authors from Livy onwards, and Tacitus in particular, use this type of dat. far more freely, not only extending it to use with other verbs than those noted above, but employing the colloquial and poetic licence of using it with nouns, e.g. *Ann*. I, 23, *centurionem morti deposcere*; *Ann*. XIV, 15, 2, *posita ueno*; Livy IX, 19, 7, *corpori tegumentum*; *Ann*. I, 3, *subsidia dominationi*; XIV, 3, 3, *cetera ostentandae pietati*; 59, 2, *nudus exercitando corpori*; cf. also cc., 4, 2;

39, 3. This use of the dat. of the gerund or gerundive is very rare in classical authors, apart from legal formulae such as *Decemuiri legibus scribendis*, and is first used as a regular construction by Livy. Tacitus goes farthest in the use of it.

4. ABLATIVE

The ablative case in Latin combines the functions of three original cases, viz. the true abl. or ' from ' case; the sociative-instrumental or ' with ' case (i.e. denoting both instrumentality and accompaniment—all the senses of the preposition ' with ') ; and the locative or ' in ' case (denoting position both in time and space). These distinctions must always be kept in mind when trying to understand any given usage.

(i) *Omission of Prepositions*

Tacitus sometimes uses the freedom of poetry in omitting prepositions with the abl. of source and the locat. In classical prose the bare abl. of source is confined to place-names, *domo, rure*, &c., which are survivals. Occasionally the abl. may depend on a preposition contained in the verb, but as a rule classical prose repeats the preposition. For instances of omission in *Ann.* XIV, see cc. 10, 2, *sonitum tubae collibus circum editis planctusque tumulo matris audiri*; 45, 2, *ut . . . Italia deportarentur*; 50, 2, *Veientonem Italia depulit* (source). 14, 2, *clausumque ualle Vaticana spatium*; 20, 2, *si consideret theatro*; 38, 2, *cohortes alaeque nouis hibernaculis locatae*; 61, 1, *foroque ac templis statuunt* (place ' where ').

(ii) *Ablative Absolute used Impersonally*

The impersonal use of a neuter past participle in the abl. abs. is found even in early Latin, e.g. Plaut., *Pers.* 607 *auspicato*, ' the auspices having been taken ', but what is rare before Livy is the use of such an abl. with an acc. and infin. or subordinate clause depending on it. There are one or two examples of the latter type in Cicero, none in Caesar, a few in Sallust, many in Livy, and still more in

Tacitus, e.g. *Ann.* XIV, 7, 4, *audito uenisse nuntium*; 57, 1, *compertoque Plautum et Sullam maxime timeri.*

(iii) *Ablative of Quality*

The abl. of quality originates in the abl. of attendant circumstances, which has become detached from the verb and loosely attached to the noun. In classical Latin it rarely qualifies a proper name, but usually a common noun in apposition. Tacitus frequently attaches it straight on to a proper name, as *Ann.* XIV, 57, 3, *Plautum magnis opibus*; and he extends its use in other ways, often separating it at some distance from the word it qualifies, and using it so loosely that sometimes it is difficult to know whether the abl. is one of quality, or whether the phrase is absolute, or whether it should be taken as abl. of att. circ. with the verb. Other examples in this book are: 11, 3, *Seneca aduerso rumore erat*; 22, 1, *ipse placita maiorum colebat, habitu seuero, casta et secreta domo*; 29, 1, *Veranius . . . magna, dum uixit, seueritatis fama*; 62, 2, *Anicetus . . . leui post admissum scelus gratia.*

(iv) *Ablative of the Gerund*

Tacitus often uses the abl. of the gerund as a complete equivalent to a pres. participle agreeing with the subject, e.g. 31, 2 *exturbabant agris, captiuos, seruos appellando.* The origin of this usage is seen plainly in such examples as 20, 3, *degeneretque iuuentus, gymnasia et otia exercendo*, where the abl. may be alternatively construed as a sheer instrumental abl. with *degeneret*, ' degenerates by means of ', or ' owing to '. Other exx. may be 7, 1, *siue . . . peruaderet . . . interfectos amicos obiciendo*; 22, 4, *fontem . . . nando incesserat*; but in these two examples the case may be dat. of purpose. The corresponding use of the abl. of the gerundive is very rare, see n. on c. 4, 3 *explenda simulatione.*

(v) *Locative Ablative of ' Time throughout which '*

The use of the abl. instead of the acc., to denote duration of time, is very frequent in Tacitus, e.g. *Ann.* XIV, 10, 1, *reliquo noctis . . . lucem opperiebatur*, ' *for* the remainder of the night . . . he awaited daylight'; 29, 1, *si biennio proximo uixisset*, 'had he lived *for* the next two years'; 32, 3, *templum* . . . *biduo obsessum expugnatumque*, where, however, the abl. may refer chiefly to *expugnatum*, 'was stormed *within* two days'. In 21, 1, *nec quemquam . . . ad theatrales artes degenerauisse ducentis iam annis a L. Mummii triumpho*, the abl. may possibly be absolute, 'it being now two hundred years since . . .'. This use of the abl. is an obvious outgrowth of the abl. denoting time 'within' or 'during which', cf. *biduo obsessum expugnatumque*. The fundamental distinction between the abl. and the acc. in expressions of time or space is that the acc. denotes progression and answers the question 'how far?', 'how long did the action go on?' The abl. fixes position in time or space, answering the question 'when?' or 'where?' But this question may be answered by denoting two limits between which an event happened or went on, even if it filled the whole space between the limits. Accordingly there are bound to be border-line cases where either the abl. or the acc. may be used, according to the point of view of the speaker. Nevertheless, this use of the abl. had not yet developed in early Latin. There are no examples in Plautus. It is still rare in classical Latin, though cf. Cic., *De Or.* 3, 138, (*Pericles*) *quadraginta annis praefuit Athenis*; Caes., *B.G.* 1, 26, 5, *tota nocte continenter ierunt*, and about half a dozen other examples. It is noteworthy that in all instances quoted from these authors the tense of the verb is one of complete action, so that the abl. denotes completion 'within certain limits'. The imperf. tense seems naturally to demand the acc., so the example from c. 10, 1 above seems to indicate deterioration in the purity of Latin. The old distinctions are breaking down and the cases are losing their significance. This use of the abl. is common in Livy, but most common in Tacitus.

5. THE INFINITIVE

In colloquial Latin (e.g. Plautus, Terence, letter-writers, technical treatises such as those of Varro), in poetry, and in literary prose of the Silver Age, the infinitive is used far more extensively than in good prose of the Golden Age. Consequently many verbs will be found in Tacitus constructed with an infin. which in Cicero or Caesar would have their meaning amplified by a subj. *ut*-clause or other form of subordinate clause. Occasionally also the infin. will be found boldly attached to a noun or to an adj. to amplify or complete its meaning. These uses are not to be considered bold innovations by Tacitus or as contrary to the nature of the Latin language. The only rules they violate are those laid down in school text-books, which are founded rather too exclusively on Cicero and Caesar.

In classical Latin the infin. is regarded as an indeclinable neuter noun of either nom. or accus. case. But, as is shown by its terminations, it was originally a third declension noun in the locat. or dat. case. E.g. the prolate infin. with verbs of incomplete meaning is not an acc. object, but an adverbial complement. *Possum uincere* originally meant ' I am powerful *in* (locat.) or *for* (dat.) conquering.' Nor is it surprising to find the infin. performing the function of a dat. ' of the end aimed at ' or ' result achieved ' (cf. III, 4 above). In colloquial Latin the infin. can even be used after verbs of motion for a purpose clause, as in English; cf., for instance, Plaut., *Bacch.* 631 *uenerat aurum petere*, ' he had come to seek the gold ' with *auxilio uenire*, or with the dat. of the gerund expressing purpose. It would seem that Cicero and Caesar, in setting their rigid canons of style, delayed the logical development of the infin.

The following uses of the infin. which occur in *Ann.* XIV may be regarded as unclassical, though precedent may be found for some of them even in Cicero and Caesar:

(i) *The Infinitive explanatory of Nouns or Adjectives (Epexegetic Infinitive)*

See c. 14, 1, *Vetus illi cupido erat curriculo . . . . insistere, nec minus foedum studium . . . canere.* With *cupido insistere, studium canere,* cf. the colloquial attachment of datives to nouns referred to in III, 4, though doubtless Tacitus used the infin. because *cupido erat* = *cupiebat* and *studium erat* = *studebat*. 56, 3 *factus natura et consuetudine exercitus uelare odium*. The infin. explanatory of adjectives is a Grecism (cf. δέξιος λέγειν, 'clever at speaking') which Tacitus probably introduced into Latin prose under the influence of the poets. But it could not have been adopted, were it contrary to the genius of Latin. Cf. the use of the dat. in *nudus exercitando corpori*, 'stripped for exercising his body'; so above, ' fashioned and practised *for veiling* his hatred '.

(ii) ' *Prolate ' Infinitive with Verbs which in Classical Latin would Require a Subordinate Clause*

Adigo, 24, 1, *carne pecudum propulsare famem adacti* (only in poets and later prose). *concedo*, 55, 2, *Maecenati usurpare otium concessit* (found also in Cicero, but mostly after impers. pass., e.g. *T. D.* 2, 55, *ingemiscere non numquam uiro concessum est*). *impello*, 60, 1, *quendam impulit seruilem ei amorem obicere* (found also in Livy). *paciscor*, 31, 2, *resumere libertatem pepigerant* (Livy and poets). *permitto*, 12, 4, *sepulcrum extrui permisit* (occasionally in Cicero and Nepos, frequent in Livy). *subigo*, 14, 4; 26, 1 (also in Sallust and Livy).

Tacitus sometimes (not always) uses an infin. after some verbs of ' asking ', viz. *exposco, expostulo, oro* (though *not* after *posco, peto, rogo*), all of which normally require an *ut*-clause as object in classical Latin, e.g. *Ann.* XIV, 13, 1, *praegredi exposcunt* (for *ut praegrederentur*). For *expostulo* with infin., see *Hist.* I, 82; III, 83; *Ann.* XV, 17 (with which cf. *Ann.* XII, 46, *ut . . . decedant expostulat*); for *oro*, see *Ann.* VI, 2, *principem orabat deligere senatores*; XI, 32; XII, 9; XIII, 13; with acc. and infin., XI, 10. There is no precedent in classical prose for the infin. with *oro*, which is poetic and post-Augustan, as also is that with *posco, peto, rogo*. But examples are found in classical prose of the infin. with *postulo* and *expostulo*, though they are mostly confined to the *passive* infin., e.g. Cic., *De Inv.* I, 53, *postulabimus nobis illud concedi*; *Verr.* 3, 138, *hic postulat se Romae absolui*; Caes.,

B.G. 4, 16, 4, *cur sui quicquam esse . . . trans Rhenum postularet?*

After *non dubito*, in the sense ' not to doubt that ', the acc. and infin. is used about half a dozen times by Tacitus where classical Latin demands a *quin*-clause, e.g. *Ann.* XIV, 43, 1, *non quia dubitarem melius olim prouisum* (sc. *esse*) *et quae conuerterentur ad deterius mutari* . . . Livy also often uses the infin., but more often *quin*. There are no examples of this in Caesar, and only one certain in Cicero. Cornelius Nepos, on the other hand, prefers the infin. Care must be taken to distinguish between this sense of *dubito* and the sense ' to hesitate ', after which the infin. is regular and classical.

(iii) *Historic Infinitive*

This is a favourite device of the historians, particularly Sallust and Tacitus, but it is already quite common in early Latin. The hist. infin. is generally a substitute for the imperf. indic., not for the aorist perf. It is used to describe a state of feeling or a tense scene. Even when it describes a series of rapid events, it represents them as a progression, as part of a changing scene, and the effect is not the same as that of the hist. pres. indic. The latter is equivalent in sense to an aorist perf. In classical Latin the hist. infin. is used only in main clauses. Sallust is the first to use it in a connective *qui*-clause or in an ' inverted ' *cum*-clause, e.g. *Jug.* 70, 5, *litteras ad eum . . . mittit; in quis . . . accusare; Jug.* 98, 2, *iam dies consumptus erat, cum tamen barbari nihil remittere.* There are two parallel examples in *Ann.* XIV, viz. 1, 1, *scelus non ultra distulit Nero . . . flagrantior in dies amore Poppaeae, quae . . . incusare principem et pupillum uocare;* 5, 1, *Acerronia . . . memorabat, cum dato signo ruere tectum.* It should be noted that in these cases the hist. infin. is really a main verb, since *quae = nam ea*, and *cum = et tum*. Tacitus is the first to use the hist. infin. in clauses that are really subordinate, e.g. after *ubi, ut, postquam,* see *Ann.* II, 4; XI, 37; XII, 51, &c. There are, however, no examples of the latter type in *Ann.* XIV.

6. THE SUBJUNCTIVE

i. As Tacitus' use of the subjunctive independently in main clauses does not differ from classical usage, little need be said on this score, except that Tacitus is very fond of the use of the perfect tense of the so-called ' potential ' subj. in mild assertions, suggesting possibility, e.g. *dicat quispiam, dixerit quispiam*. In such cases the perf. subj. is ' aoristic ' and refers to the future. It is commonest in the first person, e.g. *crediderim*, ' I am inclined to think '; in the third person it is usually used in combination with an indefinite pronoun (*aliquis, quispiam*); the second person (= ' one ') is also common. For examples in *Ann.* XIV, see 44, 3, *colluuiem istam non nisi metu coercueris*, ' one *cannot* restrain . . .'; 56, 2, *non . . . decorum fuerit*, ' it would not be becoming '. But such a perf. potential subj. is very rarely found in classical Latin depending on *ut* or *ne*, as in c. 53, 3, *ut sic dixerim*, ' so to speak '. Cf. *Ann.* VI, 22, *ne . . . longius abierim*. Possibly the fairly frequent *ut sic, ut ita dixerim* (cf. *Agr.* 3; *Germ.* 2) arose from a conflation of an expression like *paene dixerim*, ' I might almost say ', with *ut sic dicam*.

ii. *Subjunctive in Subordinate Clauses*

(a) *Temporal Clauses.* In classical Latin the subj. can only be used after conjunctions like *donec* and *priusquam* if they are quasi-oblique, indicating intention on the part of the subject of the main verb. The fondness of classical Latin for this nuance, however, caused it to become outworn, so that from Livy onwards the subj. is sometimes used instead of the indic. to denote nothing but a ' Time ' relationship, e.g. *Ann.* I, 13, *neque . . . mitigatus est, donec Haterius Augustam oraret* . . . Cf. *Germ.* 1, 35; *Ann.* II, 6; and often. In *Ann.* XIV, 8, 2, *obuios seruorum abripit donec ad fores cubiculi ueniret*, the idea of purpose is possibly present.

(b) *Indefinite Clauses and Clauses of Repeated Action.* In generalizing clauses, i.e. those introduced by words like ' whoever ', ' whenever ', classical Latin normally uses the indic., the commonest tenses being the perf. and pluperf., e.g. Cic. *Verr.* 5, 10, *cum rosam uiderat, tum incipere uer arbitrabatur*; Livy 21, 42, *ut cuiusque sors exciderat, alacer arma raptim capiebat.* But the fondness which Latin developed for the ' characterizing ' (generic) subj. caused it to be extended to these clauses also, since ' whenever ' really = ' on *such* occasions *as* ', ' whoever ' = ' *such* persons *as* ', and so on. The subj. in such clauses becomes increasingly common from Livy on, e.g. Livy 1, 32, *id fetialis ubi dixisset, hastam in fines eorum emittebat* (describing the formula used whenever war was declared). Both Livy and Tacitus seem to use the indic. or the subj. indiscriminately. Cf. Tac., *Hist.* II, 27, *ut cuiusque legionis tentoria accessissent, superbe agebant*; *Ann.* VI, 21, *quotiens super tali negotio consultaret, edita domus parte utebatur*; and many other examples, with *Ann.* XIV, 8, 1, *ut quisque acceperat, decurrere ad litus*; so also cc. 5, 3; 35, 1; 64, 3. There are no clear examples of the subj. so used in *Ann.* XIV. See notes on cc. 13, 2; 52, 2.

(c) *Simple Form for Periphrastic.* If the verb in a subordinate clause requiring the subj. denotes an action which is future in relation to the time of the governing verb, classical Latin requires the use of the periphrastic fut. subj. (*-urus sim, essem*), except in cases where the sense of the governing verb makes ambiguity impossible, e.g. in *rogo ut uenias*, ' I ask you to come ', *uenias* must refer to the future, and it would be ridiculous to say *rogo ut uenturus sis.* On the other hand, to ask a question about a past, present, or future happening, clearer tense distinctions are required in the subj. clause, so that one must say *rogo quid facturus sis* for ' I ask what you will do ', in order to avoid ambiguity. The periphrastic form, however, was the product of literary precision, and the simple tense was often used in colloquial Latin and in poetry, and becomes increasingly common in prose from Livy on. Cf. Ter., *Heaut.* 715, *quid me fiat parui pendis* (for *futurum sit*); Caes., *B.G.* 1, 31, 15, *non dubitare quin . . . supplicium sumat* (for *sumpturus sit*); Livy 2, 55, 9; 3, 4, 2, &c. Examples are rare in Cicero, and are either from his *earliest* works, or else the verb is passive. In many examples that are quoted from various authors, the subj.

can be construed as an indirect deliberative (cf. note on c. 13, 1, *ingrederetur*). In the passive, periphrases like *rogauit num futurum esset ut laudaretur* for ' he asked whether he would be praised ' are not found except in grammar-books, but are represented by *num laudari posset, num postea laudaretur*, &c., or else turned actively. For examples of the simple form for the periphrastic in *Ann.* XIV, see cc. 13, 1, *an studia plebis reperiret anxius* (for *reperturus esset*); 58, 3, *multa secutura quae adusque bellum eualescerent*; 61, 3, *ducem tantum defuisse, qui motis rebus facile reperiretur*. Notice that in two out of these three exx., one verb is passive, and the other has no fut. part.

(d) *Concessive Clauses of Fact*. Tacitus regularly uses the subj. after *quamquam*, probably on the analogy of *quamuis*, e.g. c. 36, 1, *quamquam confideret uirtuti, tamen exhortationes et preces miscebat*.

(e) *Tamquam* and *Quasi*. Although in classical Latin *tamquam* and *quasi* with the subj. can only introduce clauses of unreal comparison (e.g. Cic. *Fin.* 5, 42, *parui iacent tamquam omnino sine animo sint*, ' babies lie as if they had no mind at all '), in Silver Latin the meaning ' as if ' in a sentence like ' he put him to death *as if* he had done wrong ' is made to mean ' *on the ground that* '; i.e. the subj. is treated as if it were not a conditional subj., but a subj. of virtual o.o. This use is then extended still further, and the meaning ' on the ground that ' passes over to ' to the effect that ', so that in some sentences *tamquam* and *quasi* with the subj. seem to be used almost as an alternative to the acc. and infin. to quote thought or speech obliquely, e.g. 21, 1, *cometes . . . de quo uulgi opinio est tamquam mutationem regis portendat*, ' a comet . . . about which the common belief is to the effect that it portends a change of ruler '. Here *id mutationem portendere* would give the same sense. 52, 1, *criminationibus Senecam adoriuntur, tamquam opes augeret*; 59, 1. *nuntios uenisse . . . tamquam nihil atrox immineret*; 8, 1, *uulgato Agrippinae periculo, quasi casu euenisset*; perhaps also 10, 2, *fuisse eam poenam conscientia, quasi scelus parauisset*. The use of *quasi* in this way is very rare in other authors, and in

Tacitus occurs only in the Annals. *Tamquam* is so used by Quintilian, Juvenal, Pliny the Younger, and Suetonius, among others.

(f) *Quod-clauses.* An adverbial (causal) *quod*-clause, with the verb in the subj., is very often used in all periods of Latin to give an alleged reason. This is the regular construction after *accuso* and other verbs of 'accusing'. A substantival *quod*-clause, however, standing as object of verbs of 'saying', 'thinking', or 'perceiving', is a great rarity in literary Latin. Nevertheless it must have been very common, if not the regular construction, in the spoken language of the lower classes, since it became the regular method of reporting speech in the Romance languages (e.g. *il dit que* . . .). Examples such as *Ann.* XIV, 6, 1, *reputans ideo se . . . accitam . . . , quodque . . . nauis . . . concidisset*; and *Ann.* III, 54, *nemo refert quod Italia externae opis indiget*, 'no one mentions that Italy needs foreign resources', suggest that the *sermo plebeius* was beginning to influence literary Latin in the first century A.D.

7. THE PARTICIPLES

(i) *Perfect Passive*

Although the form of the past participle passive in *-atus*, *-tus* was originally merely a verbal adj. with no particular voice or tense significance (cf. the corresponding form in *-ητος* in Greek, and similar adjectival forms such as *taci-tus*, *sceles-tus* which survive in Latin), it had long before the time of Cicero become narrowed down to a passive significance (except in the case of deponent verbs) and had come to denote *priority* in time in relation to the main verb. However, there are instances even in classical Latin of the past part. loosely used to denote circumstances not prior, but even posterior to the time of the main verb. This is very rare in classical Latin, but occurs a number of times in Livy, and is very common in Tacitus. See *Ann.* XIV, 24, 1; 50, 2 (where see note); 63, 2.

Another use of the past part. of which Tacitus is fonder

than any author before him is to put it in agreement with a noun to give the sense of an abstract noun with the gen., or of a substantival clause; e.g. c. 14, 3, *euulgatus pudor non satietatem . . . attulit = euulgatio pudoris . . .* Cf. also 7, 1; 23, 1; 29, 2; 32, 1. The similar use of the pres. part. is far less common in classical Latin, and that of the fut. part. does not occur before Livy. Tacitus uses both freely, e.g., *Ann.* IV, 12, *quod principium fauoris et mater Agrippina spem male tegens perniciem accelerauere = quod Agrippina spem male tegebat; Ann.* I, 36, *augebat metum . . . inuasurus hostis = quod hostis inuasuras erat;* possibly also *Ann.* XIV, 11, 1, *adiciebat crimina . . . quod consortium imperii iuraturasque in feminae uerba praetorias cohortes sperauisset* (cf. Kühner-Stegmann I, 769).

(ii) *Future Participle*

The most probable history of the form in *-urus* is that it was originally an indeclinable fut. infin. in *-urum*. The likeness of the termination to the 2nd declension acc. sing. would cause it to be thought that it agreed with its subject, and so it came to be declined like a 2nd declension adj. The meaning now was ' (that which is) about to do . . . ', and the addition of *esse* was now necessary to make a periphrastic fut. infin. Finite forms of *esse* could also be used with it to make a periphrastic fut. tense (*facturus sum*). This was as far as the development had gone by the time of Cicero and Caesar, neither of whom uses the form in *-urus* as an adj. or as freely as the other participles. Logically there was no reason why they should not have done so, but they probably refrained merely because there was as yet no precedent for such a usage. The introduction of it may have been due to Sallust, who was fond of innovating. From the time of Livy onwards the form is employed freely as an adj. with several shades of meaning, e.g. to denote intention, likelihood, potentiality. Uses such as the following, therefore, are not to be found in Cicero or Caesar: *Ann.* XIV, 8, 3, *si ad uisendum uenisset, refotam nuntiaret, sin facinus patraturus . . .* (where *patraturus =*

NERO

' with the intention of committing . . .' and is an alternative to *ad* with the gerund); 41, 1, *quod reos . . . ad praetorem detulisset . . . ultionem elusurus*; 4, 3, *periturae matris supremus aspectus*; 20, 1, *quod mansuram theatri sedem posuisset*; 33, 2, *tamquam reddituri supplicium* (cf. Greek ὡς with fut. part.); 38, 3, *nouum legatum opperiendum esse, sine hostili ira deditis consulturum* (= *qui consulturus esset*).

IV

THE REIGN OF NERO

The emperor Claudius, having been persuaded by his last wife Agrippina formally to adopt her son, L. Domitius Ahenobarbus, and to bestow on him honours that marked him out for promotion over his own son Britannicus, was poisoned before he could change his mind. Nevertheless no reign began with greater promise than that of the young prince, now called Nero Claudius Drusus Germanicus Caesar, who in A.D. 54, at the age of seventeen, was hailed as Imperator by the Praetorian Guards and unanimously accepted by the Senate. Guided by the good counsels of his tutor Seneca and the Praetorian Prefect, Burrus, he set out to restore the confidence of the senatorial aristocracy, which had suffered much from the wives and freedmen of Claudius, and to secure their goodwill and collaboration in the government of the Empire.[1]

At the beginning of the reign Seneca and Burrus had to contend with the ambitions of Agrippina, who as dowager-empress desired to reap the reward of power from her successful intrigues. The extent of her pretensions can be judged from the fact that her head appears on coins on an equality with Nero's;[2] from her removal without Nero's knowledge of persons obnoxious to her;[3] from her continued

---

[1] For evidence of the continuance of Nero's policy of deference towards the Senate at least up to A.D. 60, see *Ann.* XIV, 28.

[2] See illustration opposite p. 65. Cf. *Ann.* XIV, 11.

[3] Ibid., XIII, 1; XIV, 11.

violation of Roman propriety in attempting to preside with
Nero at interviews with foreign envoys; and from the fact
that she forced the Senate to meet on the Palatine in order
that she might hear a debate in which she was interested.[1]
Seneca and Burrus undermined her influence with Nero
and won his acceptance of their advice in matters of state by
winking at his youthful excesses, and even encouraging him
to form connexions of which Agrippina had sufficient
maternal instinct to disapprove. By representing their
policy of deference towards the Senate as an act of grace
from a superior being from whom alone all authority
derived, they caused him to resent any claim to independent
authority. The emperor is, as it were, the vicegerent of
God on earth.[2] To those who blame Seneca for thus
securing temporary good government at the expense of
Nero's character, and hold him indirectly responsible for
the tragedy of the reign, it may be answered that Seneca
had studied his pupil and thought that external influence
would make little difference in the long run to a
temperament like Nero's, whose inheritance of the vices of
the Domitii combined with those of the Julio-Claudians
was probably already visible.[3]

Agrippina, seeing her power slipping, was foolish enough
to lose her temper. Her nagging merely attached Nero
more closely to the more indulgent advisers. Her belated
attempt to recover lost ground by outdoing Seneca in
indulgence was worse than useless, for it opened Nero's
eyes to her intentions. In her baffled rage she next tried
to frighten him by pretending to espouse the cause of her
stepson Britannicus.[4] When that unfortunate youth
immediately died by poison, it became obvious that Seneca
and Burrus were in charge of something they could not
control. They were forced to accept the crime as an

[1] *Ann.*, XIII, 5.
[2] Seneca, *De Clem.* I, 1, *et passim*.
[3] Cf. Suetonius, *Nero*, cc. 4–5. Nero was, through his mother, the
great-great-grandson of Augustus. His Claudian blood came from his
grandfather, Germanicus Caesar.
[4] *Ann.* XIII, 14 sqq.

accomplished fact. Their complacent acceptance of such deeds did at least secure for the Empire at large five years of reasonably efficient government, the famous *quinquennium Neronis*,[1] during which Nero indulged his tastes for art, music, and sensuality, while leaving the cares of State to them.

But Agrippina, though the death of Britannicus had deprived her of her last political weapon, continued to exercise a check on Nero in his private affairs. Unscrupulous and headstrong as she was, she had a sense of the dignity of the imperial position, which Nero had not. She was unable to prevent him from drunken brawling in the streets at night, or from neglecting his unhappy wife Octavia, but she still dominated him enough to prevent him from scandalizing Roman society by appearing in public as a jockey or an opera-singer. To indulge these tastes in private was of no use at all to one with a stage-struck craving for the limelight. Nero felt himself bursting with talent and longed for the applause of an adoring public. If the public preferred wild-beast hunts and gladiatorial combats, then their taste must be educated to higher things; and who was in a better position to do this than the lord of the world, himself the most talented exponent of the arts? Meanwhile Agrippina and Octavia seemed to be the greatest obstacles to his self-expression. To make matters worse, in A.D. 58 he fell in love with Poppaea Sabina, wife of M. Salvius Otho, one of his Bohemian friends. This wicked beauty, not content to be the emperor's mistress, but seeing no chance of becoming empress while Agrippina lived to protect Octavia, worked to bring about an open breach between Nero and his mother.

This is the point which Tacitus' narrative has reached at the beginning of *Ann.* XIV. There we read how Nero

---

[1] It is possible, however, that Trajan, the author of this phrase (see Aurelius Victor, *Caes.* V, 2), was not referring to good government in the early part of Nero's reign, but to his rebuilding of Rome after the fire. See J. G. C. Anderson, *J.R.S.* 1, 1911, pp. 173 sqq.

murdered his mother and broke loose from all restraint. Not only does he go on the stage, but he begins to change the temper of the government. However, the turning-point of the reign is the death of Burrus in 62. Burrus is replaced by Tigellinus, and Seneca's policy of deference to the aristocracy is thrown overboard. There follow in quick succession the senseless murders of Plautus and Sulla, the horribly cruel death of Octavia, and the marriage with Poppaea. The poisoning of a rich freedman for his money seems almost too unimportant for anything but a passing mention. The book ends on an ominous note of fear for the future.

By this time Nero's extravagant behaviour had exhausted his credits both in money and popularity. The resort to treason-trials and confiscation to refill the treasury did not restore his popularity, which by A.D. 64 had sunk so low that, when Rome was devastated by the great fire, the mob credited him with being the incendiary. Nero, with his temperament at once sensitive and brutal, looking round for a scapegoat to divert attention from himself, lit upon the new Christian sect, the persecution of which further ensured his posthumous fame. The continued profligacy of the court and the growing hatred of all classes produced in A.D. 65 the conspiracy of Piso, after the detection and suppression of which nineteen persons, including Seneca himself and the poet Lucan, lost their lives. Now began a real reign of terror, in which victims were not confined to the nobles in the city. During Nero's celebrated tour of Greece, the governors of Upper and Lower Germany and even the great Corbulo were summoned to kill themselves, and obeyed.

But when the terror reached out to the provinces, the end was near. Early in A.D. 68 news of serious unrest in the West at last persuaded Nero to tear himself away from his appreciative audiences in Greece. He had not been back long when news came that C. Julius Vindex, governor of Gallia Lugdunensis, was in open revolt. This was mainly a Gallic nationalist movement and was easily put down by Verginius Rufus, governor of Upper Germany, but not before Servius Sulpicius Galba with the legions of Spain had made common cause with it. Galba proclaimed himself legate of the Senate and Roman people. Verginius did not defend Nero against this new enemy, but placed himself at the disposal of the Senate. Nero, deserted by Tigellinus, was quite incapable of organizing resistance. When the praetorians were tricked into betraying him, he tried to escape, but hearing that the Senate had recognized Galba as emperor and proclaimed himself a public enemy, he made up his mind to die. ' What an artist perishes in me! ' he said. When the tramp of pursuing horsemen was heard, he plunged a dagger into his throat with the aid of one of his freedmen Epaphroditus. So died, at the age of thirty years and six months, on the 9th June, A.D. 68, the last of the Julio-Claudian Caesars.

For Nero's reputation in modern times as ' one of the worst men who ever occupied a throne ',[1] Tacitus more than any one is responsible. But all ancient literary authorities are hostile. Pliny the Elder, as mentioned above, called Nero ' an off-scouring of humanity and its enemy '. He trampled on the most cherished traditions of the Roman aristocracy in the very act of trying to conciliate them, and, unable to understand their lack of appreciation, replaced his desire to conciliate by a ferocious hatred. He made them tremble and reveal, to themselves as well as to the world, their cowardice, incompetence, and degeneracy, and they have retaliated by damning him to all eternity. There is no reason to doubt that the portrait of Nero that has been handed down to us shows him as he really appeared to the contemporary resident in Rome. If his murders of step-brother, mother, and wife, to name only a few of his crimes, are facts, any attempt to whitewash him is vain.[2]

[1] Sir Samuel Dill.
[2] The most reasonable is that of B. W. Henderson, *Life and Principate of the Emperor Nero*.

Yet outside Rome a different scene presents itself. The provinces for the greater part of the reign were prosperous and contented, and their governors generally well chosen.[1] Diplomatic relations with foreign powers were conducted wisely. The old feud with Parthia was settled for the time being without loss of Roman prestige, and after Nero's death Vologaeses actually sent an embassy to ask the Senate to honour his memory. It is difficult to reconcile this with the literary tradition and with the Christian identification of Nero with Antichrist. The efficiency of the system set up by Augustus and the advice of Seneca and Burrus may account for much, but not for all. Nero must be given credit for his choice of ministers and agents, and for recognizing good advice when it was given. In some corner of his wayward, wanton heart he must have had a real regard for the welfare of the Empire at large. Tacitus, with his eyes glued on Rome, could see nothing but a ruthless attempt to degrade or eliminate the former ruling class, to which he himself belonged.

V

CORBULO IN ARMENIA [2]

A glance at the map of the eastern frontier of the Roman Empire (p. 39) will show that the river Euphrates is the natural boundary. The peoples to the east of the river had more affinities with Parthia than with Rome, and control over any part of them by Rome was precarious and could only be maintained at the cost of Parthian hostility. Not

---

[1] Admittedly there was oppression in Britain, and much maladministration is necessary to account for the revolt of Vindex, but for this Nero was not entirely to blame. In the East, at any rate, he seems to have been regretted.
[2] The chronology here followed is that of B. W. Henderson in *Life and Principate of the Emperor Nero*, ch. 5. Tacitus, falling a victim to the disadvantages of the annalistic method, omits to mention Corbulo under the year 59, but distributes his activities of that year between the years 58 and 60. The re-distribution is still a matter of dispute. For a different view, see *C. A. H.* X, ch. xxii, 5.

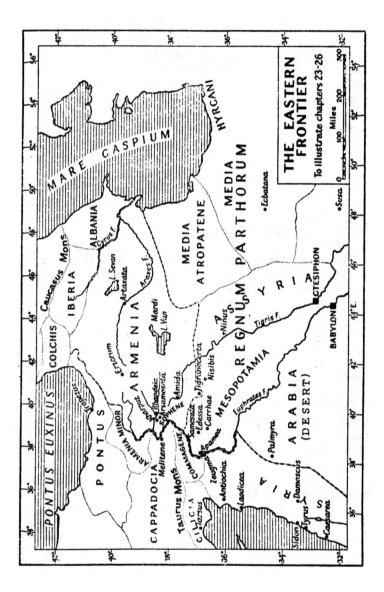

THE EASTERN
FRONTIER

To illustrate chapters 23–26

Miles

0   100   200   300

MARE CASPIUM

PONTUS EUXINUS

HYRCANI

MEDIA PARTHORUM

MEDIA
ATROPATENE

•Ecbatana

•Susa

ALBANIA

IBERIA

Caucasus Mons

Cyrus F.

L. Sevan

Araxes F.

Artaxata

COLCHIS

ARMENIA

Mardi

L. Van

Erzerum

Ninus

CTESIPHON

Tigris F.

Tigranocerta

Bagadeia

Arsamosata

Amida

Nisibis

Edessa

Carrhae

BABYLON

ARMENIA MINOR

Sophene

Samosata

MESOPOTAMIA

REGNUM

SYRIA

ARABIA
(DESERT)

PONTUS

CAPPADOCIA

COMMAGENE

Euphrates F.

•Palmyra

Melitene

Zeugma

Apamea

Taurus Mons

Antiochia

•Laodicea

•Damascus

CILICIA

•Tarsus

Sidon

Tyrus

Caesarea

all the territories immediately to the west of the river were yet, at Nero's accession, governed directly by Rome, but they were in process of Romanization, and as soon as they were ripe for it, would be annexed and organized as provinces. Pontus and Armenia Minor were client-kingdoms, Cappadocia had been annexed by Tiberius, Commagene was a client-kingdom, Syria was a major province and contained the only standing army of the East. The large kingdom of Armenia, stretching from Cappadocia to the Caspian Sea, never would be Romanized, and it was considered by the Parthians as a perquisite of their royal house. There could be no lasting peace with Parthia unless an Arsacid ruled Armenia, yet for over 100 years Rome had claimed the right to appoint its kings.

The author of this perverse policy had been Pompey the Great, who, after the overthrow of Mithridates of Pontus, had reduced the latter's great ally, Tigranes of Armenia, to vassalage, and had at the same time gone out of his way to irritate Parthia. Pride in Pompey's achievement and humiliation at the defeat of Crassus at Carrhae in 53 B.C. had conspired to make the Romans obstinate. No Roman government before Nero had dared to brave the popular indignation which would have greeted the cession of Armenia.

But granted the fact of Parthian hostility, there was a more sensible reason for exercising suzerainty over Armenia. The long frontier stretching from the eastern end of the Black Sea to the Red Sea, was difficult to defend except at great expense. The Euphrates could be crossed at Zeugma in the north-east corner of Syria, at Samosata on the frontier of Commagene, and opposite Melitene in Cappadocia. The army of Syria could not be relied upon to catch an invader trying to enter Asia Minor via Commagene or Cappadocia. Therefore, if the government could not afford to raise Cappadocia to the status of a first-class province with an army of its own, it must control Armenia. Armenia could be controlled by installing a client-king on the throne, or by annexing it and sending out a Roman governor. The latter course was likely to be too expensive, and would, besides, result in a frontier even more difficult to defend than the previous one. Thus it was that every Roman government from the time of Pompey to the reign of Nero had chosen the policy of suzerainty, in spite of the trouble that was bound to arise whenever Parthia was strong enough to induce the Armenians to change their allegiance. Annexation was not given a real trial till the time of Trajan. To sum up, the three policies open to Rome were: (a) Appeasement of Parthia and cession of Armenia. This could only be done by hoodwinking the Roman public, and would therefore obviously require the collaboration of the Parthian king. (b) Annexation. (c) The continuance of effective suzerainty. The government of Nero, faced with the necessity in A.D. 54 of settling the problem one way or another, tried all three policies, beginning and ending with the first.

The course of events, as far as can be gathered from the narrative of Tacitus in books XII–XV, was briefly as follows. In A.D. 51 the Armenian king Mithridates, who had ruled in the Roman interest since A.D. 35, was murdered by his nephew Radamistus. In the same year a strong king of Parthia arose in Vologaeses. The cruelty of Radamistus caused the Armenians to turn to Parthia for assistance, and by A.D. 54 Vologaeses had succeeded in installing his brother Tiridates as king of Armenia.[1] Nero and his advisers, called upon to face a crisis at the outset of the reign, prepared to act vigorously. The army of Syria, consisting of four legions, was brought up to full strength by recruiting, and the governor, Ummidius Quadratus, was ordered to move it up towards Zeugma, to defend the entry into Syria, and to hand over two of his legions to a new general specially appointed for the conduct of the war. This was Cn. Domitius Corbulo, who had been consul in A.D. 39 and had later distinguished himself

[1] Tac., *Ann.* XII, 44–51.

in campaigning on the Rhine, where he had acquired a reputation as a strict disciplinarian. He arrived in the East early in A.D. 55, took over Quadratus' two legions in Cilicia, and marched north to make Cappadocia his base for an invasion of Armenia. A joint embassy from Corbulo and Quadratus to warn Vologaeses to remain neutral during the coming war and to give hostages as a pledge of this met with unexpected success. Tacitus suggests that the reason was that Vologaeses had got wind of a rebellion brewing amongst his nobles, and seized the occasion to get rid of those whom he most suspected by handing them over as hostages to Rome. In any case his hands were tied by his son Vardanes, who was already in revolt, and he was unable to support Tiridates for another three years.[1]

This was extremely lucky, for Corbulo found that Quadratus had allowed the army of Syria to get into a parlous state, and the two legions which he had taken over were quite unfit for service. He spent the years 55-7 in reorganizing the troops and restoring discipline, ending by marching them into Armenia at the end of 57, and submitting them to the ordeal of a winter under canvas on the 6,000 ft. high plateau of Erzerum. The soldiers suffered severely from frost-bite and sentries died at their posts, but attempts at desertion were immediately punished with death. But this was a good position from which to begin the campaign in the spring of 58, for supplies could be drawn from the port of Trapezus (Trebizond) on the Black Sea. A chain of fortified posts secured communication in that direction.

During all this time Tiridates had remained inactive, but early in 58 he bestirred himself. As he now had Parthian troops sent by Vologaeses to aid him, we are justified in concluding that the latter had at last freed himself from entanglements in his own realm. But Vologaeses was not able to lend his support for long, for presently we hear that the Hyrcanians, a people who

[1] *Ann.* XIII, 5-9.

dwelt to the south of the Caspian, were in revolt behind his back. In the campaign of 58, Tiridates won no successes except against an isolated Roman detachment, but neither was Corbulo able to bring him to battle, so at last the latter changed his tactics, and divided his forces so as to attack as many districts as possible at the same time. Neighbouring kings were encouraged to invade Armenia from the west and north, so that by the end of the year Tiridates, harried on all sides, was ready to negotiate for peace. It is evident, however, that he had not yet had a very severe lesson, for he was still in a truculent mood. He implies that Vologaeses has only been restrained from taking the field in person because he believed in the possibility of a reasonable settlement acceptable to both sides, which would leave Tiridates in possession of Armenia. Whether this change of policy on the part of Rome really had already been foreshadowed is not clear,[1] but at any rate Corbulo's reply revealed it now. If Tiridates wished to retain his crown, he must approach the emperor in a suppliant mood. But Tiridates' pride was not yet humbled to such an extent. After attempting to bring Corbulo to a parley under circumstances which indicated treachery, he broke off negotiations and disappeared into the wilds.

There is nothing in the account of Tacitus [2] to indicate that the campaigning season of 58 was yet over, but as the activities already related were enough to occupy an untried army for many months, and as Corbulo now proceeds to a radical change of plan, it probably was. The army probably wintered in the old camp near Erzerum, and in the spring of 59 Corbulo gave up chasing Tiridates and

---

[1] See *Ann.* XIII, 37, *cur . . . redintegrata amicitia . . . quae nouis quoque beneficiis locum aperiret, uetere Armeniae possessione depelleretur ?* Cf. c. 34, *nec Vologaeses sinebat fratrem Tiridatem . . . alienae id potentiae donum habere.* It seems possible that B. W. Henderson (pp. 163, 169) is wrong in supposing that Rome's change of policy was revealed now for the first time. Had it been suggested by the envoys of Quadratus and Corbulo in A.D. 55, it would have given Vologaeses an additional inducement to keep quiet.

[2] *Ann.* XIII, 34-41.

set about storming the fortified places one by one, in the hope that the enemy might be forced to defend them. But as Tiridates, deprived of Parthian help through the Hyrcanian revolt, was unable to hinder him, he met with such rapid success that he soon found himself able to march on the old capital city of Artaxata. The opposition of Tiridates was so feeble that the city opened its gates. But Corbulo, having got it, did not know what to do with it. He had not, after all, brought the enemy to battle, and he had not enough troops to garrison so large a town and still prosecute the war. But a success so spectacular was not to be wasted, and Corbulo hit on the bold plan of burning the stronghold, cutting himself adrift from his communications, and marching through 300 miles of difficult country upon a still more important objective, the new capital, Tigranocerta. This strongly fortified city guarded the entrance into Armenia from Mesopotamia, and, if held by the Romans, would deprive Vologaeses of the strategic advantages of the re-entrant angle between the Syrian and the Armenian frontiers.

It is at this point that Tacitus takes up the narrative again in *Ann.* XIV, 23. Here and in *Ann.* XIII, 41, the language makes it clear that Artaxata was burned soon after its capture, and that the march on Tigranocerta was begun straight away. It must have been late autumn before the weary army, after a march of terrible hardship, emerged into the plain of Tigranocerta. But their fame had obviously preceded them, for they did not have to fight to win this comfortable city in which to spend the winter. Next year (A.D. 60), from his new base, Corbulo proceeded to pacify the country. Tiridates, having been driven out, made an attempt to re-enter from Media, but was prevented, and retired baffled to the court of Vologaeses. It appears that at this point the policy of Nero's government underwent a change. Armenia was without a ruler, and as no further overtures had come from Tiridates or Vologaeses, Corbulo was proceeding to annex the country, when there arrived one Tigranes, grandson of Archelaus, former King of Cappadocia, with orders from Nero that he should be installed on the throne. This was a return to the old unsatisfactory policy of effective suzerainty. But it is hard to blame Nero. Corbulo's success had been so complete and Parthian interference so ineffective that there was every hope that the new king, aided by a small Roman garrison, would be left alone. Corbulo accordingly installed him as king, after ensuring him foreign allies and the hostility of his own subjects by assigning parts of the Armenian territory to each of the neighbouring client-kings. Leaving him a detachment of 1,000 legionaries, three allied cohorts, and two squadrons of cavalry, Corbulo then retired to keep watch from the province of Syria, which had been entrusted to him on the death of Ummidius Quadratus. Such was the state of things at the end of A.D. 60, which is as far as the narrative of *Ann.* XIV takes us.

In *Ann.* XV, 1–17 and 24–31, and XVI, 23, we learn how the incredible folly of Tigranes caused the old policy to fail once more. In A.D. 61 he tried to show off to his new subjects by invading Parthian territory. Unluckily for him and for Rome, Vologaeses, having crushed the Hyrcanian revolt, was free to exact vengeance. In A.D. 61 he crowned Tiridates King of Armenia and sent him with a strong Parthian force to turn Tigranes out, while he himself attacked the province of Syria. Tigranes was besieged in Tigranocerta, and Corbulo, fully employed with the defence of Syria, could do no more than send his two weakest legions to hold what they could of Armenia, while he wrote and begged Nero to send another army and general to enter the country from the side of Cappadocia. Meanwhile Tigranocerta held out, and Vologaeses, in difficulties owing to lack of supplies and Corbulo's able conduct, offered to negotiate. Corbulo, seeing a chance at last of putting into effect Nero's first and wisest policy, obtained the withdrawal of the Parthians, probably on condition that the Romans also evacuated Armenia pending Nero's decision. But Nero had now decided on annexation,

and sent out Caesennius Paetus to effect it. This
appointment was the worst he ever made, and it is
significant that it was made in the year in which Burrus
died and Seneca fell from power. By a series of blunders
and inexcusable cowardice, Paetus allowed himself to be
trapped into surrender at Rhandeia, when Corbulo with a
rescuing force was only three days' march away. Nevertheless Vologaeses graciously consented to allow Nero to
ratify Tiridates' kingship. This was now the only wise
course for Nero, but it had to come as a concession from
him, after the disgrace at Rhandeia had been repaired.
Accordingly Corbulo was put in sole charge of the forces
of the East with power to act as he thought fit. In A.D. 63
he marched ravaging into Armenia. Tiridates and
Vologaeses, convinced that resistance would mean the
final loss of Armenia, came to terms. At Rhandeia, the
site of Paetus' disgrace, Tiridates laid his crown at the
feet of Nero's statue, and agreed to come to Rome to
receive it back from the emperor in person. After much
preparation, he finally arrived in Rome in A.D. 66, and the
spectacle of an eastern prince doing homage to the emperor
in the forum delighted the Roman public and blinded them
to the real fact that Armenia had been ceded to a Parthian
nominee. But this wise settlement secured peace for half
a century, and accounts for the honour in which Nero's
name was held in Parthia.

VI

THE ROMANS IN BRITAIN

It is not to be supposed that the inhabitants of the part of
Britain which was reduced to the form of a Roman province
by the Emperor Claudius in the years following A.D. 43
were uncivilized savages. The Britons were of the same
Celtic stock as the Gauls. When we realize that many
famous Romans, including, perhaps, Virgil, were of
Gallic origin, we can understand why anthropologists

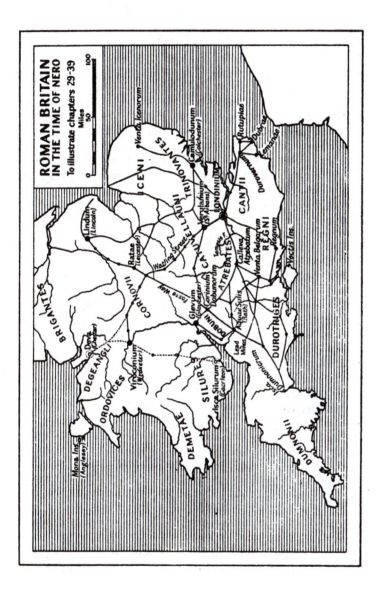

ROMAN BRITAIN
IN THE TIME OF NERO

To illustrate chapters 29-39

Miles
0   50   100

are unable to distinguish between Roman and British skeletons. Neither were the Britons much inferior in intellect to the Romans, though they were behind them in developing the amenities of civilization. Since the time of Julius Caesar's invasion, which was little more than a reconnaissance in force, the Britons had been growing more and more like the Romans. After Caesar's departure, the confederacy of tribes which had been his chief enemy recovered its ascendancy over the other tribes of the south-east. By the time of Augustus, King Cunobelinus (Shakespeare's Cymbeline) of the Catuvellauni, reigning from his capital at Colchester (Camulodunum), was regarded as king of Britain, though it is likely that his claims to overlordship were resented by powerful tribes like the Iceni.

But though this powerful kingdom of southern Britain was growing rich by exporting corn, cattle, gold, silver, iron, hides, slaves, and hunting-dogs to Gaul and the Empire, and imbibing Roman culture through the presence of Roman merchants and the importation of Roman goods, its ruling house was politically opposed to Rome, and looked with favour on any attempts by Gallic kinsmen across the Channel to throw off the Roman yoke. At the same time there was a pro-Roman opposition, so that if the Romans ever decided to subdue Britain, they were sure of allies in the country itself.

This decision was finally taken by Claudius in A.D. 43. Gaul was now pacified, but Claudius was bent on destroying the influence of the priestly Druid caste over the minds of the Gallic people, and this could not be done so long as fresh priests could always be obtained from Britain, the last stronghold of Druidism. Also Cunobelinus had just died, and had been succeeded by his sons Togodumnus and Caratacus, who were fanatically anti-Roman. The task of subduing the island was assigned to Aulus Plautius with four legions, viz. IInd Augusta (commanded by Vespasian, the future emperor), IXth Hispana, XIVth Gemina, and XXth Valeria. Caratacus was defeated and

DOMITIUS CORBULO

fled to the Silures of Wales, the Iceni and Regni came over to Rome, and by A.D. 47, when Aulus Plautius was succeeded as governor by P. Ostorius Scapula, the frontier of the new Roman province had been pushed forward to a line running from Lincoln to south Devon—the line of the Fosse Way. On the western side of this line, Caratacus continued to stir up such hostility to Rome that, although he was defeated again and fled to Queen Cartimandua of the Brigantes, who gave him up to Ostorius, no considerable advance was made for another thirty years. On the eastern side of the line the work of Romanization went on rapidly—too rapidly, as events proved. The friendship of King Prasutagus of the Iceni and of Cogidubnus of the Regni was rewarded by allowing them to keep their kingdoms as vassals of Rome, the latter with the title of *rex et legatus Augusti*. As usual, the Romans were making use of the native tribal organization until such time as the infiltration of Roman ideas would make it possible to substitute the Roman system of government without arousing too much resentment. Unfortunately the apparently civilized condition of the country deceived them into acting too quickly. Ostorius thought that a colony of disbanded veterans at Camulodunum would provide sufficient security for the province while the regular troops pushed on into the west and north. The IInd Legion had now established its permanent base at Glevum (Gloucester), the XIVth and XXth at Viroconium (Wroxeter), and the IXth at Lindum (Lincoln). No further advance was made under Ostorius' successors, A. Didius Gallus, Q. Veranius, and C. Suetonius Paulinus.[1] Indeed, under the last-named, who became governor in A.D. 59, the territory already won was almost lost in the great rebellion of Boudicca, which Tacitus relates in *Ann.* XIV, 29–39.

The immediate causes of the revolt are given by Tacitus in c. 31. Discontent had been growing ever since Ostorius

---

[1] The establishment of military bases at Isca Silurum (Caerleon-on-Usk), Deva (Chester), and Eburacum (York) probably belongs to the next phase of advance in the time of Vespasian.

had, in A.D. 51, arrogantly disregarded British rights by confiscating land for the Roman colony at Camulodunum. The insolent behaviour of the settlers made matters worse. Then, about A.D. 60–61, when King Prasutagus of the Iceni died, Nero made a premature attempt to dispense with the system of client-kingdoms, which Claudius had retained. Prasutagus had evidently suspected some such design on the part of the emperor, for in his will he had named him co-heir along with his widow, Boudicca, and his two daughters, doubtless hoping that, in return for this smoothing of his path, Nero would allow them to keep at least part of the crown lands. Perhaps a good procurator [1] would have been able to arrange such a concession. But Catus Decianus was not a good procurator. From his office in London he sent out his bailiffs to give Boudicca notice to quit. Her palace and landed property now belonged to the emperor, and Catus was doubtless eager to begin collecting her rents, some of which might find their way into his own pockets, before he began his official returns. Boudicca, being a lady of spirit, refused to quit; whereupon she was arrested and scourged, and her daughters were insulted. Not content with the crown lands, Catus seized the property of the chief nobles as well. To add to the popular indignation, the centurions, who acted on behalf of the political governor, omitted no circumstance of indignity in taking over the political administration from Boudicca.

These incredible acts of folly let loose a flood of hate that had been gathering for ten years. We read in these chapters of Tacitus how every Briton of military age answered Boudicca's call to arms. The terrified settlers sent messengers for help to London and to the legions. Catus sent them merely 200 men poorly armed; the two nearest legions were over 100 miles away, and the legate of one of them was absent; Suetonius himself was 250

---

[1] The *procuratores* were the emperor's finance ministers in the provinces. Though inferior in dignity to the military governors, they seem to have been independent of them.

miles away, with his legions involved in operations in
Anglesey; the only legion that could immediately answer
the call was the IXth under Petilius Cerealis from Lincoln.
But it was too late. Camulodunum was sacked and
burned, the population, men, women, and children,
massacred with every atrocity. Then Boudicca turned
to meet Petilius Cerealis, cut his legion to pieces, and
chased him back with the remnant of his cavalry to
Lincoln. But there is no doubt that the escape of Cerealis
himself saved the Roman power in Britain, for it drew the
Britons north in pursuit and saved the commander-in-chief
from being trapped. Suetonius, hurrying by forced
marches down Watling Street, reached London before
Boudicca. London had already grown into the largest
commercial town in the country; it was thronged with
merchants of all nationalities, and packed with stores of
merchandise, an obvious prize for the victorious rebels.
But it was unwalled and would require a large army to
defend it. Suetonius had arrived with less than 10,000
men.[1] He had set out down Watling Street with the XIVth
Legion and half of the XXth, leaving the other half to
defend his base. Messengers had been sent to Lincoln and
to Gloucester to order the IXth and IInd to join him on the
march. Both failed him, the IXth because it no longer
existed as an effective force, the IInd because its commander
was absent, for what reason we do not know. A subordinate, Poenius Postumus, Prefect of the Camp, was
temporarily in charge. On this unfortunate officer was
laid a grave responsibility. The Silures were seething
with revolt around him, and if he marched out, he was
leaving his commanding officer and whatever troops were

---

[1] It is usually assumed that he galloped ahead with the cavalry,
leaving the main body of infantry to follow. But in view of the state
of the country, it is most unlikely that he would thus separate himself
from them, nor is this necessarily to be inferred from the account of
Tacitus. He received the refugees *in partem agminis*, which suggests an
infantry column of route. *Iam*, at the beginning of the next chapter,
may not refer to an accretion of strength through the meeting with
the main body, but to the gathering in of auxiliaries from the minor
posts along the line of retreat.

with him to certain destruction.   On the other hand, if he disobeyed orders and remained to protect Gloucester, Suetonius might not have enough troops to win the day. It evidently did not occur to him that, in such a case, the fate of Gloucester and the IInd legion was sealed anyway. Possibly he did not know that Suetonius' available field army was already reduced by the loss of the IXth.   However that may be, he made the wrong decision, and when the truth was revealed later, he committed suicide to avoid ·being cashiered.

Thus left in the lurch, Suetonius was in a perilous plight. To allow himself to be caught with his little army in an indefensible town like London was suicide.   If retreat might by any means save the military situation, he must not let pity for the helpless civil population stand in his way.   But which way could he go?   To make for the Channel coast would not help him, for he would miss the IInd legion, which, if it was moving at all, was advancing up the Fosse Way, or else along the road to Verulamium, to join him on Watling Street.   If he missed it, it would suffer the fate of the IXth; so might he and the half-legion he had left at Wroxeter.   The only course left was to fall back along Watling Street towards his base, hoping to pick up the missing IInd, or, if the worst came to the worst, to remain on the defensive at Wroxeter until such time as a new army could be sent from the continent.   Moreover, he had probably noticed places on the way down, where advantage of ground might counterbalance superiority of numbers, should his pursuers press him too hard.   So, shutting his ears to the prayers of those whom he was leaving to certain death, and taking into his column of route only those refugees who could march, he went back along Watling Street, gathering in as he went auxiliaries who had been called in from minor posts along the great roads.

No sooner had he gone than the furious Britons entered London behind him, sacked it, and massacred the inhabitants.   Then they set off to pursue Suetonius, but stopped to burn and slaughter at Verulamium.   Here and in Camulodunum and in London 70,000 are said to have been butchered.[1] This should have given Suetonius a good start, but the refugees retarded his march and consumed his provisions. Possibly this persuaded him to fight when the Britons came up with him. He had now about 10,000 men when, at some point on the line of Watling Street between Wroxeter and St. Albans, he turned to face his pursuers. The number of Britons said to have been killed in the decisive battle that followed bears a suspicious resemblance to the number of Roman settlers who had fallen in the massacre. Nevertheless Boudicca's army may well have numbered at least 100,000, and it was destroyed as an effective force. Guerrilla warfare was now all that the Romans had to fear, and Suetonius gathered together all the Roman troops in the island to stamp out the remnants of the revolt.

But the soldier was embittered by his experiences, and to such ruthless lengths did he go in exacting vengeance, that between famine and the Roman swords the British race was like to be extirpated. The province was saved by the new procurator, Julius Classicianus, a man of very different stamp from Catus, his disgraced predecessor. Seeing all hope of revenue gone for years to come, and that the return of prosperity was being indefinitely delayed by Suetonius' ruthless policy, he protested. He was over-ruled, but bravely stuck to his guns in face of the governor's superior authority. Tacitus' disparaging remarks about him betray the historian's lack of statesmanship and his personal bias. Suetonius was a brave soldier of the type that Tacitus admired. He had saved the Roman power in Britain, but the island now needed peace and a mild administration. That is why the general who was haunted by the memory of the atrocities he had been forced to witness had to be replaced. The inscription from the tomb of the man whose representations brought this home

---

[1] A large collection of pottery and glass, fire-stained and fused, which was found at Colchester some years ago and which belongs to this period, forms a material record of the disaster. [D. A.]

to the emperor has been dug up in London, and is now in the British Museum.[1] Suetonius was succeeded by Petronius Turpilianus, ' who, not provoking the enemy and not provoked by him, claimed the honourable name of peace for his slothful inactivity '. With this undeserved sneer Tacitus ends his account of that terrible year in Britain.

[1] See illustration, facing p. 80.

CORNELII TACITI

AB EXCESSV DIVI AVGVSTI
ANNALIVM

LIBER XIV

1. GAIO VIPSTANO *C.* Fonteio consulibus diu meditatum
scelus non ultra Nero distulit, uetustate imperii coalita
audacia et flagrantior in dies amore Poppaeae, quae sibi
matrimonium et discidium Octauiae incolumi Agrippina
haud sperans crebris criminationibus, aliquando per facetias
incusare [1] principem et pupillum uocare, qui iussis alienis
obnoxius non modo imperii sed libertatis etiam indigeret.
2 cur enim differri nuptias suas? formam scilicet displicere
et triumphalis auos. an fecunditatem et uerum animum?
timeri ne uxor saltem iniurias patrum, iram populi aduersus
superbiam auaritiamque matris aperiat. quod si nurum
Agrippina non nisi filio infestam ferre posset, redderetur
ipsa Othonis coniugio: ituram quoquo terrarum, ubi
audiret potius contumelias imperatoris quam uiseret peri-
3 culis eius immixta. haec atque talia lacrimis et arte
adulterae penetrantia nemo prohibebat, cupientibus cunc-
tis infringi potentiam matris et credente nullo usque ad
caedem eius duratura filii odia.

2. Tradit Cluuius ardore retinendae Agrippinam potentiae eo usque prouectam ut medio diei, cum id temporis
Nero per uinum et epulas incalesceret, offerret se saepius
temulento comptam et incesto paratam; iamque lasciua
oscula et praenuntias flagitii blanditias adnotantibus proxi-

---

[1] incusaret . . . uocaret *O.T.*

55

mis, Senecam contra muliebris inlecebras subsidium a
femina petiuisse, immissamque Acten libertam quae simul
suo periculo et infamia Neronis anxia deferret peruulgatum
esse incestum gloriante matre, nec toleraturos milites pro-
2 fani principis imperium. Fabius Rusticus non Agrippinae
sed Neroni cupitum id memorat eiusdemque libertae astu
disiectum. sed quae Cluuius eadem ceteri quoque auctores prodidere, et fama huc inclinat, seu concepit animo
tantum immanitatis Agrippina, seu credibilior nouae
libidinis meditatio in ea uisa est quae puellaribus annis
stuprum cum Lepido spe dominationis admiserat, pari
cupidine usque ad libita Pallantis prouoluta et exercita ad
omne flagitium patrui nuptiis.

3. Igitur Nero uitare secretos eius congressus, absce-
dentem in hortos aut Tusculanum uel Antiatem in agrum
laudare quod otium capesseret. postremo, ubicumque
haberetur, praegrauem ratus interficere constituit, hactenus
2 consultans, ueneno an ferro uel qua alia ui. placuitque
primo uenenum. sed inter epulas principis si daretur, re-
ferri ad casum non poterat tali iam Britannici exitio; et
ministros temptare arduum uidebatur mulieris usu scelerum
aduersus insidias intentae; atque ipsa praesumendo remedia
munierat corpus. ferrum et caedes quonam modo occulta-
retur nemo reperiebat; et ne quis illi tanto facinori delectus
3 iussa sperneret metuebat. obtulit ingenium Anicetus libertus, classi apud Misenum praefectus et pueritiae Neronis
educator ac mutuis odiis Agrippinae inuisus. ergo nauem
posse componi docet cuius pars ipso in mari per artem
soluta effunderet ignaram: nihil tam capax fortuitorum
quam mare; et si naufragio intercepta sit, quem adeo
iniquum ut sceleri adsignet quod uenti et fluctus deliquerint? additurum principem defunctae templum et aras et
cetera ostentandae pietati.

4. Placuit sollertia, tempore etiam iuta, quando Quinquatruum festos dies apud Baias frequentabat. illuc matrem elicit, ferendas parentium iracundias et placandum
animum dictitans quo rumorem reconciliationis efficeret
acciperetque Agrippina facili feminarum credulitate ad

gaudia. uenientem dehinc obuius in litora (nam Antio
aduentabat) excepit manu et complexu ducitque Baulos.
id uillae nomen est quae promunturium Misenum inter et
2 Baianum lacum flexo mari adluitur. stabat inter alias
nauis ornatior, tamquam id quoque honori matris daretur:
quippe sueuerat triremi et classiariorum remigio uehi. ac
tum inuitata ad epulas erat ut occultando facinori nox
adhiberetur. satis constitit extitisse proditorem et Agrippinam auditis insidiis, an crederet ambiguam, gestamine
3 sellae Baias peruectam. ibi blandimentum subleuauit
metum, comiter excepta superque ipsum conlocata. iam
pluribus sermonibus modo familiaritate iuuenili Nero et
rursus adductus, quasi seria consociaret, tracto in longum
conuictu, prosequitur abeuntem, artius oculis et pectori
haerens, siue explenda simulatione, seu periturae matris
supremus aspectus quamuis ferum animum retinebat.

5. Noctem sideribus inlustrem et placido mari quietam
quasi conuincendum ad scelus dii praebuere. nec multum
erat progressa nauis, duobus e numero familiarium Agrippinam comitantibus, ex quis Crepereius Gallus haud procul
gubernaculis adstabat, Acerronia super pedes cubitantis
reclinis paenitentiam filii et reciperatam matris gratiam per
gaudium memorabat, cum dato signo ruere tectum loci
multo plumbo graue, pressusque Crepereius et statim exani-
2 matus est: Agrippina et Acerronia eminentibus lecti parie-
tibus ac forte ualidioribus quam ut oneri cederent protectae
sunt. nec dissolutio nauigii sequebatur, turbatis omnibus
et quod plerique ignari etiam conscios impediebant. uisum
dehinc remigibus unum in latus inclinare atque ita nauem
submergere: sed neque ipsis promptus in rem subitam
consensus, et alii contra nitentes dedere facultatem lenioris
3 in mare iactus. uerum Acerronia, imprudentia dum se
Agrippinam esse utque subueniretur matri principis clami-
tat, contis et remis et quae fors obtulerat naualibus telis
conficitur: Agrippina silens eoque minus adgnita (unum
tamen uulnus umero excepit) nando, deinde occursu
lenunculorum Lucrinum in lacum uecta uillae suae
infertur.

6. Illic reputans ideo se fallacibus litteris accitam et
honore praecipuo habitam, quodque litus iuxta non uentis
acta, non saxis impulsa nauis summa sui parte ueluti ter-
restre machinamentum concidisset; obseruans etiam Acerroniae necem, simul suum uulnus aspiciens, solum insidiarum remedium esse sensit,[1] si non intellegerentur;
misitque libertum Agerinum qui nuntiaret filio benignitate
deum et fortuna eius euasisse grauem casum; orare ut
quamuis periculo matris exterritus uisendi curam differret;
2 sibi ad praesens quiete opus. atque interim securitate
simulata medicamina uulneri et fomenta corpori adhibet;
testamentum Acerroniae requiri bonaque obsignari iubet,
id tantum non per simulationem.

7. At Neroni nuntios patrati facinoris opperienti adfertur
euasisse ictu leui sauciam et hactenus adito discrimine ne
auctor dubitaretur. tum pauore exanimis et iam iamque
adfore obtestans uindictae properam, siue seruitia armaret
uel militem accenderet, siue ad senatum et populum peruа-
deret, naufragium et uulnus et interfectos amicos obiciendo:
2 quod contra subsidium sibi? nisi quid Burrus et Seneca
expedirent; quos statim acciuerat, incertum an et ante ignaros.[2] igitur longum utriusque silentium ne inriti dis-
suaderent, an eo descensum credebant, *ut*, nisi praeueniretur
3 Agrippina, pereundum Neroni esset. post Seneca hactenus promptius *ut* respiceret Burrum ac sciscitaretur an
militi imperanda caedes esset. ille praetorianos toti
Caesarum domui obstrictos memoresque Germanici nihil
aduersus progeniem eius atrox ausuros respondit: perpetraret Anicetus promissa. qui nihil cunctatus poscit summam sceleris. ad eam uocem Nero illo sibi die dari
imperium auctoremque tanti muneris libertum profitetur:
4 iret propere duceretque promptissimos ad iussa. ipse
audito uenisse missu Agrippinae nuntium Agerinum,
scaenam ultro criminis parat gladiumque, dum mandata
perfert, abicit inter pedes eius, tum quasi deprehenso
uincla inici iubet, ut exitium principis molitam matrem

---

[1] sensit *post* esse *om. O.T.*
[2] Seneca; quos expergens: gnaros *O.T.*

et pudore deprehensi sceleris sponte mortem sumpsisse confingeret.

8. Interim uulgato Agrippinae periculo, quasi casu euenisset, ut quisque acceperat, decurrere ad litus. hi molium obiectus, hi proximas scaphas scandere; alii quantum corpus sinebat uadere in mare; quidam manus protendere; questibus, uotis, clamore diuersa rogitantium aut incerta respondentium omnis ora compleri; adfluere ingens multitudo cum luminibus, atque ubi incolumem esse pernotuit, ut ad gratandum sese expedire, donec aspectu armati et mini-
2 tantis agminis disiecti sunt. Anicetus uillam statione circumdat refractaque ianua obuios seruorum abripit, donec ad foris cubiculi ueniret; cui pauci adstabant, ceteris terrore inrumpentium exterritis. cubiculo modicum lumen inerat et ancillarum una, magis ac magis anxia Agrippina quod nemo a filio ac ne Agerinus quidem: aliam fore laetae rei faciem; nunc solitudinem ac repentinos strepitus
3 et extremi mali indicia. abeunte dehinc ancilla ' tu quoque me descris ' prolocuta respicit Anicetum trierarcho Herculeio et Obarito centurione classiario comitatum : ac, si ad uisendum uenisset, refotam nuntiaret, sin facinus patraturus, nihil se de filio credere; non imperatum parri-
4 cidium. circumsistunt lectum percussores et prior trierarchus fusti caput eius adflixit. iam in mortem centurioni ferrum destringenti protendens uterum ' uentrem feri ' exclamauit multisque uulneribus confecta est.

9. Haec consensu produntur. aspexeritne matrem exanimem Nero et formam corporis eius laudauerit, sunt qui tradiderint, sunt qui abnuant. cremata est nocte eadem conuiuali lecto et exequiis uilibus; neque, dum Nero rerum potiebatur, congesta aut clausa humus. mox domesticorum cura leuem tumulum accepit, uiam Miseni propter et uillam Caesaris dictatoris quae subiectos sinus
2 editissima prospectat. accenso rogo libertus eius cognomento Mnester se ipse ferro transegit, incertum caritate in patronam an metu exitii. hunc sui finem multos ante annos crediderat Agrippina contempseratque. nam consulenti super Nerone responderunt Chaldaei fore ut

imperaret matremque occideret; atque illa 'occidat' inquit, 'dum imperet.'

10. Sed a Caesare perfecto demum scelere magnitudo eius intellecta est. reliquo noctis modo per silentium defixus, saepius pauore exsurgens et mentis inops lucem opperiebatur tamquam exitium adlaturam. atque eum auctore Burro prima centurionum tribunorumque adulatio ad spem firmauit, prensantium manum gratantiumque quod discrimen improuisum et matris facinus euasisset. amici dehinc adire templa et coepto exemplo proxima Campaniae 2 municipia uictimis et legationibus laetitiam testari: ipse diuersa simulatione maestus et quasi incolumitati suae infensus ac morti parentis inlacrimans. quia tamen non, ut hominum uultus, ita locorum facies mutantur, obuersaba-turque maris illius et litorum grauis aspectus (et erant qui crederent sonitum tubae collibus circum editis planctusque tumulo matris audiri), Neapolim concessit litterasque ad senatum misit quarum summa erat repertum cum ferro percussorem Agerinum, ex intimis Agrippinae libertis, et luisse eam poenas conscientia quasi scelus parauisset.

11. Adiciebat crimina longius repetita, quod consortium imperii iuraturasque in feminae uerba praetorias cohortis idemque dedecus senatus et populi sperauisset, ac postquam frustra habita sit, infensa militi patribusque et plebi dissua-sisset donatiuum et congiarium periculaque uiris inlustribus struxisset. quanto suo labore perpetratum ne inrumperet 2 curiam, ne gentibus externis responsa daret. temporum quoque Claudianorum obliqua insectatione cuncta eius dominationis flagitia in matrem transtulit, publica fortuna extinctam referens. namque et naufragium narrabat: quod fortuitum fuisse quis adeo hebes inueniretur ut cre-deret? aut a muliere naufraga missum cum telo unum 3 qui cohortis et classis imperatoris perfringeret? ergo non iam Nero, cuius immanitas omnium questus antibat, sed Seneca aduerso rumore erat quod oratione tali confessionem scripsisset.

12. Miro tamen certamine procerum decernuntur suppli-cationes apud omnia puluinaria, utque Quinquatrus quibus

apertae insidiae essent ludis annuis celebrarentur; aureum
Mineruae simulacrum in curia et iuxta principis imago sta-
tuerentur; dies natalis Agrippinae inter nefastos esset.
Thrasea Paetus silentio uel breui adsensu priores adulationes
transmittere solitus exiit tum senatu ac sibi causam peri-
2 culi fecit, ceteris libertatis initium non praebuit. prodigia
quoque crebra et inrita intercessere: anguem enixa mulier
et alia in concubitu mariti fulmine exanimata; iam sol
repente obscuratus et tactae de caelo quattuordecim urbis
regiones. quae adeo sine cura deum eueniebant ut
multos post annos Nero imperium et scelera continuauerit.
3 ceterum quo grauaret inuidiam matris eaque demota
auctam lenitatem suam testificaretur, feminas inlustris
Iuniam et Calpurniam, praetura functos Valerium Capitonem et Licinium Gabolum sedibus patriis reddidit, ab
4 Agrippina olim pulsos. etiam Lolliae Paulinae cineres
reportari sepulcrumque extrui permisit; quosque ipse
nuper relegauerat, Iturium et Caluisium poena exoluit.
nam Silana fato functa erat, longinquo ab exilio Tarentum
regressa labante iam Agrippina, cuius inimicitiis conci-
derat, uel mitigata.

13. Tamen cunctari in oppidis Campaniae, quonam
modo urbem ingrederetur, an obsequium senatus, an studia
plebis reperiret anxius: contra deterrimus quisque,
quorum non alia regia fecundior extitit, inuisum Agrippinae nomen et morte eius accensum populi fauorem dis-
serunt: iret intrepidus et uenerationem sui coram ex-
2 periretur; simul praegredi exposcunt. et promptiora
quam promiserant inueniunt, obuias tribus, festo cultu
senatum, coniugum ac liberorum agmina per sexum et
aetatem disposita, extructos, qua incederet, spectaculorum
gradus, quo modo triumphi uisuntur. hinc superbus ac
publici seruitii uictor Capitolium adiit, grates exoluit seque
in omnis libidines effudit quas male coercitas qualiscumque
matris reuerentia tardauerat.

14. Vetus illi cupido erat curriculo quadrigarum insistere nec minus foedum studium cithara ludicrum in modum
canere. concertare equis regium et antiquis ducibus facti-

tatum memorabat idque uatum laudibus celebre et deorum
honori datum. enimuero cantus Apollini sacros, talique
ornatu adstare non modo Graecis in urbibus sed Romana
2 apud templa numen praecipuum et praescium. nec iam
sisti poterat, cum Senecae ac Burro uisum ne utraque
peruinceret alterum concedere. clausumque ualle Vaticana spatium in quo equos regeret haud promisco spectaculo: mox ultro uocari populus Romanus laudibusque
extollere, ut est uulgus cupiens uoluptatum et, si eodem
3 princeps trahat, laetum. ceterum euulgatus pudor non
satietatem, ut rebantur, sed incitamentum attulit. ratusque
dedecus molliri, si pluris foedasset, nobilium familiarum
posteros egestate uenalis in scaenam deduxit; quos fato
perfunctos ne nominatim tradam, maioribus eorum tri-
4 buendum puto. nam et eius flagitium est qui pecuniam
ob delicta potius dedit quam ne delinquerent. notos
quoque equites Romanos operas arenae promittere subegit
donis ingentibus, nisi quod merces ab eo qui iubere potest
uim necessitatis adfert.

15. Ne tamen adhuc publico theatro dehonestaretur,
instituit ludos Iuuenalium uocabulo, in quos passim nomina
data. non nobilitas cuiquam, non aetas aut acti honores
impedimento, quo minus Graeci Latiniue histrionis artem
2 exercerent usque ad gestus modosque haud uirilis. quin
et feminae inlustres deformia meditari; extructaque apud
nemus, quod nauali stagno circumposuit Augustus, conuenticula et cauponae et posita ueno inritamenta luxui.
dabanturque stipes quas boni necessitate, intemperantes
3 gloria consumerent. inde gliscere flagitia et infamia, nec
ulla moribus olim corruptis plus libidinum circumdedit
quam illa conluuies. uix artibus honestis pudor retinetur,
nedum inter certamina uitiorum pudicitia aut modestia aut
quicquam probi moris reseruaretur. postremus ipse scaenam incedit, multa cura temptans citharam et praemeditans adsistentibus phonascis. accesserat cohors militum,
centuriones tribunique et maerens Burrus ac laudans.
4 tuncque primum conscripti sunt equites Romani cognomento Augustianorum, aetate ac robore conspicui et pars

ingenio procaces, alii in·spem potentiae. ii dies ac noctes plausibus personare, formam principis uocemque deum uocabulis appellantes; quasi per uirtutem clari honoratique agere.

16. Ne tamen ludicrae tantum imperatoris artes notescerent, carminum quoque studium adfectauit, contractis quibus aliqua pangendi facultas necdum insignis erat. hi cenati considere simul et adlatos uel ibidem repertos uersus conectere atque ipsius uerba quoquo modo prolata supplere, quod species ipsa carminum docet, non 2 impetu et instinctu nec ore uno fluens. etiam sapientiae doctoribus tempus impertiebat post epulas, utque contraria adseuerantium discordia frueretur. nec deerant qui ore uultuque tristi inter oblectamenta regia spectari cuperent.

17. Sub idem tempus leui initio atrox caedes orta inter colonos Nucerinos Pompeianosque gladiatorio spectaculo quod Liuineius Regulus, quem motum senatu rettuli, edebat. quippe oppidana lasciuia in uicem incessentes probra, dein saxa, postremo ferrum sumpsere, ualidiore Pompeianorum plebe, apud quos spectaculum edebatur. ergo deportati sunt in urbem multi e Nucerinis trunco per uulnera corpore, ac plerique liberorum aut parentum 2 mortis deflebant. cuius rei iudicium princeps senatui, senatus consulibus permisit. et rursus re ad patres relata, prohibiti publice in decem annos eius modi coetu Pompeiani collegiaque quae contra leges instituerant dissoluta; Liuineius et qui alii seditionem conciuerant exilio multati sunt.

18. Motus senatu et Pedius Blaesus, accusantibus Cyrenensibus uiolatum ab eo thesaurum Aesculapii dilectumque militarem pretio et ambitione corruptum. idem Cyrenenses reum agebant Acilium Strabonem, praetoria potestate usum et missum disceptatorem a Claudio agrorum, quos regis Apionis quondam auitos et populo Romano cum regno relictos proximus quisque possessor inuaserant, diutinaque licentia et iniuria quasi iure et aequo nite-2 bantur. igitur abiudicatis agris orta aduersus iudicem inuidia; et senatus ignota sibi esse mandata Claudii et

consulendum principem respondit. Nero probata Strabonis sententia se nihilo minus subuenire sociis et usurpata concedere scripsit.

19. Sequuntur uirorum inlustrium mortes, Domitii Afri et M. Seruilii, qui summis honoribus et multa eloquentia uiguerant, ille orando causas, Seruilius diu foro, mox tradendis rebus Romanis celebris et elegantia uitae quam clariorem effecit, ut par ingenio, ita morum diuersus.

20. Nerone quartum Cornelio Cosso consulibus quinquennale ludicrum Romae institutum est ad morem Graeci certaminis, uaria fama, ut cuncta ferme noua. quippe erant qui Gn. quoque Pompeium incusatum a senioribus
2 ferrent quod mansuram theatri sedem posuisset. nam antea subitariis gradibus et scaena in tempus structa ludos edi solitos, uel si uetustiora repetas, stantem populum spectauisse, ne, si consideret theatro, dies totos ignauia continuaret. spectaculorum quidem antiquitas seruaretur, quoties praetores ederent, nulla cuiquam ciuium necessitate
3 certandi. ceterum abolitos paulatim patrios mores funditus euerti per accitam lasciuiam, ut quod usquam corrumpi et corrumpere queat in urbe uisatur, degeneretque studiis externis iuuentus, gymnasia et otia et turpis amores exercendo, principe et senatu auctoribus, qui non modo licentiam uitiis permiserint, sed uim adhibeant *ut* proceres Romani specie orationum et carminum scaena polluantur.
4 quid superesse nisi ut corpora quoque nudent et caestus adsumant easque pugnas pro militia et armis meditentur? an iustitiam auctum iri et decurias equitum egregium iudicandi munus melius[1] expleturos, si fractos sonos et dulcedinem uocum perite audissent? noctes quoque dedecori adiectas ne quod tempus pudori relinquatur, sed coetu promisco, quod perditissimus quisque per diem concupiuerit, per tenebras audeat.

21. Pluribus ipsa licentia placebat, ac tamen honesta nomina praetendebant. maiores quoque non abhorruisse spectaculorum oblectamentis pro fortuna quae tum erat, eoque a Tuscis accitos histriones, a Thuriis equorum certa-

[1] melius *om. O.T.*

COINS OF NERO (slightly enlarged)

(Notice that on one of them, from the early part of the reign, the head of Agrippina is portrayed on an equality with Nero's.)

mina; et possessa Achaia Asiaque ludos curatius editos.
nec quemquam Romae honesto loco ortum ad theatralis
artes degenerauisse, ducentis iam annis a L. Mummii
triumpho qui primus id genus spectaculi in urbe praebuerit.
2 sed et consultum parsimoniae quod perpetua sedes theatro
locata sit potius quam immenso sumptu singulos per annos
consurgeret ac destrueretur.   nec perinde magistratus rem
familiarem exhausturos aut populo efflagitandi Graeca certamina a magistratibus causam fore, cum eo sumptu res pu-
3 blica fungatur.   oratorum ac uatum uictorias incitamentum
ingeniis adlaturas; nec cuiquam iudici graue auris studiis
honestis et uoluptatibus concessis impertire.   laetitiae
magis quam lasciuiae dari paucas totius quinquennii
noctes, quibus tanta luce ignium nihil inlicitum occultari
4 queat.   sane nullo insigni dehonestamento id spectaculum transiit; ac ne modica quidem studia plebis
exarsere, quia redditi quamquam scaenae pantomimi
certaminibus sacris prohibebantur.   eloquentiae primas
nemo tulit, sed uictorem esse Caesarem pronuntiatum.
Graeci amictus quis per eos dies plerique incesserant tum
exoleuerunt.

22. Inter quae sidus cometes effulsit; de quo uulgi
opinio est tamquam mutationem regis portendat.   igitur
quasi iam depulso Nerone, quisnam deligeretur anquire-
bant; et omnium ore Rubellius Plautus celebratur, cui
nobilitas per matrem ex Iulia familia. ipse placita
maiorum colebat, habitu seuero, casta et secreta domo,
quantoque metu occultior, tanto plus famae adeptus.
2 auxit rumorem pari uanitate orta interpretatio fulguris.
nam quia discumbentis Neronis apud Simbruina stagna
in uilla cui Sublaqueum nomen est ictae dapes mensaque
disiecta erat idque finibus Tiburtum acciderat, unde
paterna Plauto origo, hunc illum numine deum destinari
credebant, fouebantque multi quibus noua et ancipitia
3 praecolere auida et plerumque fallax ambitio est.   ergo
permotus his Nero componit ad Plautum litteras, consuleret
quieti urbis seque praua diffamantibus subtraheret: esse
illi per Asiam auitos agros in quibus tuta et inturbida

iuuenta frueretur. ita illuc cum coniuge Antistia et paucis familiarium concessit.

4 Isdem diebus nimia luxus cupido infamiam et periculum Neroni tulit, quia fontem aquae Marciae ad urbem deductae nando incesserat; uidebaturque potus sacros et caerimoniam loci corpore loto polluisse. secutaque anceps ualetudo iram deum adfirmauit.

23. At Corbulo post deleta Artaxata utendum recenti terrore ratus ad occupanda Tigranocerta, quibus excisis metum hostium intenderet uel, si pepercisset, clementiae famam adipisceretur, illuc pergit, non infenso exercitu ne spem ueniae auferret, neque tamen remissa cura, gnarus facilem mutatu gentem, ut segnem ad pericula ita infidam 2 ad occasiones. barbari, pro ingenio quisque, alii preces offerre, quidam deserere uicos et in auia digredi; ac fuere qui se speluncis et carissima secum abderent. igitur dux Romanus diuersis artibus, misericordia aduersum supplices, celeritate aduersus profugos, immitis iis qui latebras insederant ora et exitus specuum sarmentis uirgultisque com-3 pletos igni exurit. atque illum finis suos praegredientem incursauere Mardi, latrociniis exerciti contraque inrumpentem montibus defensi; quos Corbulo immissis Hiberis uastauit hostilemque audaciam externo sanguine ultus est.

24. Ipse exercitusque ut nullis ex proelio damnis ita per inopiam et labores fatiscebant, carne pecudum propulsare famem adacti; ad hoc penuria aquae, feruida aestas, longinqua itinera sola ducis patientia mitigabantur, eadem pluraque gregario milite tolerantis. uentum dehinc in locos cultos demessaeque segetes, et ex duobus castellis in quae confugerant Armenii alterum impetu captum; qui 2 primam uim depulerant, obsidione coguntur. unde in regionem Tauraunitium transgressus improuisum periculum uitauit. nam haud procul tentorio eius non ignobilis barbarus cum telo repertus ordinem insidiarum seque auctorem et socios per tormenta edidit, conuictique et 3 puniti sunt qui specie amicitiae dolum parabant. nec multo post legati Tigranocerta missi patere moenia adferunt, intentos popularis ad iussa: simul hospitale donum, coronam auream, tradebant. accepitque cum honore, nec quicquam urbi detractum quo promptius obsequium integri retinerent.

25. At praesidium Legerda quod ferox iuuentus clauserat non sine certamine expugnatum est: nam et proelium pro muris ausi erant et pulsi intra munimenta aggeri demum et inrumpentium armis cessere. quae facilius proueniebant, 2 quia Parthi Hyrcano bello distinebantur. miserantque Hyrcani ad principem Romanum societatem oratum, attineri a se Vologesen pro pignore amicitiae ostentantes. eos regredientis Corbulo, ne Euphraten transgressi hostium custodiis circumuenirentur, dato praesidio ad litora maris rubri deduxit, unde uitatis Parthorum finibus patrias in sedes remeauere.

26. Quin et Tiridaten per Medos extrema Armeniae intrantem praemisso cum auxiliis Verulano legato atque ipse legionibus citis abire procul ac spem belli amittere subegit; quosque nobis auersos animis cognouerat, caedibus et incendiis perpopulatus possessionem Armeniae usurpabat, cum aduenit Tigranes a Nerone ad capessendum imperium delectus, Cappadocum ex nobilitate, regis Archelai nepos, sed quod diu obses apud urbem fuerat, usque ad 2 seruilem patientiam demissus. nec consensu acceptus, durante apud quosdam fauore Arsacidarum: at plerique superbiam Parthorum perosi datum a Romanis regem malebant. additum et praesidium mille legionarii, tres sociorum cohortes duaeque equitum alae, et quo facilius nouum regnum tueretur, pars Armeniae, ut cuique finitima, Pharasmani Polemonique et Aristobulo atque Antiocho parere iussae sunt. Corbulo in Syriam abscessit, morte Vmmidii legati uacuam ac sibi permissam.

27. Eodem anno ex inlustribus Asiae urbibus Laodicea tremore terrae prolapsa nullo *a* nobis remedio propriis opibus reualuit. at in Italia uetus oppidum Puteoli ius coloniae et cognomentum a Nerone apiscuntur. ueterani Tarentum et Antium adscripti non tamen infrequentiae locorum subuenere, dilapsis pluribus in prouincias in quibus stipendia expleuerant; neque coniugiis suscipiendis neque

alendis liberis sueti orbas sine posteris domos relinquebant.
2 non enim, ut olim, uniuersae legiones deducebantur cum
tribunis et centurionibus et sui cuiusque ordinis militibus ut
consensu et caritate rem publicam efficerent, sed ignoti
inter se, diuersis manipulis, sine rectore, sine adfectibus
mutuis, quasi ex alio genere mortalium repente in unum
collecti, numerus magis quam colonia.

28. Comitia praetorum arbitrio senatus haberi solita,
quod acriore ambitu exarserant, princeps composuit, tres
qui supra numerum petebant legioni praeficiendo. auxitque patrum honorem statuendo ut, qui a priuatis iudicibus
ad senatum prouocauissent, eiusdem pecuniae periculum
facerent cuius si qui imperatorem appellarent; nam antea
2 uacuum id solutumque poena fuerat. fine anni Vibius
Secundus eques Romanus accusantibus Mauris repetundarum damnatur atque Italia exigitur, ne grauiore
poena adficeretur Vibii Crispi fratris opibus enisus.

29. Caesennio Paeto et Petronio Turpiliano consulibus
grauis clades in Britannia accepta; in qua neque A. Didius
legatus, ut memoraui, nisi parta retinuerat, et successor
Veranius modicis excursibus Siluras populatus, quin ultra
bellum proferret, morte prohibitus est, magna, dum uixit,
seueritatis fama, supremis testamenti uerbis ambitionis
manifestus: quippe multa in Neronem adulatione addidit
subiecturum ei prouinciam fuisse, si biennio proximo uixisset. sed tum Paulinus Suetonius obtinebat Britannos,
scientia militiae et rumore populi qui neminem sine aemulo
sinit, Corbulonis concertator, receptaeque Armeniae decus
aequare domitis perduellibus cupiens. igitur Monam in-
sulam, incolis ualidam et receptaculum perfugarum,
adgredi parat, nauisque fabricatur plano alueo aduersus
breue et incertum. sic pedes; equites uado secuti aut
altiores inter undas adnantes equis tramisere.

30. Stabat pro litore diuersa acies, densa armis uirisque,
intercursantibus feminis; in modum Furiarum ueste ferali,
crinibus deiectis faces praeferebant; Druidaeque circum,
preces, diras sublatis ad caelum manibus fundentes, nouⁱ-
tate aspectus perculere militem ut quasi haerentibus

2 membris immobile corpus uulneribus praeberent. dein cohortationibus ducis et se ipsi stimulantes ne muliebre et fanaticum agmen pauescerent, inferunt signa sternuntque obuios et igni suo inuoluunt. praesidium posthac impositum uictis excisique luci saeuis superstitionibus sacri: nam cruore captiuo adolere aras et hominum fibris consulere deos fas habebant. haec agenti Suetonio repentina defectio prouinciae nuntiatur.

31. Rex Icenorum Prasutagus, longa opulentia clarus, Caesarem heredem duasque filias scripserat, tali obsequio ratus regnumque et domum suam procul iniuria fore. quod contra uertit, adeo ut regnum per centuriones, domus per seruos uelut capta uastarentur. iam primum uxor eius Boudicca uerberibus adfecta et filiae stupro uiolatae sunt: praecipui quique Icenorum, quasi cunctam regionem muneri accepissent, auitis bonis exuuntur, et propinqui
2 regis inter mancipia habebantur. qua contumelia et metu grauiorum, quando in formam prouinciae cesserant, rapiunt arma, commotis ad rebellationem Trinouantibus et qui alii nondum seruitio fracti resumere libertatem occultis coniurationibus pepigerant, acerrimo in ueteranos odio. quippe in coloniam Camulodunum recens deducti pellebant domibus, exturbabant agris, captiuos, seruos appellando, fouentibus impotentiam ueteranorum militibus
3 similitudine uitae et spe eiusdem licentiae. ad hoc templum diuo Claudio constitutum quasi arx aeternae dominationis aspiciebatur, delectique sacerdotes specie religionis omnis fortunas effundebant. nec arduum uidebatur excindere coloniam nullis munimentis saeptam; quod ducibus nostris parum prouisum erat, dum amoenitati prius quam usui consulitur.

32. Inter quae nulla palam causa delapsum Camuloduni simulacrum Victoriae ac retro conuersum quasi cederet hostibus. et feminae in furorem turbatae adesse exitium canebant, externosque fremitus in curia eorum auditos; consonuisse ululatibus theatrum uisamque speciem in aestuario Tamesae subuersae coloniae: iam Oceanus cruento aspectu, dilabente aestu humanorum corporum effigies

relictae, ut Britannis ad spem, ita ueteranis ad metum
2 trahebantur. sed quia procul Suetonius aberat, petiuere
a Cato Deciano procuratore auxilium. ille haud amplius
quam ducentos sine iustis armis misit; et inerat modica
militum manus. tutela templi freti et impedientibus qui
occulti rebellionis conscii consilia turbabant, neque fossam
aut uallum praeduxerunt, neque motis senibus et feminis
iuuentus sola restitit: quasi media pace incauti multitudine
3 barbarorum circumueniuntur. et cetera quidem impetu
direpta aut incensa sunt: templum in quo se miles conglo-
bauerat biduo obsessum expugnatumque. et uictor Bri-
tannus Petilio Ceriali, legato legionis nonae, in subsidium
aduentanti obuius fudit legionem et quod peditum interfecit: Cerialis cum equitibus euasit in castra et munimentis
defensus est. qua clade et odiis prouinciae quam auaritia
eius in bellum egerat trepidus procurator Catus in Galliam
transiit.

33. At Suetonius mira constantia medios inter hostis
Londinium perrexit, cognomento quidem coloniae non
insigne, sed copia negotiatorum et commeatuum maxime
celebre. ibi ambiguus an illam sedem bello deligeret, circumspecta infrequentia militis, satisque magnis documentis
temeritatem Petilii coercitam, unius oppidi damno seruare
uniuersa statuit. neque fletu et lacrimis auxilium eius
orantium flexus est quin daret profectionis signum et comitantis in partem agminis acciperet: si quos imbellis sexus
aut fessa aetas uel loci dulcedo attinuerat ab hoste oppressi
2 sunt. eadem clades municipio Verulamio fuit, quia barbari
omissis castellis praesidiisque militarium, quod uberrimum
spolianti et defendentibus intutum, laeti praeda et aliorum
segnes petebant. ad septuaginta milia ciuium et sociorum
iis quae memoraui locis cecidisse constitit. neque enim
capere aut uenundare aliudue quod belli commercium, sed
caedes patibula ignes cruces, tamquam reddituri supplicium
at praerepta interim ultione, festinabant.

34. Iam Suetonio quarta decima legio cum uexillariis
uicesimanis et *e* proximis auxiliares, decem ferme milia
armatorum erant, cum omittere cunctationem et congredi

acie parat. deligitque locum artis faucibus et a tergo silua
clausum, satis cognito nihil hostium nisi in fronte et aper-
2 tam planitiem esse sine metu insidiarum. igitur legionarius
frequens ordinibus, leuis circum armatura, conglobatus pro
cornibus eques adstitit. at Britannorum copiae passim per
cateruas et turmas exultabant, quanta non alias multitudo,
et animo adeo feroci ut coniuges quoque testis uictoriae
secum traherent plaustrisque imponerent quae super extremum ambitum campi posuerant.

35. Boudicca curru filias prae se uehens, ut quamque
nationem accesserat, solitum quidem Britannis feminarum
ductu bellare testabatur, sed tunc non ut tantis maioribus
ortam regnum et opes, uerum ut unam e uulgo libertatem
amissam, confectum uerberibus corpus, contrectatam filia-
2 rum pudicitiam ulcisci. eo prouectas Romanorum cupi-
dines ut non corpora, ne senectam quidem aut uirginitatem
impollutam relinquant. adesse tamen deos iustae uindictae: cecidisse legionem quae proelium ausa sit; ceteros
castris occultari aut fugam circumspicere. ne strepitum
quidem et clamorem tot milium, nedum impetus et manus
perlaturos: si copias armatorum, si causas belli secum
expenderent, uincendum illa acie uel cadendum esse. id
mulieri destinatum: uiuerent uiri et seruirent.

36. Ne Suetonius quidem in tanto discrimine silebat:
quamquam confideret uirtuti, tamen exhortationes et preces
miscebat ut spernerent sonores barbarorum et inanis minas:
plus illic feminarum quam iuuentutis aspici. imbellis,
inermis cessuros statim ubi ferrum uirtutemque uincentium
2 toties fusi adgnouissent. etiam in multis legionibus paucos
qui proelia profligarent; gloriaeque eorum accessurum
quod modica manus uniuersi exercitus famam adipisceren-
tur. conferti tantum et pilis emissis post umbonibus et
gladiis stragem caedemque continuarent, praedae im-
3 memores: parta uictoria cuncta ipsis cessura. is ardor
uerba ducis sequebatur, ita se ad intorquenda pila expe-
dierat uetus miles et multa proeliorum experientia ut
certus euentus Suetonius daret pugnae signum.

37. Ac primum legio gradu immota et angustias loci pro

munimento retinens, postquam in propius suggressos hostis
certo iactu tela exhauserat, uelut cuneo erupit. idem auxiliarium impetus; et eques protentis hastis perfringit quod
obuium et ualidum erat. ceteri terga praebuere, difficili
effugio, quia circumiecta uehicula saepserant abitus. et
miles ne mulierum quidem neci temperabat, confixaque
2 telis etiam iumenta corporum cumulum auxerant. clara et
antiquis uictoriis par ea die laus parta: quippe sunt qui
paulo minus quam octoginta milia Britannorum cecidisse
tradant, militum quadringentis ferme interfectis nec multo
3 amplius uulneratis. Boudicca uitam ueneno finiuit. et
Poenius Postumus, praefectus castrorum secundae legionis,
cognitis quartadecimanorum uicesimanorumque prosperis
rebus, quia pari gloria legionem suam fraudauerat abnue-
ratque contra ritum militiae iussa ducis, se ipse gladio
transegit.

38. Contractus deinde omnis exercitus sub pellibus
habitus est ad reliqua belli perpetranda. auxitque copias
Caesar missis ex Germania duobus legionariorum milibus,
octo auxiliarium cohortibus ac mille equitibus, quorum
2 aduentu nonani legionario milite suppleti sunt. cohortes
alaeque nouis hibernaculis locatae quodque nationum am-
biguum aut aduersum fuerat igni atque ferro uastatur.[1]
sed nihil aeque quam fames adfligebat serendis frugibus
incuriosos, et omni aetate ad bellum uersa, dum nostros
3 commeatus sibi destinant. gentesque praeferoces tardius
ad pacem inclinabant, quia Iulius Classicianus, successor
Cato missus et Suetonio discors, bonum publicum priuatis
simultatibus impediebat disperseratque nouum legatum
opperiendum esse, sine hostili ira et superbia uictoris cle-
menter deditis consulturum. simul in urbem mandabat,
nullum proeliorum finem expectarent, nisi succederetur
Suetonio, cuius aduersa prauitati ipsius, prospera ad fortunam referebat.

39. Igitur ad spectandum Britanniae statum missus est
e libertis Polyclitus, magna Neronis spe posse auctoritate
eius non modo inter legatum procuratoremque concordiam

uastatum *O.T.*

2 gigni, sed et rebellis barbarum animos pace componi. nec defuit Polyclitus quo minus ingenti agmine Italiae Galliaeque grauis, postquam Oceanum transmiserat, militibus quoque nostris terribilis incederet. sed hostibus inrisui fuit apud quos flagrante etiam tum libertate nondum cognita libertinorum potentia erat; mirabanturque quod dux et 3 exercitus tanti belli confector seruitiis oboedirent. cuncta tamen ad imperatorem in mollius relata; detentusque rebus gerundis Suetonius, quod postea paucas nauis in litore remigiumque in iis amiserat, tamquam durante bello tradere exercitum Petronio Turpiliano qui iam consulatu abierat iubetur. is non inritato hoste neque lacessitus honestum pacis nomen segni otio imposuit.

40. Eodem anno Romae insignia scelera, alterum senatoris, seruili alterum audacia, admissa sunt. Domitius Balbus erat praetorius, simul longa senecta, simul orbitate 2 et pecunia insidiis obnoxius. ei propinquus Valerius Fabianus, capessendis honoribus destinatus, subdidit testamentum adscitis Vinicio Rufino et Terentio Lentino equitibus Romanis. illi Antonium Primum et Asinium Marcellum sociauerant. Antonius audacia promptus, Marcellus Asinio Pollione proauo clarus neque morum spernendus habebatur nisi quod paupertatem praecipuum malorum 3 credebat. igitur Fabianus tabulas ascitis [1] quos memoraui et aliis minus inlustribus obsignat. quod apud patres conuictum et Fabianus Antoniusque cum Rufino et Terentio lege Cornelia damnantur. Marcellum memoria maiorum et preces Caesaris poenae magis quam infamiae exemere.

41. Perculit is dies Pompeium quoque Aelianum, iuuenem quaestorium, tamquam flagitiorum Fabiani gnarum, eique Italia et Hispania in qua ortus erat interdictum est. pari ignominia Valerius Ponticus adficitur quod reos ne apud praefectum urbis arguerentur ad praetorem detulisset, interim specie legum, mox praeuaricando ultionem elusurus. additur senatus consulto, qui talem operam emptitasset uendidissetue perinde poena teneretur ac publico iudicio calumniae condemnatus.

[1] ascitis *Kiessling*: sociis *O.T.*

42. Haud multo post praefectum urbis Pedanium Secundum seruus ipsius interfecit, seu negata libertate cui
pretium pepigerat siue amore exoleti incensus et dominum
2 aemulum non tolerans. ceterum cum uetere ex more
familiam omnem quae sub eodem tecto mansitauerat ad
supplicium agi oporteret, concursu plebis quae tot innoxios
protegebat usque ad seditionem uentum est. senatu[1] quoque
in ipso erant studia nimiam seueritatem aspernantium,
pluribus nihil mutandum censentibus. ex quis C. Cassius
sententiae loco in hunc modum disseruit:

43. 'Saepe numero, patres conscripti, in hoc ordine
inter.ui, cum contra instituta et leges maiorum noua
senatus decreta postularentur; neque sum aduersatus, non
quia dubitarem super omnibus negotiis melius atque rectius
olim prouisum et quae conuerterentur ad [2] deterius mutari,
sed ne nimio amore antiqui moris studium meum extollere
2 uiderer. simul quidquid hoc in nobis auctoritatis est
crebris contradictionibus destruendum non existimabam,
ut maneret integrum si quando res publica consiliis eguisset.
quod hodie uenit consulari uiro domi suae interfecto per
insidias seruilis, quas nemo prohibuit aut prodidit quamuis
nondum concusso senatus consulto quod supplicium toti
3 familiae minitabatur. decernite hercule impunitatem: ut[3]
quem dignitas sua defendat, cum praefecto urbis non profuerit? quem numerus seruorum tuebitur, cum Pedanium
Secundum quadringenti non protexerint? cui familia
opem feret, quae ne in metu quidem pericula nostra
4 aduertit? an, ut quidam fingere non erubescunt, iniurias
suas ultus est interfector, quia de paterna pecunia trans-
egerat aut auitum mancipium detrahebatur? pronuntiemus
ultro dominum iure caesum uideri.

44. Libet argumenta conquirere in eo quod sapientioribus deliberatum est? sed et si nunc primum statuendum
haberemus, creditisne seruum interficiendi domini animum
sumpsisse ut non uox minax excideret, nihil per temeritatem
proloqueretur? sane consilium occultauit, telum inter

---

[1] senatusque *obsessus* in quo ipso *O.T.*
[2] in *O.T.* ad *Koestermann, om. M.*   [3] at . . . defendet *O.T.*

ignaros parauit: num excubias transire, cubiculi foris re-
cludere, lumen inferre, caedem patrare *poterat* omnibus
2 nesciis? multa sceleris indicia praeueniunt: serui si prodant possumus singuli inter pluris, tuti inter anxios,
postremo, si pereundum sit, non inulti inter nocentis agere.
suspecta maioribus nostris fuerunt ingenia seruorum etiam
cum in agris aut domibus isdem nascerentur caritatemque
3 dominorum statim acciperent. postquam uero nationes
in familiis habemus, quibus diuersi ritus, externa sacra aut
nulla sunt, conluuiem istam non nisi metu coercueris. at
quidam insontes peribunt. nam et ex fuso exercitu cum
decimus quisque fusti feritur, etiam strenui sortiuntur.
habet aliquid ex iniquo omne magnum exemplum quod
contra singulos utilitate publica rependitur.'

45. Sententiae Cassii ut nemo unus contra ire ausus est,
ita dissonae uoces respondebant numerum aut aetatem aut
sexum ac plurimorum indubiam innocentiam miserantium:
praeualuit tamen pars quae supplicium decernebat. sed
obtemperari non poterat, conglobata multitudine et saxa
2 ac faces minante. tum Caesar populum edicto increpuit
atque omne iter quo damnati ad poenam ducebantur militaribus praesidiis saepsit. censuerat Cingonius Varro ut
liberti quoque qui sub eodem tecto fuissent Italia deportarentur. id a principe prohibitum est ne mos antiquus
quem misericordia non minuerat per saeuitiam intenderetur.

46. Damnatus isdem consulibus Tarquitius· Priscus repetundarum Bithynis interrogantibus, magno patrum
gaudio quia accusatum ab eo Statilium Taurum pro con-
2 sule ipsius meminerant. census per Gallias a Q. Volusio
et Sextio Africano Trebellioque Maximo acti sunt, aemulis
inter se per nobilitatem Volusio atque Africano: Trebellium dum uterque dedignatur, supra tulere.

47. Eo anno mortem obiit Memmius Regulus, auctoritate
constantia fama, in quantum praeumbrante imperatoris
fastigio datur, clarus, adeo ut Nero aeger ualetudine et adu-
lantibus circum, qui finem imperio adesse dicebant, si quid
fato pateretur, responderit habere subsidium rem publicam.

rogantibus dehinc in quo potissimum, addiderat in Memmio
2 Regulo. uixit tamen post haec Regulus quiete defensus et
quia noua generis claritudine neque inuidiosis opibus erat.
gymnasium eo anno dedicatum a Nerone praebitumque
oleum equiti ac senatui Graeca facilitate.

48. P. Mario L. Afinio consulibus Antistius praetor,
quem in tribunatu plebis licenter egisse memoraui, probrosa
aduersus principem carmina factitauit uulgauitque celebri
conuiuio dum apud Ostorium Scapulam epulatur. exim a
Cossutiano Capitone, qui nuper senatorium ordinem preci-
bus Tigellini soceri sui receperat, maiestatis delatus est.
2 tum primum reuocata ea lex; credebaturque haud perinde
exitium Antistio quam imperatori gloriam quaeri, ut con-
demnatum a senatu intercessione tribunicia morti eximeret.
et cum Ostorius nihil audiuisse pro testimonio dixisset,
aduersis testibus creditum; censuitque Iunius Marullus
consul designatus adimendam reo praeturam necandumque
3 more maiorum. ceteris inde adsentientibus Paetus Thrasea, multo cum honore Caesaris et acerrime increpito
Antistio, non quidquid nocens reus pati mereretur, id
egregio sub principe et nulla necessitate obstricto senatui
4 statuendum disseruit: carnificem et laqueum pridem
abolita et esse poenas legibus constitutas quibus sine
iudicum saeuitia et temporum infamia supplicia decernerentur. quin in insula publicatis bonis quo longius sontem
uitam traxisset, eo priuatim miseriorem et publicae clementiae maximum exemplum futurum.

49. Libertas Thraseae seruitium aliorum rupit et postquam discessionem consul permiserat, pedibus in sententiam eius iere, paucis exceptis, in quibus adulatione
promptissimus fuit A. Vitellius, optimum quemque iurgio
lacessens et respondenti reticens, ut pauida ingenia solent.
at consules perficere decretum senatus non ausi de con-
2 sensu scripsere Caesari. ille inter pudorem et iram cunctatus, postremo rescripsit nulla iniuria prouocatum Antis-
tium grauissimas in principem contumelias dixisse; earum
ultionem a patribus postulatam et pro magnitudine delicti
poenam statui par fuisse. ceterum se, qui seueritatem

decernentium impediturus fuerit, moderationem non pro-
hibere: statuerent ut uellent, datam et absoluendi licen-
3 tiam. his atque talibus recitatis et offensione manifesta,
non ideo aut consules mutauere relationem aut Thrasea
decessit sententia ceteriue quae probauerant deseruere,
pars, ne principem obiecisse inuidiae uiderentur, plures
numero tuti, Thrasea sueta firmitudine animi et ne gloria
intercideret.

50. Haud dispari crimine Fabricius Veiento conflictatus
est, quod multa et probrosa in patres et sacerdotes compo-
suisset iis libris quibus nomen codicillorum dederat. adiciebat Tullius Geminus accusator uenditata ab eo munera
2 principis et adipiscendorum honorum ius. quae causa Neroni fuit suscipiendi iudicii, conuictumque Veientonem
Italia depulit et libros exuri iussit, conquisitos lectitatosque
donec cum periculo parabantur: mox licentia habendi
obliuionem attulit.

51. Sed grauescentibus in dies publicis malis subsidia
minuebantur, concessitque uita Burrus, incertum ualetudine an ueneno. ualetudo ex eo coniectabatur quod in
se tumescentibus paulatim faucibus et impedito meatu
spiritum finiebat. plures iussu Neronis, quasi remedium
adhiberetur, inlitum palatum eius noxio medicamine
adseuerabant, et Burrum intellecto scelere, cum ad uisendum eum princeps uenisset, aspectum eius auersatum
sciscitanti hactenus respondisse: ʽ ego me bene habeo.ʼ
2 ciuitati grande desiderium eius mansit per memoriam uir-
tutis et successorum alterius segnem innocentiam, alterius
flagrantissima flagitia. quippe Caesar duos praetoriis
cohortibus imposuerat, Faenium Rufum ex uulgi fauore,
quia rem frumentariam sine quaestu tractabat, Ofonium
Tigellinum, ueterem impudicitiam atque infamiam in eo
3 secutus. atque illi pro cognitis moribus fuere, ualidior
Tigellinus in animo principis et intimis libidinibus adsump-
tus, prospera populi et militum fama Rufus, quod apud
Neronem aduersum experiebatur.

52. Mors Burri infregit Senecae potentiam quia nec
bonis artibus idem uirium erat altero uelut duce amoto et

Nero ad deteriores inclinabat. hi uariis criminationibus
Senecam adoriuntur, tamquam ingentis et priuatum modum
euectas opes adhuc augeret, quodque studia ciuium in se
uerteret, hortorum quoque amoenitate et uillarum magni-
2 ficentia quasi principem supergrederetur. obiciebant
etiam eloquentiae laudem uni sibi adsciscere et carmina
crebrius factitare, postquam Neroni amor eorum uenisset.
nam oblectamentis principis palam iniquum detrectare
uim eius equos regentis, inludere uoces, quoties caneret.
quem ad finem nihil in re publica clarum fore quod non
ab illo reperiri credatur? certe finitam Neronis pueritiam
et robur iuuentae adesse: exueret magistrum satis amplis
doctoribus instructus maioribus suis.

53. At Seneca criminantium non ignarus, prodentibus iis
quibus aliqua honesti cura et familiaritatem eius magis
aspernante Caesare, tempus sermoni orat et accepto ita in-
cipit: ' quartus decimus annus est, Caesar, ex quo spei
tuae admotus sum, octauus ut imperium obtines: medio
temporis tantum honorum atque opum in me cumulasti ut
2 nihil felicitati meae desit nisi moderatio eius. utar magnis
exemplis nec meae fortunae sed tuae. abauus tuus Augustus Marco Agrippae Mytilenense secretum, C. Maecenati
urbe in ipsa uelut peregrinum otium permisit; quorum
alter bellorum socius, alter Romae pluribus laboribus
iactatus ampla quidem sed pro ingentibus meritis praemia
3 acceperant. ego quid aliud munificentiae tuae adhibere
potui quam studia, ut sic dixerim, in umbra educata, et
quibus claritudo uenit, quod iuuentae tuae rudimentis
4 adfuisse uideor, grande huius rei pretium. at tu gratiam
immensam, innumeram pecuniam circumdedisti adeo ut
plerumque intra me ipse uoluam: egone equestri et pro-
uinciali loco ortus proceribus ciuitatis adnumeror? inter
nobilis et longa decora praeferentis nouitas mea enituit?
ubi est animus ille modicis contentus? talis hortos extruit
et per haec suburbana incedit et tantis agrorum spatiis,
tam lato faenore exuberat? una defensio occurrit quod
muneribus tuis obniti non debui.

54. Sed uterque mensuram impleuimus, et *tu*, quantum

princeps tribuere amico posset, et ego, quantum amicus a principe accipere: cetera inuidiam augent. quae quidem, ut omnia mortalia, infra tuam magnitudinem iacet, sed 2 mihi incumbit, mihi subueniendum est. quo modo in militia aut uia fessus adminiculum orarem, ita in hoc itinere uitae senex et leuissimis quoque curis impar, cum opes meas ultra sustinere non possim, praesidium peto. iube rem per procuratores tuos administrari, in tuam 3 fortunam recipi. nec me in paupertatem ipse detrudam, sed traditis quorum fulgore praestringor, quod temporis hortorum aut uillarum curae seponitur in animum reuocabo. superest tibi robur et tot per annos uisum *summi* fastigii regimen: possumus seniores amici quietem reposcere. hoc quoque in tuam gloriam cedet, eos ad summa uexisse qui et modica tolerarent.'

55. Ad quae Nero sic ferme respondit: ' quod meditatae orationi tuae statim occurram id primum tui muneris habeo, qui me non tantum praeuisa sed subita expedire 2 docuisti. abauus meus Augustus Agrippae et Maecenati usurpare otium post labores concessit, sed in ea ipse aetate cuius auctoritas tueretur quidquid illud et qualecumque tribuisset; ac tamen neutrum datis a se praemiis exuit. bello et periculis meruerant; in iis enim iuuenta Augusti 3 uersata est: nec mihi tela et manus tuae defuissent in armis agenti; sed quod praesens condicio poscebat, ratione consilio praeceptis pueritiam, dein iuuentam meam fouisti. et tua quidem erga me munera, dum uita suppetet, aeterna erunt: quae a me habes, horti et faenus et uillae, casibus 4 obnoxia sunt. ac licet multa uideantur, plerique haudquaquam artibus tuis pares plura tenuerunt. pudet referre libertinos qui ditiores spectantur: unde etiam mihi rubori est quod praecipuus caritate nondum omnis fortuna antecellis.

56. Verum et tibi ualida aetas rebusque et fructui rerum sufficiens, et nos prima imperii spatia ingredimur, nisi forte aut te Vitellio ter consuli aut me Claudio postponis et quantum Volusio longa parsimonia quaesiuit, tantum in te mea liberalitas explere non potest. quin, si qua in parte

lubricum adulescentiae nostrae declinat, reuocas orna-
2 tumque robur subsidio impensius regis? non tua moderatio, si reddideris pecuniam, nec quies, si reliqueris
principem, sed mea auaritia, meae crudelitatis metus in
ore omnium uersabitur. quod si maxime continentia tua
laudetur, non tamen sapienti uiro decorum fuerit unde
3 amico infamiam paret inde gloriam sibi recipere.' his
adicit complexum et oscula, factus natura et consuetudine
exercitus uelare odium fallacibus blanditiis. Seneca, qui
finis omnium cum dominante sermonum, grates agit:
sed instituta prioris potentiae commutat, prohibet coetus
salutantium, uitat comitantis, rarus per urbem, quasi
ualetudine infensa aut sapientiae studiis domi attineretur.

57. Perculso Seneca promptum fuit Rufum Faenium im-
minuere Agrippinae amicitiam in eo criminantibus. uali-
diorque in dies Tigellinus et malas artes, quibus solis
pollebat, gratiores ratus si principem societate scelerum
obstringeret, metus eius rimatur; compertoque Plautum
et Sullam maxime timeri, Plautum in Asiam, Sullam in
Galliam Narbonensem nuper amotos, nobilitatem eorum
et propinquos huic Orientis, illi Germaniae exercitus
2 commemorat. non se, ut Burrum, diuersas spes sed solam
incolumitatem Neronis spectare; cui caueri utcumque ab
urbanis insidiis praesenti opera: longinquos motus quonam
modo comprimi posse? erectas Gallias ad nomen dicta-
torium nec minus suspensos Asiae populos claritudine aui
3 Drusi. Sullam inopem, unde praecipuam audaciam, et
simulatorem segnitiae dum temeritati locum reperiret.
Plautum magnis opibus ne fingere quidem cupidinem otii
sed ueterum Romanorum imitamenta praeferre, adsumpta
etiam Stoicorum adrogantia sectaque quae turbidos et
4 negotiorum adpetentis faciat. nec ultra mora. Sulla
sexto die peruectis Massiliam percussoribus ante metum
et rumorem interficitur cum epulandi causa discumberet.
relatum caput eius inlusit Nero tamquam praematura
canitie deforme.

58. Plauto parari necem non perinde occultum fuit, quia

DIS MANIBVS
C·IVL·C·F·FAB·ALPINI·CLASSICIANI
PROC·PROVINC·BRITANN
IVLIA·INDI·FILIA·PACATA·I·NFELIX
VXOR

SEPULCHRAL INSCRIPTION OF JULIUS CLASSICIANUS, RESTORED FROM TRACINGS OF THE TWO BLOCKS FOUND ON TOWER HILL IN 1852 AND 1935

['To the immortal soul of Gaius Julius Alpinus Classicianus, son of Gaius, of the Fabian Tribe, procurator of the province of Britain, his sorrowing wife, Julia Pacata, daughter of Indus (set up this monument).']

pluribus salus eius curabatur et spatium itineris ac maris
tempusque interiectum mouerat famam; uulgoque fingebant petitum ab eo Corbulonem, magnis tum exercitibus
praesidentem et, clari atque insontes *si* interficerentur,
praecipuum ad pericula. quin et Asiam fauore iuuenis
arma cepisse, nec milites ad scelus missos aut numero uali-
dos aut animo promptos, postquam iussa efficere nequi-
2 uerint, ad spes nouas transisse. uana haec more famae
credentium otio augebantur; ceterum libertus Plauti
celeritate uentorum praeuenit centurionem et mandata
L. Antistii soceri attulit: effugeret segnem mortem, dum
suffugium esset: magni nominis miseratione reperturum
bonos, consociaturum audacis: nullum interim subsidium
3 aspernandum. si sexaginta milites (tot enim adueniebant)
propulisset, dum refertur nuntius Neroni, dum manus alia
permeat, multa secutura quae adusque bellum eualescerent.
denique aut salutem tali consilio quaeri, aut nihil grauius
audenti quam ignauo patiendum esse.

59. Sed Plautum ea non mouere, siue nullam opem pro-
uidebat inermis atque exul, seu taedio ambiguae spei, an
amore coniugis et liberorum, quibus placabiliorem fore
principem rebatur nulla sollicitudine turbatum. sunt qui
alios a socero nuntios uenisse ferant, tamquam nihil atrox
immineret; doctoresque sapientiae, Coeranum Graeci,
Musonium Tusci generis, constantiam opperiendae mortis
2 pro incerta et trepida uita suasisse. repertus est certe per
medium diei nudus exercitando corpori. talem eum centurio trucidauit coram Pelagone spadone quem Nero centurioni et manipulo, quasi satellitibus ministrum regium,
3 praeposuerat. caput interfecti relatum; cuius aspectu
(ipsa principis uerba referam) 'cur', inquit, 'Nero,
hominem nasutum timuisti?' et posito metu nuptias Poppaeae
ob eius modi terrores dilatas maturare parat Octauiamque
coniugem amoliri, quamuis modeste ageret, nomine patris
4 et studiis populi grauem. sed ad senatum litteras misit
de caede Sullae Plautique haud confessus, uerum utriusque
turbidum ingenium esse et sibi incolumitatem rei publicae
magna cura haberi. decretae eo nomine supplicationes

utque Sulla et Plautus senatu mouerentur, grauioribus iam
ludibriis quam malis.

60. Igitur accepto patrum consulto, postquam cuncta
scelerum suorum pro egregiis accipi uidet, exturbat Octauiam, sterilem dictitans; exim Poppaeae coniungitur. ea
diu paelex et adulteri Neronis, mox mariti potens, quendam
ex ministris Octauiae impulit seruilem ei amorem obicere.
2 destinaturque reus cognomento Eucaerus, natione Alex-
andrinus, canere per tibias[1] doctus. actae ob id de ancillis
quaestiones et ui tormentorum uictis quibusdam ut falsa
adnuerent, plures perstitere sanctitatem dominae tueri; ex
quibus una instanti Tigellino castiora esse muliebria Octa-
3 uiae respondit quam os eius. mouetur tamen primo ciuilis
discidii specie domumque Burri, praedia Plauti, infausta
dona accipit: mox in Campaniam pulsa est addita militari
custodia. inde crebri questus nec occulti per uulgum, cui
minor sapientia *et* ex mediocritate fortunae pauciora pericula sunt. his . . . tamquam Nero paenitentia flagitii
coniugem reuocarit Octauiam.

61. Exim laeti Capitolium scandunt deosque tandem
uenerantur. effigies Poppaeae proruunt, Octauiae imagines
gestant umeris, spargunt floribus foroque ac templis
statuunt. itur etiam in principis laudes strepitu[2] uenerantium. iamque et Palatium multitudine et clamoribus
complebant, cum emissi militum globi uerberibus et in-
2 tento ferro turbatos disiecere. mutataque quae per seditionem uerterant et Poppaeae honos repositus est. quae
semper odio, tum et metu atrox ne aut uulgi acrior uis
ingrueret aut Nero inclinatione populi mutaretur, prouoluta genibus eius, non eo loci res suas agi ut de matrimonio
certet, quamquam id sibi uita potius, sed uitam ipsam in
extremum adductam a clientelis et seruitiis Octauiae quae
plebis sibi nomen indiderint, ea in pace ausi quae uix
3 bello euenirent. arma illa aduersus principem sumpta;
ducem tantum defuisse qui motis rebus facile reperiretur,
omitteret modo Campaniam et in urbem ipsa pergeret ad
4 cuius nutum absentis tumultus cierentur. quod alioquin

[1] tibiis *O.T.*   [2] strepitu *Andresen :* repetitum *M et O.T.*

suum delictum? quam cuiusquam offensionem? an quia
ueram progeniem penatibus Caesarum datura sit? malle
populum Romanum tibicinis Aegyptii subolem imperatorio
fastigio induci? denique, si id rebus conducat, libens quam
coactus acciret dominam, uel consuleret securitati[1] iusta
ultione. et modicis remediis primos motus consedisse: at
si desperent uxorem Neronis fore Octauiam, illi maritum
daturos.

62. Varius sermo et ad metum atque iram accommodatus
terruit simul audientem et accendit. sed parum ualebat
suspicio in seruo et quaestionibus ancillarum elusa erat.
ergo confessionem alicuius quaeri placet cui rerum quoque
2 nouarum crimen adfingeretur. et uisus idoneus maternae
necis patrator Anicetus, classi apud Misenum, ut memoraui,
praefectus, leui post admissum scelus gratia, dein grauiore
odio, quia malorum facinorum ministri quasi exprobrantes
3 aspiciuntur. igitur accitum eum Caesar operae prioris
admonet: solum incolumitati principis aduersus insidian-
tem matrem subuenisse; locum haud minoris gratiae
instare si coniugem infensam depelleret. nec manu aut
telo opus: fateretur Octauiae adulterium. occulta quidem
ad praesens sed magna ei praemia et secessus amoenos
4 promittit, uel, si negauisset, necem intentat. ille insita
uaecordia et facilitate priorum flagitiorum plura etiam
quam iussum erat fingit fateturque apud amicos quos uelut
consilio adhibuerat princeps. tum in Sardiniam pellitur
ubi non inops exilium tolerauit et fato obiit.

63. At Nero praefectum in spem sociandae classis corruptum et incusatae paulo ante sterilitatis oblitus, abactos
partus conscientia libidinum, eaque sibi comperta edicto
memorat insulaque Pandateria Octauiam claudit. non
alia exul uisentium oculos maiore misericordia adfecit.
2 meminerant adhuc quidam Agrippinae a Tiberio, recentior
Iuliae memoria obuersabatur a Claudio pulsae: sed illis
robur aetatis adfuerat; laeta aliqua uiderant et praesentem
saeuitiam melioris olim fortunae recordatione adleuabant.
huic primum nuptiarum dies loco funeris fuit, deductae in

[1] . . . securitati. iusta . . . O.T.

domum in qua nihil nisi luctuosum haberet, erepto per
uenenum patre et statim fratre; tum ancilla domina ualidior
et Poppaea non nisi in perniciem uxoris nupta, postremo
crimen omni exitio grauius.

64. Ac puella uicesimo aetatis anno inter centuriones
et milites, praesagio malorum iam uitae exempta, nondum
tamen morte adquiescebat. paucis dehinc interiectis diebus mori iubetur, cum iam uiduam se et tantum sororem
testaretur communisque Germanicos et postremo Agrippinae nomen cieret, qua incolumi infelix quidem matri-
2 monium sed sine exitio pertulisset. restringitur uinclis
uenaeque eius per omnis artus exoluuntur; et quia pressus
pauore sanguis tardius labebatur, praeferuidi balnei uapore
enecatur. additurque atrocior saeuitia quod caput am-
3 putatum latumque in urbem Poppaea uidit. dona ob
haec templis decreta quem ad finem memorabimus?
quicumque casus temporum illorum nobis uel aliis auctoribus noscent, praesumptum habeant, quoties fugas et caedes
iussit princeps, toties grates deis actas, quaeque rerum
secundarum olim, tum publicae cladis insignia fuisse.
neque tamen silebimus si quod senatus consultum adulatione nouum aut patientia postremum fuit.

65. Eodem anno libertorum potissimos ueneno inter-
fecisse creditus est, Doryphorum quasi aduersatum nuptiis
Poppaeae, Pallantem, quod immensam pecuniam longa
senecta detineret. Romanus secretis criminationibus in-
cusauerat Senecam ut C. Pisonis socium, sed ualidius a
Seneca eodem crimine perculsus est. unde Pisoni timor et
orta insidiarum in Neronem magna moles et improspera.

NOTES

1. § 1. Gaio Vipstano, C. Fonteio coss., i.e. A.D. 59. C. Vipstanus Apronianus became proconsul of Africa in A.D. 69, see *Hist.* I, 76. For the character of C. Fonteius Capito, see *Hist.* I, 7. As *legatus* of Lower Germany in A.D. 68 he was murdered by his own officers.

meditatum. Though *meditor*, ' reflect upon,' ' meditate,' ' practise ', is deponent, the perfect participle is frequently used in a passive sense in all periods of Latin.

uetustate . . . Poppaeae, ' his audacity increasing with the length of his reign, and as he was becoming every day more violently in love with Poppaea. . . .' *coalesco* = lit. ' to grow together ', hence ' harden', ' become rooted '. The pf. part. is not in use before Tacitus. *uetustate*, either causal or instr. abl.

quae . . . incusare . . . uocare. The relative here is not really subordinate, but introduces a new statement (= *haec enim*). The hist. infin. is therefore permissible.

criminationibus . . . per facetias. For the variation, see Introd. ch. III, p. 11. *criminationibus* refers to *incusare*, *per facetias* to *uocare*; therefore trans. ' she began to assail the emperor with frequent reproaches, at times, in jest, calling him a mere ward who was subject to the bidding of others and not only lacking sovereignty, but destitute of personal freedom '. Notice the sense of the hist. infin., which = imperf. indic., and has quite a different effect from the hist. pres. indic.

§ 2. cur . . . differri . . . ? The infin. is due to the fact that the question was rhetorical and did not await an answer. Poppaea said *cur differuntur ?*, implying that there was no reason. Such a question is equivalent to a statement, and is accordingly quite logically reported by means of acc. and infin. in Latin.

triumphalis auos. Only her maternal grandfather, Poppaeus Sabinus, had gained triumphal honours, for victories in Thrace during the reign of Tiberius. See *Ann.* IV, 46; V, 10; VI, 39; XIII, 45.

uerum animum, ' sincere affection '. ' . . . was he not satisfied as to the sincerity of her affection? '

timeri ne uxor saltem . . . ' It was feared (i.e. by Agrippina) that as his wife, at any rate, she would open his eyes to the wrongs inflicted on the Senate, &c.' The point of *saltem* is that, so as long as Poppaea was struggling for possession of Nero against Agrippina's influence, Nero might regard her accusations as nothing but attempts to undermine his mother's position; but if Poppaea once became his wife, there would be no point in her continuing such attacks, unless they were true. Then, *at least*, Nero would have no cause to disbelieve when he was told that Agrippina's behaviour was making his government unpopular.

patrum, obj. gen.   Agrippina's attacks on senators are mentioned in c. 11.

Othonis coniugio.   She had been married first to Rufrius Crispinus, by whom she had a son (*Ann.* XIII, 45).   After her divorce from him, she married Otho, whom she was now deserting in turn for Nero.

ituram quoquo terrarum.   Nero had made Otho governor of Lusitania to get him out of the way, so that, if Poppaea rejoined him, she had a long way to go.

audiret, final subj.

imperatoris, obj. gen.

§ 3. ad caedem eius duratura. . . ' that her son's hatred would steel itself to her murder '.   For this use of *duro* with *ad* or *in* with acc. to denote result or purpose, cf. *Ann.* I. 6, *in nullius unquam suorum necem durauit.*

2. § 1. Cluuius.   See Introd. ch. II, p. 9.

ardore retinendae . . . potentiae.   For the gen., see Introd. III, 2, (v).   In this case it is clearly an obj. gen., since *ardore = cupiditate.*

medio diei.   Although the classical rule is for adjectives like *medius, summus, extremus,* &c., to agree with their noun, the neut. adj. with part. gen. is found occasionally, and is used freely by Sallust and Livy. See Introd. III, 2, (iv).

id temporis.   In phrases like *id temporis, id aetatis, illud aetatis* (which are classical) the acc. is adverbial.   The usage is extended by Tacitus, e.g. *Ann.* XII, 8 *nemo id auctoritatis aderat.*

per uinum et epulas.   The Romans considered it a mark of depravity to begin drinking at mid-day.

immissamque Acten . . . matre, ' his freedwoman Acte, who was alarmed by the danger to herself and the infamy which threatened Nero, was sent in to tell him that the scandal was noised abroad through his mother's actually boasting of it '.   *deferret*, final subj., though the subj. would be required in any case in o. o.

profani = quite literally ' beyond the pale '.

§ 2. Fabius Rusticus.   See Introd. ch. II, p. 9.

ceteri auctores, ' all the other authorities ', i.e. except Fabius Rusticus.   For an account of Tacitus' authorities, see Introd. ch. II.

seu . . . seu . . . ' either because Agrippina actually did conceive such a monstrous design, or else because it seemed more credible in the woman who . . .'

Lepido.   This M. Aemilius Lepidus was the son of Augustus' grand-daughter Julia and L. Aemilius Paullus.   He had been the husband of Agrippina's sister Drusilla.   He was put to death by Gaius in A.D. 39 as being connected with the conspiracy of Lentulus Gaetulicus.   Probably Agrippina made up to him as being the likeliest candidate for the throne, if the conspiracy succeeded.

patrui nuptiis.   A marriage of uncle and niece was considered incestuous until rendered legal by Claudius (Suet. *Claud.* 26).

3. § 1. uitare . . . laudare, hist. infin.

in hortos aut . . . in agrum.   The former refers to a park in Rome, the latter to country estates.

praegrauem ratus, ' considering her a great nuisance '.

hactenus consultans, i.e. he did not deliberate on the advisability of murdering her at all, but only on the method of doing it. **qua alia.** *qua* is here the indef. adj. = *aliqua.*

§ 2. **si daretur . . . non poterat.** The protasis is oblique, but not the apodosis. Nero said to himself *si dabitur* (or *detur*) . . . *non potest.* . . . Tacitus says *poterat,* speaking from his own point of view.

tali iam Britannici exitio, abl. abs., giving cause, 'such having been the fate of Britannicus already'. Britannicus was the son of Claudius and Messalina, and had been deprived of the succession by the machinations of Agrippina. His murder is described in *Ann.* XIII, 16.

praesumendo remedia, 'by taking antidotes beforehand'. *praesumere* is often used in the metaphorical sense of 'to anticipate', 'assume', cf. c. 64, 3 *praesumptum habeant.*

ferrum et caedes, probably hendiadys for 'violent death', 'death by the sword'.

reperiebat. The tense of incomplete action must be rendered, e.g. 'no one was able to discover'.

metuebat, sc. *Nero.*

§ 3. **obtulit ingenium Anicetus.** Notice the order, which emphasizes both *obtulit* and *Anicetus,* 'It was Anicetus who produced a scheme'. The effect of putting the verb first is staccato, and accounts for the absence of an introductory particle. For *ingenium* in this sense, cf. *Hist.* III. 28, though the more usual sense of 'ingenuity', i.e. 'he offered the service of his ingenuity', is also possible.

apud Misenum. From the review of the Roman forces in the reign of Tiberius, which Tacitus gives in *Ann.* IV. 5, we learn that there were three fleets stationed in Italian waters, at Misenum, Ravenna, and Forum Julium.

educator, i.e. he had been Nero's *paedagogus.*

cuius pars . . . effunderet. The subj. may be either final or consec., 'a ship such that part might be designed to collapse while actually at sea and throw her overboard unawares'.

intercepta sit . . . deliquerint, o. o. for *si intercepta erit, quis adeo iniquus* (*erit*) . . .? Anicetus really meant *nemo adeo iniquus erit,* hence the acc. and infin. reporting a rhet. quest. *fore* is understood. Notice the change from historic (*effunderet*) to the more vivid primary sequence after *docet.*

additurum represents *addes* of o. r., the fut. indic. being often used for imperative. Cf. Eng. 'shall' 'will'.

cetera ostentandae pietati, 'the other things designed to display filial piety'. For the dat. of the gerundive denoting purpose, see Introd. III, 3, (iv).

4. § 1. **Quinquatruum.** *Quinquatrus* strictly means 'the fifth day after the Ides', and was a festival in honour of Minerva celebrated on the 19th March. A misinterpretation of the name afterwards led to the festival being prolonged for five days. It was celebrated especially by those whose work was under the protection of the goddess, hence it was a school holiday.

dies . . . frequentabat. From meaning 'to resort to a place frequently', or 'to resort to a place in great numbers', *frequento* sometimes has the same sense as *celebro,* 'to celebrate', or 'to keep in great numbers', of a festival. To use it so with a single person as the subject is an illogical extension which does not occur in classical Latin. For another ex., see *Ann*. XV, 35, *eius munus frequentanti Neroni* . . .

iracundias, 'outbreaks of temper'. The singular means 'hastiness of temper' as an abstract quality, but the plural particularizes it. Similarly *asperitas* = 'roughness', *asperitates* = 'examples of roughness', *seruitium* = 'slavery', *seruitia* = 'slaves'.

placandum animum. This is usually taken to mean 'he must calm *his own* resentment'. As Tacitus often uses *animus* in the sense of 'high spirits' or 'temper' in the sing. as well as in the plur. when referring to a number of persons, it might equally well mean 'and their (parents') temper must be humoured'. There is no means of deciding, but the latter is preferable, as it avoids the awkward change after *parentium*, which calls for *suum* for the sake of clarity.

facili . . . credulitate, rather a modal abl. than abl. abs., 'and that Agrippina might receive it with the easy credulity of women towards cheerful news'.

Misenum inter. For the anastrophe of the preposition, cf. also c. 9, 1, *uiam Miseni propter*.

Baianum lacum, i.e. the Lucrine Lake.

§ 2. **honori.** Notice that this is not a predic. dat., as it is qualified by *matris*. A predic. dat. cannot be qualified by a gen. or any other epithet, except one of quantity. If it were predic., the dat. of interest *matri* would be required (which, indeed, has been conjectured). Trans. 'as if that, too, were a tribute offered to his mother's honour'.

quippe sueuerat, 'To be sure, she had been accustomed . . .' The pluperf. tense refers to the time before her estrangement from Nero, so that the tribute to her honour consisted in the restoration of this privilege in even fuller measure. This is the only ex. in Tacitus of intrans. *suesco* with the infin.

classiariorum, 'sailors from the fleet'. Normally the rowers were slaves.

occultando facinori, see Introd. III, 3, (iv).

gestamine sellae. The gen. is the 'defining' one, which gives a more particular description of the general term, i.e. 'conveyance *consisting of* a sedan-chair'. Cf. 'city *of* London'.

Baias. This is a generally accepted correction for *Baulos* of M. The latter can hardly be right, as Tacitus has just told us that Nero had already conducted his mother to Bauli. The assumption is that he then returned himself to Baiae, after inviting her to dinner there. She was expected to use for the journey the ship which had been tampered with, but, her suspicions being aroused, she went by land in a sedan-chair. If this was not the case, the insistence on her mode of conveyance has no point, and in any case the order of Tacitus' narrative suggests that the ship was anchored at Bauli. On the other hand, we have then to explain how the ship came to be at Baiae ready for her return. We must assume that it was sent for during the banquet.

§ 3. **excepta collocata.** It is difficult to decide whether these participles are abl. abs., or whether we should understand *est*. Tacitus is quite fond of ending a period with an abl. abs. phrase, so perhaps the former is slightly preferable. In that case, only a comma is required after *metum*. **superque ipsum**, i.e. in the *locus consularis* on the *lectus medius*.

iam pluribus . . . There is something to be said for Heinsius' correction of ms. *nam* to *iam*, since the *blandimentum* has already been explained by *comiter excepta*, &c. Further illustrations of Nero's attentiveness would more naturally be introduced by *iam*, which is an easy correction.

This sentence is easier to understand and to translate than to construe, as it contains an anacoluthon. The ablatives *pluribus sermonibus* and *familiaritate iuuenili* are instr. or modal with *tracto in longum conuictu*, but Tacitus, in his fondness for variety, has joined with them the nom. part. *adductus* in agreement with the subject *Nero*, as if he were going to write *traxit in longum conuictum*. The sentence might be regularized either by substituting this for the abl. abs. *tracto . . . conuictu*, or by substituting *adducto uoltu* for *adductus*. *familiaritate iuuenili* comes near to being an adjectival abl. of quality with *Nero*, as in c. 36, 3, *uetus miles et multa proeliorum experientia*, but as it describes the manner in which Nero prolonged the feast, it is an adverbial modal abl. as well. For a sentence with a similar anacoluthon, see c. 23, 2 and note. *adductus* = lit. ' drawn tight ', so of character or demeanour ' strict ', ' serious '. Trans. ' There Nero's charm of manner relieved her fears. She was courteously received and placed in the seat of honour above the emperor. Then Nero prolonged the entertainment with many topics of conversation, now with youthful intimacy, now with a serious air, as if he were communicating important matters, and when she was going away, he saw her off. . . .'

oculis et pectori haerens. If *pectori* is right, and both words are in the dat., ' clinging to her eyes and breast ' must mean ' hanging on her gaze and clinging to her breast ', but the zeugma is rather awkward. Either *oculis haerere* or *pectori haerere* would be common enough phrases by themselves, the former having a less literal sense than the latter: cf. Ov. *Tr.* IV, 3, 19, *Vultibus illa tuis tamquam praesentibus haeret* (= ' hangs upon your gaze ', ' tries to keep your face in her mind '); Pliny, *Ep.* V, 16, 3, *illa patris ceruicibus inhaerebat*, ' clung to her father's neck '. Tacitus has combined the literal and the less literal sense in one phrase with the same verb.

explenda simulatione. Lipsius changed this to a dat. of purpose of the type of *occultando facinori* above. But there is no need for this, as this abl. is exactly parallel to that quasi-instrumental abl. of the gerund which is equivalent in sense to a nom. part. in agreement with the subject. This is not unknown in Cicero, and is common in Livy and Tacitus, e.g. c. 31, 2, *exturbabant agris, captiuos, seruos appellando* (= *appellantes*). Livy can say *gerendo solus censuram*. It is true that the gerund and not the gerundive is usually thus used, yet we do find, in Livy XXI, 2, 1, *ita se . . . in Hispania augendo Punico imperio gessit* (= *augens* or *dum auget*). Trans. ' This he did, either putting the finishing touches to his hypocrisy, or else the last sight of his mother going to her death was catching at his heart, brutalized though it was.' It is worth noting how Tacitus' psychological insight is revealed by this sentence.

5. § 1. Crepereius Gallus, not mentioned elsewhere by Tacitus.
Acerronia, probably the daughter of Cn. Acerronius Proculus,
consul in the last year of Tiberius' reign, see *Ann.* VI, 45.

cum ruere. For the hist. infin. in an 'inverted' *cum*-clause, see
Introd. III, 5, (iii). Furneaux' suggestion that the collapse of the
cabin roof was an alternative to the plan suggested in c. 3 seems hardly
likely, since, had the sea been rough enough to lend verisimilitude to a
shipwreck, Agrippina would not have returned by sea. The falling of
a weight must have been intended to knock a hole in the hull and so
sink the ship; which could have happened whether the sea was rough
or calm. As it was, the couch took the brunt of the weight, and no
leak was started. Acerronia escaped with Agrippina because, as she
reclined across the couch over Agrippina's legs, she too was lower than
the projecting sides.

§ 2. dissolutio nauigii. It was evidently hoped that, with a little
help from the crew, the crashing weight might strain the timbers
sufficiently for the ship to founder.

turbatis omnibus et quod . . . . The abl. abs. here is equivalent to
a causal clause. Notice how Tacitus avoids two parallel clauses of the
same sort, cf. Introd. p. 11.

plerique. The normal meaning of this word in Tacitus is not ' the
majority ' or ' most ', as in classical Latin, but ' very many '. Cf.
c. 53, 4 *plerumque* = ' very often ' (not ' usually ').

remigibus, i.e. only those who were *conscii*.

in rem subitam, either ' to meet the sudden emergency ' or ' to carry
through the extempore plan '.

facultatem iactus, ' the possibility of being thrown overboard less
violently '. *iactus* is a word particularly used of jettisoning cargo.

§ 3. imprudentia, causal abl. ' out of ignorance ' or ' lack of foresight ', cf. Caes. *timore defugere.* It is easiest to translate it by an adverb,
' witlessly ', ' foolishly ', though this implies that the abl. is modal, a
type which is normally accompanied by either *cum* or an epithet.
The word here signifies ' inability to put two and two together '.

quae fors obtulerat. This use of the pluperf. indic. is the normal
classical constr. in indefinite clauses, or clauses of repeated action.
Silver Latin often uses the iterative subj. (see Introd. III, 6, (*b*)).
Tacitus sometimes uses the one, sometimes the other.

occursu lenunculorum, ' by falling in with some boats '.

uillae suae infertur. For the dat., see Introd. III, 3, (iii). As
there is no other evidence that Agrippina had a villa of her own on the
Lucrine Lake, it seems safer to suppose that she was afterwards carried
back to Bauli, which Nero had placed at her disposal. She would
naturally ask the fishermen to take her northwards, for, if she tried to
return southwards to Bauli by water, she might fall in with her enemies
again.

6. § 1. reputans . . . quodque . . . concidisset. This *quod*-clause
cannot be a common adverbial (causal) clause in o.o., because -*que*
shows it to be parallel to *accitam* (*esse*), and therefore substantival,
standing as another object of *reputans.* In any case Agrippina did not
decide how to counter the plot *because* the ship had collapsed. For the
substantival *quod*-clause after verbs of 'saying' and 'thinking', see

Introd. III, 6 (*f*). Trans. 'There, reflecting that it was for this purpose that she had been summoned by the treacherous letter and treated with such distinguished honour, and *on the fact that. . . .*'

summa sui parte. The abl. is one of respect: the ship collapsed 'in the upper part of itself'. Note that the chief use of the gen. of the personal pronoun (or rather of the neut. possess. adj. which is used instead of it) is either as a partitive, as here, or as an objective gen. Cf. Cic. *Fin.* 5, 37, *Pars est nostri manus. cui proposita est conseruatio sui, necesse est huic partes quoque sui caras esse.*

solum . . . intellegerentur. Most editors follow M in omitting *sensit*, which was inserted by Bezzenberger. It might easily have dropped out between *esse* and *si.* However, the omission of the verb of thinking or speaking could also be paralleled: cf. c. 7, 1, *quod contra subsidium sibi?* *si non intellegerentur* is pregnant for *si simularet se non intellegere.* N.b. that when *si non* is used instead of *nisi*, *non* qualifies one particular word or phrase, and not the whole protasis. *nisi* here would mean almost the opposite of *si non*, i.e. ' (there was no remedy) *unless* the plot was understood '. Trans. 'she realized that the only way in which she could counter the plot was by seeming not to notice it'.

misitque, *que* here almost = *itaque*, ' and so ',' for that reason '.

fortuna eius, 'thanks to (the kindness of Providence and) his own lucky star'. Notice that the *Fortuna populi Romani* has now become *Fortuna principis*, as embodying the State.

euasisse . . . orare, sc. *se.* For the ellipse, cf. c. 1, 2, *ituram quoquo terrarum.* For the acc. after *euado*, cf. *Ann.* VI, 49, *donec minor filius lubricum iuuentae exiret.* In poetry and post-Aug. prose, verbs of motion compounded with *ex* (*egredior, euado, exeo*), meaning 'pass out of', 'pass beyond', 'escape', are used transitively on the analogy of transitive verbs of similar meaning, e.g. *relinquo.*

uisendi curam. The gen. is one of definition, 'attentiveness *consisting of* visiting her ', 'the attention of visiting her '.

§ 2. testamentum . . . obsignari iubet. Acerronia's papers and effects would be put under seal, in order that nothing might be removed, pending the execution of the will. If Acerronia had left her a legacy, Agrippina meant to have it intact. Notice the sting in the tail of the chapter, which is characteristically Tacitean. Agrippina's *cupido auri immensa* is spoken of in *Ann.* XII. 7.

7. § 1. patrati facinoris. Again the part. agreeing with the noun = an abstract noun with obj. gen. (*patratio facinoris*). The gen. is obj. with *nuntios.*

ne auctor dubitaretur. For *dubitor* used personally with nom. and infin., cf. *Ann.* III, 8, *neque dubitabantur praescripta ei a Tiberio.* The usage is classical with verbs like *dicor, uideor, nuntior, intellegor,* &c., but post-classical writers extend it to many more verbs. Trans. '. . . having come so near to death that the author of it could not be in doubt '. The explanation of *ne* instead of *ut non* in what appears to be a consecutive clause is that Tacitus wishes to imply that it was the *will* of Heaven that the villainy should be exposed.

uindictae properam. Possibly dat. of 'end aimed at ', see Introd. III, 3, (iv). It is more likely, however, to be gen. of reference, which often

implies purpose, see Introd. III, 2, (i). Cf. *Ann.* XI, 26, *Claudium
. . . irae properum ; Ann.* IV, 59, *a libertis et clientibus apiscendae potentiae
properis ; Ann.* XII, 66, *Agrippina . . . oblatae occasionis propera.* It is
safest to let the last ex. determine the case of the others, where the
inflexion is ambiguous. Trans. ' hastening to exact vengeance '.

armaret . . . accenderet . . . peruaderet. subj. because it is a
fut. condition in o. o. The apodosis is *quod contra subsidium sibi* (sc.
fore). Nero said: *siue armabit* (or *armet*), &c., *quod contra subsidium
mihi (erit)* ?

obiciendo. The case again is doubtful. It may be dat. of ' end
aimed at ' = ' for the purpose of charging him with her shipwreck
and wound and the murder of her friends '. On the other hand, this
dat. of the *gerund* is comparatively rare (there are only two other certain
exx. in Tac., viz. *Ann.* XIII, 11; XV, 16), most exx. being of the
passive gerundive adj., as c. 3, 3, *ostentandae pietati.* It seems best,
therefore, to take it as that quasi-instr. abl. of the gerund which = a
pres. part. in agreement with the subject (= *obiciens*). Cf. c. 31, 2,
and note on c. 4, 3, *explenda simulatione.*

§ 2. **nisi quid Burrus et Seneca expedirent; quos . . .** This is a
pure conjecture for the reading of M: *nisi quid Burrus et Seneca expergens.
quos statim acciuerat.* Koestermann reads *nisi quid Burrus et Seneca;
quos expergens. . . .* The omission of the verb can certainly be paralleled,
but the use of the pres. part. *expergens* for *experrectos* is not good Latin.
Tacitus does not elsewhere use either *expergo* or *expergiscor.*

incertum an et ante ignaros, ' probably not unaware (of the plot)
even before this ', or ' it is *doubtful* whether they were unaware . . .'.
Notice that *incertum an,* instead of introducing an ind. quest. clause,
has degenerated into the equivalent of a single adverb (= 'doubt-
fully') qualifying *ignaros.* Cf. the similar fate which befel *forsitan,* which
by Livy's time is used = *fortasse.* Some editors change *ignaros* to
gnaros, because they think *incertum an* must be affirmative (= ' possibly '
or ' probably '). Then ' they were probably unaware (of the plot)
even before (this revelation) ' would make nonsense. But there is no
need to alter the reading of M, because *incertum an* is non-committal
and draws any affirmative or negative implication from the context.
In *Hist.* I, 75; *Ann.* VI, 50; XI, 18 it is affirmative (= ' probably ');
in *Ann.* V, 1; XI, 22; XV, 64 it seems to be non-committal (= ' it is
really doubtful whether . . .'); in *Hist.* I, 23 it is negative and
= ' probably *not* ', as here. If *expergens* above were the right reading,
and Nero had to rouse Seneca and Burrus from sleep, Tacitus' doubt
about their ignorance of the affair would be silly. No responsible
ministers could have rested, had they known that Nero was perpetrating
such a monkeyish crime.

igitur, ' therefore ', ' accordingly ', ' the result was that . . .'
igitur refers to the whole of the previous sentence rather than merely
to the last clause. Seneca and Burrus stood for a long time in embar-
rassed silence because of Nero's panic, which made it obvious that any
attempt on their part to deter him from taking extreme criminal
measures would be in vain and would only make him hostile. Their
embarrassment would be all the greater because they were political
opponents of Agrippina and had helped to alienate Nero from her

(see c. 1, 3), not expecting that the young maniac would get so out of hand. The alternative explanation of their silence is that they were now agreed that Agrippina must die, or else she would win the political battle, but they hesitated to give advice that would make them Nero's open accomplices.

§ 3. **hactenus promptius**, sc. *egit.*

perpetraret Anicetus promissa, ' It was Anicetus who must fulfil the promises he had made '. The subj. is indir. jussive.

summam sceleris, either ' chief responsibility for ' or ' the completion of ', i.e. he asked for the privilege of being entrusted with the task of completing the crime.

§ 4. **audito,** lit. ' it having been heard that . . .' See Introd. III, 4, (ii).

scaenam ultro criminis parat, ' took the initiative and prepared a stage-setting for an accusation against her '. *Ultro* always suggests ' going beyond ' what is expected or asked, and so often = ' of one's own accord ', ' on one's own initiative ', and often in Tacitus ' unexpectedly to take the initiative in doing something '. Cf. *Hist.* I. 7, *fuere qui crederent . . . a legatis bellum suadentibus, postquam impellere (Capitonem) nequiuerint, crimen ac dolum ultro compositum.* This seems to be the sense here. Nero, in his panic, assumed that Agerinus had come with a charge against him, and decided to take the initiative.

molitam, sc. *esse.*

pudore deprehensi sceleris, ' through shame at the exposure of her crime '. The gen. of the cause with *pudor* is natural, since *pudet* itself takes the gen. of the cause (*pudet me sceleris*).

8. § 1. **quasi casu euenisset.** For *tamquam* and *quasi* with subj. in Tacitus, see Introd. III, 6, ii (*e*). Here one might translate: ' Meanwhile the *version* of Agrippina's dangerous plight which had been noised abroad was to the effect that it had been an accident '.

ut quisque acceperat. The pluperf. indic. in such an indef. clause is the regular classical constr. Silver Latin often uses the subj. See Introd. III, 6, ii (*b*).

molium obiectus, a poetic constr. = *obiectas moles,* ' the barriers of the embankments ', ' the embankments that barred out the sea '. The long dike that separated the Lucrine lake from the sea is meant. Cf. *Hist.* III, 9, *cum terga flumine, latera obiectu paludis tegerentur ;* Virg., *Aen.* I, 160, *insula portum/ efficit obiectu laterum.*

decurrere . . . scandere . . . &c., hist. infin.

pernotuit. Pernotescere ' to become known ' is a post-classical word. Cf. *Ann.* XII, 67, *cuncta mox pernotuere,* though in all other exx. in Tacitus it is used impers. with acc. and infin., as here.

ut ad gratandum. With this use of *ut* = ' as if to . . .', i.e. ' with the intention of . . .', cf. the Greek use of ὡς with a part.

§ 2. **obuios seruorum,** ' those of the slaves who stood in his way '. See Introd. III, 2, (iv).

donec . . . ueniret. See Introd. III, 6, ii (*a*).

terrore inrumpentium, obj. gen. Notice the substantival use of the part. (' fear of the intruders ').

anxia Agrippina, abl. abs., 'while Agrippina was growing more and more nervous '.

quod nemo a filio, sc. *uenisset*. Tacitus is sometimes very bold in omitting verbs, cf. *Ann.* IV, 57, *tandem Caesar in Campaniam* (sc. *abscessit*).

aliam fore laetae rei faciem. The verb of thinking for this acc. and infin. to depend on is understood out of *anxia*. Notice that *laetae* is in an emphatic position, so that the sentence = *aliam fore rei faciem, si laeta esset*.

nunc, 'as it was'; **solitudinem**, sc. *esse*.

§ 3. **respicit**, 'she looked round and saw . . .' This is the literal meaning of *respicio*, which also has the metaphorical sense of 'to look at with respect, or attention', 'to have regard for'.

trierarcho . . . centurione classiario. *Trierarchus* is the Greek title for the commander of a warship (τριήρης—ἄρχειν). At Athens the title was applied to the citizen who fitted out a trireme. In the Roman fleet the *trierarchus* commanded the ship, while the *centurio classiarius* was in charge of the marines. Notice that the abl. without *ab* is used with the part. *comitatus*, as also with *iunctus, coniunctus, stipatus*. It is the 'sociative-instrumental' abl. of accompaniment, and is not to be confused with the abl. with *ab* of a personal agent, which is really a different case.

ad uisendum . . . patraturus. Notice the variation in the methods of expressing purpose. For this use of the fut. part., see Introd. III, 7, (ii).

uenisset . . . nuntiaret. The verb of speaking or commanding is understood. She said: *si . . . uenisti . . . nuntia*. **refotam**, sc. *se esse*.

§ 4. **prior**. Cf. *primus hoc feci*, 'I was the first to do this'. N.b. Latin, more accurate than ordinary vague English, uses *prior*, when only two are spoken of.

in mortem, 'to kill her'. *In* with acc. often denotes intention, and sometimes result. Cf. 32, 1, *in furorem turbatae*, 'roused to frenzy' (result). The latter ex. shows clearly how these two senses developed from the original sense of 'movement in a direction'.

9. § 1. **aspexeritne . . . laudauerit**. As the words *sunt qui tradiderint, sunt qui abnuant* are practically equivalent in sense to *incertum est*, Tacitus substitutes an ind. qu. clause for an acc. and infin. depending on them. 'As to whether Nero gazed on his mother's lifeless body and praised her physical beauty, some have related that he did, while others deny it.' There seems to be no particular point in the change of tense from *tradiderint* to *abnuant*. As Tacitus is writing over fifty years after the events described, it is unlikely that the pres. subj. is meant to denote the continuance of oral tradition as opposed to written records.

conuiuali lecto, an ordinary couch from the dining-room, instead of the special *lectus funebris*.

dum potiebatur. Notice that the rule requiring the use of the hist. pres. indic. after *dum* applies only when it signifies a period of time in the course of which something happens. When, as here, it means 'a period throughout which' (= *quamdiu*, 'so long as'), it may be followed by either the imperf. or aorist indic.

congesta aut clausa humus, 'was not heaped into a mound or enclosed'. By *clausa* Tacitus does not mean, of course, that the grave was not filled in, but that it was not covered over with a stone monument or enclosed within the precincts of a mausoleum. Not even a mound, he says, was raised to mark the spot. *Tumulus* may signify either ' mound of earth ', or ' stone sepulchre ', ' tomb '.

mox, 'later on'. Notice that *mox* does not mean 'soon' in all senses of the English word.

uiam Miseni propter. The placing of a preposition after its case (anastrophe) is, with certain exceptions, not very common in class. Latin. Cf. *Ann*. III, 1, *litora Calabriae contra ;* XV, 47, *uiam propter ; iter iuxta*.

editissima, ' being in a very elevated position '.

§ 2. **hunc sui finem**, sc. *fore*. The gen. *sui* for *suum* can be justified on the ground that the idea is ' objective ' rather than ' possessive ', though Tacitus does not always observe classical rule, for in *Ann*. IV, 24, we find *primo sui incessu*. See on c. 6, 1, *summa sui parte*.

super Nerone. This sense of *super* with abl., = *de*, is ante-classical post-Augustan, and poetic. It was probably colloquial in classical times, for it appears in Cicero's letters. Cf. Virg., *Aen*. I, 750, *multa super Priamo rogitans, super Hectore multa*.

Chaldaei. Professional astrologers at Rome were sometimes called by the name of the inventors of this pseudo-science, sometimes by the name *mathematici*, which has reference to the astronomical calculations which they made. Astrologers were held in contempt under the Republic, but rose in reputation under the Empire. The particular astrologer who made this prediction was named Thrasyllus. See *Ann*. VI, 22.

10. § 1. **perfecto demum scelere, magnitudo eius . . .** ' Only when the crime had been committed did the emperor realize its enormity.' This is not a Tacitean irregularity. When the abl. abs. is used in a case where the part. might have been made to agree with another word in the sentence, the effect is to give greater prominence to the idea conveyed in the participial phrase. Cf. Caes. *B. G*. 6, 4, 4, *Caesar obsidibus imperatis hos Haeduis . . . tradit ;* also *B. G*. 3, 14, 4; 5, 4, 3; 5, 44, 6. Cic. *pro Caec*. 77 and often. So in the above sentence *perfecti demum sceleris magnitudo* would have been far less effective.

reliquo noctis, see Introd. III, 4, (v).

mentis inops, ' devoid of reason ', i.e. ' out of his wits '. Cf. Cic., *De Am*. 53, *inopes amicorum*, ' destitute of friends '. The gen. is that which follows adjectives denoting ' fullness ' and the reverse.

prima . . . adulatio . . . firmauit, ' It was the fawning attitude adopted, at Burrus' suggestion, by the centurions and tribunes that first restored him to hopefulness '. Cf. note on c. 8, 4 *prior*.

quod . . . euasisset, subj. of virtual o. o., giving the *soldiers'* reasons for congratulating him. Needless to say, they were being hypocritical. Burrus probably had difficulty in persuading them to do it.

discrimen . . . et . . . facinus, hendiadys for ' the unforeseen danger from his mother's crime '.

adire . . . testari, hist. infin.

municipia, ' townships ', whether *coloniae* or of Italian origin. There was no longer any difference in status between them.

§ 2. **diuersa simulatione**, lit. ' with the opposite pretence ', i.e. the centurions and tribunes pretended to be glad, when they were not; Nero pretended to be sad, when he was not. Trans. 'Nero's own hypocrisy took the opposite course, and he pretended to be sad'. The abl. is causal or modal with *maestus*, 'sad with the opposite pretence'. Notice that *diuersus* in Tacitus more often = 'opposite' than 'different'.

quasi incolumitati suae infensus, lit. 'as if hostile to his own unscathed condition', i.e. 'angry at his own deliverance'. He pretended to be heartbroken at the thought that his own escape had involved his mother's death.

obuersabaturque . . . grauis aspectus, *grauis* = 'burdensome', 'oppressive', 'unpleasant'. Notice that, coming before its noun, it is in an emphatic or predicative position (= *aspectus qui obuersabatur grauis erat*). Trans. 'and the sight of that sea and shore obtruded itself upon him with an unpleasant effect'.

collibus . . . tumulo. For the omission of prepositions, see Introd. III, 4, (i). *tumulus* must here be used in the general sense of 'grave', unless Tacitus has forgotten that he said (c. 9, 1) that no mound was raised.

summa, 'chief point', 'gist'. Contrast its sense in c. 8, 3.

repertum, sc. *esse*.

luisse . . . parauisset. Whatever is the right reading here, the meaning is the same as c. 7, 4, *pudore deprehensi sceleris sponte mortem sumpsisse. quasi* is Halm's conjecture for *qua* of M, which would mean 'she had paid the penalty through the guilty conscience with which she had plotted the crime'. But this is not equivalent to 'consciousness of having plotted', and is practically meaningless. *quasi* would = 'on the ground that', cf. c. 8, 1; 52, 1, and would explain *conscientia*. Agrippina felt conscience-stricken 'on the ground that' she had plotted a murder. This is a very easy alteration; but *quasi* normally explains a verbal phrase or clause. To explain a single word like *conscientia*, Tacitus more often uses *quia* or *quod*, e.g. *Ann.* II, 55, *ira, quia . . . non concederent. quia* has also been conjectured, and is, perhaps, preferable. Trans. '. . . and that she had paid the penalty out of remorse for having plotted to murder him'.

11. § 1. quod . . . sperauisset. A substantival *quod*-clause standing in apposition to an object (*crimina*) already present is not so rare as one standing as the sole object of a verb of speaking. Cf. Introd. III, 6, ii (*f*).

consortium imperii, 'joint sovereignty'. The appointment of a *consors imperii* or co-regent was a device instituted by Augustus in order to secure a suitable successor. The consort had conferred upon him first the *imperium proconsulare*, which entitled him to command troops, and secondly the *tribunicia potestas*, which gave him control of legislation. The *consors* was not the peer of the emperor, but was in so strong a position on the death of the *princeps* that it would have required civil war and revolution to prevent his succession. Such was the position of Tiberius on the death of Augustus. A position almost as strong had been obtained for Nero from Claudius by the intrigues of Agrippina. She obviously hoped to rule through her son. But women at Rome were not eligible for office, and the Roman people would have considered it an outrage had she claimed legal recognition of her power. However, there seems little doubt that Nero was right in saying that she tried to usurp such a position.

iuraturasque in . . . uerba. *iurare in uerba alicuius* is a regular phrase ' for ' to take the oath of allegiance to some one ', of the *sacramentum militare*. The phrase signifies the repeating of a form of words prescribed by some one. Until the reforms of Marius (*c.* 100 B.C.), troops took the oath to the general, afterwards to the State, and, after Augustus, to the emperor. This charge against Agrippina seems to belie Bury's belief (*Students' Roman Empire*, p. 47) that at this time the soldiers took the oath of fidelity to the ' whole house of the Caesars '. c. 7, 3, *toti C. domui obstrictos* refers to sentimental attachment.

praetorias cohortes. The Praetorian Guard consisted of nine cohorts under Augustus, but by Nero's time had been raised to twelve, each of 1,000 men. In theory it was the bodyguard of the emperor, just as the generals under the Republic had been attended by a personal guard called the *praetoria cohors*. But the resemblance was only in name. The rank and file were recruited mainly from central Italy, served only sixteen years as against the legionary's twenty, and received thirty-two *asses* a day as against the latter's ten. They were exempt from foreign service, except when the emperor himself took the field. They and their commanders wielded an excessive influence at this period, especially at times when the throne was vacant.

idemque dedecus . . . That the magistrates, Senate, and people, and even the provinces took an oath of obedience to the emperor we learn from *Ann.* I, 7 and 34, 1.

postquam frustra habita sit, ' when she had been baffled '. For the variation of sequence, cf. 21, 2: 35, 2.

donatiuum et congiarium. In post-Augustan authors *donatiuum* is used of the present given by the emperor to each soldier at his accession or other extraordinary occasion, *congiarium* of a similar largess to the people. The latter word strictly = ' holding a *congius* ', a measure equivalent to about six pints, and shows that the present was originally in food or oil or wine, the name being retained when money was later substituted. For the occasions referred to, see *Ann.* XII, 69; XIII, 31.

periculaque struxisset, ' and that she had plotted against the lives of important citizens '. Against the soldiers and the people Agrippina's revenge for allowing her humiliation took the form of an attempt to stop the expected largess; against the Senate, of trying to remove responsible members. For the only murder of a senator planned by Agrippina, Tacitus gives quite different reasons, i.e. of Junius Silanus, *Ann.* XIII, 1.

perpetratum, sc. *esse.* Reported exclamation.

ne inrumperet curiam, &c. The charges had some foundation. See *Ann.* XIII, 5, where the Senate is said to have been forced to meet on Mt. Palatine, that Agrippina might hear a debate in which she was interested, and where only Seneca's tact prevented her from presiding with Nero at an audience of Armenian envoys. The charge that she attempted to enter the Senate was probably an exaggeration. For the acc. alone after *inrumpere*, cf. Caes., *B. C.* 2, 13, 4, *quin oppidum inrumperent.* Cicero usually repeats the preposition.

§ 2. **obliqua insectatione,** modal abl., ' with an indirect attack on the Claudian epoch, he laid all the crimes of that reign at his mother's door, representing that her death was due to the good luck which attended the Roman State '.

publica fortuna. At first sight this looks like an abl. of attendant circumstances (i.e. ' her death was lucky for the common weal '), cf. *Ann.* IV, 1, *cuius (rei Romanae) pari exitio uiguit ceciditque ;* Livy XXI, 35, 1, *maiore iumentorum quam hominum pernicie superatus.* On the other hand, it would make it easier to explain the following *namque* if Tacitus meant it as instr. abl. of cause, i.e. ' *due to* the public good luck ', cf. *Ann.* IV, 1, *ut sibi uni incautum efficeret, non tam sollertia . . . quam deum i r a in rem Romanam,* ' . . . not so much by cunning as *owing to* the anger of Heaven '. See next note.

namque, &c. The conj. *nam* (strengthened form *namque*) always introduces a sentence explaining, illustrating, or amplifying what precedes. Nero must therefore have dragged in the shipwreck as a further example of the working of Providence, which had made a previous attempt to rid the State of his mother's pernicious influence. Trans. ' for he even related her shipwreck as an example of this '.

quod fortuitum fuisse, &c. Although one might expect a further report of Nero's absurd arguments, this question must be construed as sarcastic comment by Tacitus. In Nero's mouth, the question *quis . . . inuenietur . . .?* would be rhetorical, and would have to be reported by *quem adeo hebetem inueniri posse . . .?* *inueniretur* is a past potential subj., cf. Cic., *pro l. Man.* 31, *quis unquam arbitraretur?* 'who would ever have thought . . .?'; *Ann.* IV, 11, *quis . . . inaudito filio exitium offerret?* 'who would have offered . . .?' Trans. ' but who could have been found stupid enough to believe that this was due to luck?' Notice that *quod* here = *sed id.* The connective *qui* contains in itself the sense of whatever connective particle is needed.

unum, ' one solitary man '.

cohortes et classes, rhetorical exaggeration, to emphasize the absurdity of the charge. Nero had only one cohort of the Praetorian Guard with him.

§ 3. **immanitas,** ' enormity '. It is used in both senses of the English word.

anteibat, ' surpassed ', i.e. his character was too black for adequate remonstrance to be formulated.

aduerso rumore, abl. of qual., ' was of evil reputation ', i.e. ' became unpopular ', ' was unfavourably spoken of '. For this sense of *rumor,* cf. also *fama, Hist.* I, 73, *aduersa . . . principis fama.*

quod scripsisset, ' for having written ', subj. of virtual o. o., giving his detractors' reason. The absurdity of the story invited suspicion and was tantamount to a confession. For other evidence that Nero relied on Seneca to compose his speeches, see *Ann.* XIII, 3, 11. Seneca was clever enough to have written a more plausible defence. Perhaps he hoped that, by veiling the crime so thinly, his own disgust might be read between the lines.

12. § 1. **tamen,** i.e. in spite of the fact that they well understood Nero's guilt.

decernuntur supplicationes . . . utque. The substantival *ut*-clauses stand as joint subjects to *decernuntur* with *supplicationes.*

supplicationes ... puluinaria. *Supplicationes* were originally days of fasting and humiliation in times of distress, when the people supplicated the gods for relief. Thanksgivings decreed by the Senate after great victories or the aversion of disasters were celebrated in a similar manner. Priests and laymen marched in procession, singing hymns, to all the shrines. Images of gods were laid on a couch (*lectus* or *puluinar*) at the shrine, and a table with an offering of food laid before it. This ceremony was called *lectisternium*. Here *puluinaria* may be translated 'shrines'.

Quinquatrus, see on c. 4, 1.

dies nefastos. The Roman calendar was divided into *dies fasti et nefasti*, on which the *praetor* could or could not pronounce judgement in the law-courts. Cf. Ov. *Fasti*, 1, 48, *ille* (*dies*) *nefastus erit per quem tria uerba* (i.e. *do, dico, addico*) *silentur : / fastus erit per quem lege licebit agi.* The words are derived from the root of *fa-ri*, ' to speak ', and came to mean simply ' lucky ' and ' unlucky '.

Thrasea Paetus, one of the small group of Stoic philosophers who scorned the growing servility to the emperors. The republican opposition centred round these men. Cf. *Ann.* XIII, 49; XIV, 48, 49; XV, 20, 23; XVI, 21, 22, 24, 25 ff. (a servile Senate condemns him for treason).

ac sibi, &c., ' thus causing danger to himself without imparting to the rest an impulse to assert their freedom '.

§ 2. prodigia ... intercessere, ' prodigies also, numerous but ineffective, intervened '. The choice of the verb *intercedo* for *euenio* is intentional, as it is the technical term for the interposition of a veto. It looked as if the prodigies were divine signs sent to forbid and condemn the servile acceptance of the emperor's crime. But they were *irrita*, ' invalid ', ' ineffective ', ' purposeless ', since the crime went unpunished.

iam sol ... obscuratus, ' then, too, the sun was suddenly eclipsed ', on 30 April, A.D. 59, soon after noon.

quattuordecim regiones. The city was divided by Augustus into fourteen *regiones* about 7 B.C., and subdivided into 265 wards, for the purposes of local administration.

quae adeo, &c., ' But the hand of Providence was so far from appearing in these things that actually Nero continued his reign and his crimes for many years after this .' Tacitus' religious beliefs seem to have been vague and undecided. He sometimes adopts a sceptical and scientific attitude, as *Hist.* I, 10, where he says that Destiny and portents are human inventions after the event. Cf. *Hist.* IV, 26, *quod in pace fors seu natura, tunc fatum et ira deum uocabatur.* On the other hand, *Hist.* I, 18; *Ann.* I, 55; III, 18 imply the belief that the course of events is fixed by a Destiny which mocks and renders nugatory human effort. Yet *Ann.* IV, 20; V, 4 admit the possibility that the human mind can affect the course of fate, and that a higher power can influence human behaviour. This belief in a combination of Destiny and free will is stated at greater length in *Ann.* VI, 22, in a discussion arising out of the amazing skill of the astrologer Thrasyllus (on whom see c. 9, 2). There Tacitus, after stating his own inability to decide, sets forth the diverse views of the philosophers. Some say the gods have no care for mankind at all; others (i.e. the Stoics) think that we are allowed a free choice, but after that there follows an inevitable chain of cause and effect. Such a view admits a controlling Providence and denies the validity of astrology. Probably Tacitus inclined to this Stoic view, though his attitude to Providence is bitter. See *Hist.* I, 3; *Ann.* IV, 1; the above passage; and *Ann.* XVI, 16.

continuauerit. Notice that the perf. subj. may be used in a consecutive clause, even of a long-continued action. The difference between the imperf. and the perf. subj. is that the former expresses the cause and the effect as a single indivisible idea, while the latter represents the result as something actual, but incidental, and not inevitable, e.g. Cic., *Fin.* II, 63, *erat . . . ita non superstitiosus ut . . . sacrificia et fana contemneret, ita non timidus ad mortem ut in acie sit . . . interfectus.* Lack of religious feeling involves contempt for ritual, but bravery does not necessarily entail death in battle.

§ 3. **ceterum,** ' However that may be . . .' *ceterum* is often used when resuming after a digression, or in changing the subject.

grauaret. *Grauo* = ' weigh down ', ' burden ', hence metaph. ' to add to ', ' to aggravate '. This active form is mostly poet. and post-Aug., but the passive (or deponent) form (= *moleste ferre*) is Ciceronian.

Iuniam, Junia Calvina, sister of L. Silanus (see *Ann.* XII, 4). Silanus was betrothed to Octavia, whom Agrippina wished to marry to Nero. Hence Silanus' ruin was contrived, and he committed suicide on the day of Claudius' marriage to Agrippina, Junia being driven into exile (*Ann.* XII, 8).

Calpurniam, see *Ann.* XII, 22. She was exiled simply because Claudius had praised her beauty.

Valerium Capitonem, Licinium Gabolum, not elsewhere mentioned by Tacitus.

§ 4. **Lolliae Paulinae.** She was hated by Agrippina as having been her rival for the hand of Claudius (*Ann.* XII, 1; 22). She was driven into exile, and then forced to commit suicide.

extrui permisit. For the infin. see Introd. III, 5, (ii).

relegauerat. *Relēgatio* was a milder punishment than *exilium*, since it did not involve confiscation of goods or *capitis deminutio*, and was often only imposed for a fixed time. Iturius and Calvisius were *clientes* of Junia Silana, an enemy of Agrippina, who had set them on to accuse Agrippina of treason. Agrippina, however, refuted the charge and obtained the exile of Silana and the relegation of Iturius and Calvisius (*Ann.* XIII, 19; 21; 22).

nam Silana. See previous note, which accounts for the use of *nam.*

13. § 1. **tamen cunctari,** hist. infin. The subject *Nero* is easily understood. *tamen,* i.e. even after the above-mentioned efforts to secure popular favour.

ingrederetur . . . reperiret. Both depend on *anxius. quonam modo . . . ingrederetur* is an indir. delib. qu., ' worried as to what his mode of entry into the city should be '. O. r. *quonam modo ingrediar* (subj.). *an reperiret,* on the other hand, is an ordinary indir. qu., ' wondering anxiously whether he would find . . .', o. r. *reperiam-ne ?* (fut. indic.). In strict Ciceronian Latin this would be represented in o. o. by *num reperturus esset.* See Introd. III, 6, ii, (*c*).

quorum. The gen. with *fecundus* is mostly poetic and post-Aug. It is on the analogy of gen. with adjectives denoting fullness. The abl. is usual in class. prose.

iret . . . experiretur, indir. jussive subj., ' Let him go without misgivings and make trial in person of the veneration in which he was held .'

uenerationem sui. See on c. 6, 1.

praegredi. For the infin. after verbs of ' asking ' see Introd. III, 5, (ii).

§ 2. **tribus.** The word *tribus* can only be used for ' tribe ' in the sense of one of the divisions into which all Roman citizens were divided by King Servius. Servius instituted four city (*tribus urbanae*) and twenty-six country tribes (*tribus rusticae*). In 241 B.C. the number was raised to thirty-five. The word for ' tribe ' in the sense of ' native clan ' is *natio*.

qua incederet, certainly not ' frequentative subjunct.' (i.e. = *quacumque incesserat*), as Pitman, for Nero's friends have gone ahead and Nero himself has not yet arrived. The subj. is due to virtual o. o., being either final, as representing the purpose in the minds of the builders of the stands, or, more likely, it represents their expectation, standing for *incessurus esset* (o.r. *gradus extruamus qua incedet* or *incessurus est*). Cf. Introd. III, 6, ii (*c*). Trans. ' (they found) tiers of seats built along the route by which he would proceed, like the arrangements for viewing triumphal processions '.

hinc superbus, &c., ' Hence in a spirit of haughtiness and having triumphantly secured the servility of the people, he approached the Capitol, &c.' *publici seruitii* is an obj. gen. with *uictor*, but represents an ' internal ' not an ' external ' obj. of the verb, i.e. it corresponds to *uincere publicum seruitium*, ' win public servility ' (cf. *uincere uictoriam*, ' win a victory ', where the acc. is truly ' cognate ').

Capitolium adiit, to make a sacrifice of thanksgiving to Jupiter for his escape. Since a general celebrating a triumph also went in procession to the Capitol to offer sacrifice, the use of the phrase *publici seruitii uictor* is particularly pointed.

qualiscumque matris reuerentia. Owing to an ellipse of the verb ' to be ', the rel. adj. *qualiscumque*, ' of whatever sort ', has come to be used as an indefinite adj. = ' of *some* sort or other '. *matris* is obj. gen., ' he abandoned himself to every sort of licentious pleasure, which, though restrained with difficulty, some sort of reverence for his mother had formerly postponed '. Perhaps the relative force might be retained by saying ' reverence for his mother, *such as it was* '. The indefinite use is Ciceronian, but rare till after Livy.

14. § 1. **cupido . . . insistere, studium . . . canere.** Classical Latin would require here *cupido insistendi, studium canendi.* See Introd. III, 5, (i).

ludicrum in modum, ' in a theatrical manner ', i.e. ' as a theatrical performer '. Nero wished to become a professional actor. For *ludicer* in this sense, cf. c. 16, 1 *ludicrae imperatoris artes,* ' theatrical accomplishments '. The neut. is used as a noun, = ' a show ', ' a spectacle ', see c. 20, 1 *quinquennale ludicrum.*

regium, ' a royal pursuit.'

antiquis ducibus factitatum, ' regularly engaged in by the princes of old '. For the dat. of the agent, see Introd. II, 3, (ii). Nero is thinking chiefly of the Olympian, Pythian, Nemean, and Isthmian games in Greece, celebrated in honour of Zeus, Apollo, Zeus, and Poseidon respectively. The chief poets who celebrated victories at these games were Pindar and Bacchylides.

honori. See on c. 4, 2.

enimuero . . . ' Yes, and song, moreover, was sacred to Apollo . . .' Like *enim*, the strengthened form *enimuero* explains what goes before, but corroborates it much more strongly. It is used in corroborating replies, e.g. Plaut., *Amph.* 344 *ain uero ?—Aio enimuero,* ' Do you say so ? '—' To be sure I do ! ' It is regularly used in passing from what is less to what is more important, and implies that, if what goes before is true, what follows is much more so. So here, the thought that chariot races, celebrated by the poets, took place at religious festivals, suggests to Nero the more important consideration that music especially was sacred to Apollo. ' Yes, and what was more . . .'

§ 2. **cum** . . . **uisum,** sc. *est.* ' Inverted ' *cum*-clause.

ne utraque peruinceret, ' in order that he might not win his way in both matters '. *utraque* is neut. pl. acc. and is an ' internal ' acc. The use of the plur. when each of two single things is spoken of is a careless colloquialism. Exx. occur in Cicero's letters, and become more frequent later.

ualle Vaticana, Locatival abl. For omission of prep. see Introd. III. 4, (i). St. Peter's now stands on the site.

haud promisco spectaculo, abl. of att. circs. (or abs.), ' the sight not being open to all '.

ultro uocari . . . **extollere,** hist. infin., ' actually began to be invited, &c.'. For *ultro*, see on c. 7, 4, *ultro* . . . *parat.*

ut est . . . **laetum,** ' as one might expect from a mob greedy of pleasure and happy whenever the emperor influences it in the same direction '. *ut* = ' just *as* ' comes to have several different shades of meaning. Here the sense is ' in accordance with the fact that . . .', or ' as one might expect from the fact that . . .' *si eodem trahat* is difficult, since, if *traho* has its usual trans. sense of ' draw ', with the obj. *eos* or *uulgus* understood, one would expect *eo,* ' in that direction ', sc. *ad uoluptates. Eodem* seems to require an intrans. sense for *trahat,* i.e. ' tends ', ' inclines ', but this sense is difficult to parallel. Notice that the pres. subj. with *si,* ' should the emperor draw . . .', amounts to ' whenever the emperor draws . . .'.

§ 3. **euulgatus pudor,** cf. Introd. III, 7, (i).

dedecus. Although famous actors sometimes won to positions of social distinction (e.g. S. Roscius, whom Cicero defended), yet the profession always carried with it a social stigma and was considered taboo for a true-born Roman. Julius Caesar humiliated the Roman knight Laberius in a similar way, by making him act in one of his own mimes. Laberius inserted these lines in his prologue:

ego bis trecenis annis actis sine nota
eques Romanus Lare egressus meo,
domum reuertar mimus, nimirum hoc die
uno plus uixi mihi quam uiuendum fuit.

molliri, si plures foedasset. The pres. infin. may possibly be explained as a general reflection—'Shame is always lessened, the greater the numbers affected', but as the statement is particularized by the *si*-clause, Nero probably said to himself, *dedecus mollietur, si . . . foedauero*, so that *molliri* is used loosely for *mollitum iri*. But colloquial Latin was capable of the same carelessness in the use of the pres. for the fut. as Eng. is. Exx. of the type *aibat reddere* for *se redditurum* are very common in Plautus and are even found in Caesar. Cf. c. 18, 2, *se . . . subuenire . . . scripsit ;* 58, 3, *denique aut salutem . . . quaeri . . .*

ne nominatim, &c., 'I think that, out of respect for their ancestors, I ought to refrain from recording their names.' The *ne*-clause = an acc. substantive which, with the infin. *tribuendum* (*esse*), stands as obj. of *puto,* ' I think that (that I should not report them by name) is to be paid as a tribute to their ancestors .'

§ 4. **nam et . . .,** ' For also . . .', giving an additional reason for silence. ' In any case, the guilt is his who . . .'.

ob delicta, = *ut delinquerent.* Notice the striving for variation.

promittere subegit, see Introd. III, 5, (ii).

nisi quod . . ., ' except that a reward from one who can command is tantamount to compulsion '. The intention of *nisi quod,* ' except for the fact that . . .', is to remove any false impression that may have been conveyed by the use of the word *donis.* Greed need not have been their motive for degrading themselves, for they had no choice.

15. § 1. **ludos Iuuenalium uocabulo.** For the 'defining' gen. with *nomen,* &c., cf. c. 50, 1, *quibus nomen codicillorum dederat,* and Introd. III, 2, (iii). The first clipping of a Roman's beard had always been the occasion of a festival in the family, and Nero now made it the excuse for the institution of public *ludi Iuuenales* or *Iuuenalia.* After Nero the *Iuuenalia* were changed in character, chariot-races and *uenationes* supplanting the theatrical performances.

passim nomina data. *nomen dare* is the reg. phrase for ' to enlist ', of a soldier. The point of *passim* is explained by the next sentence.

impedimento, sc. *erant.* predic. dat.

quin et, ' Nay, even . . .'.

§ 2. **deformia meditari,** ' studied degrading parts '. hist. infin.

nauali stagno. Augustus had constructed a lake on the far side of the Tiber on which to stage a mimic naval battle. Cf. *Ann.* XII, 56.

conuenticula et cauponae, ' assembly rooms and shops '.

posita ueno irritamenta luxui, ' incitements to vice were exposed for sale '. *ueno* is dat. of purpose or ' end aimed at '. Tacitus has even *ueno dedisse* (*Ann.* IV, 1), whereas the classical usage is to use the acc. of goal of motion in the phrase *uēnum dare* (whence *uendere*), and *uēnum ire* (whence *uēnire*). For the dat. *luxui* with a noun, cf. Introd. III, 3, (iv).

dabanturque . . . consumerent, ' doles (of money) were given for people to spend, decent folk under compulsion, the vicious in a spirit of vainglory '. *consumerent* must be taken as final subj., in spite of the fact that the manner in which the various characters should spend the money formed no part of the purpose of the donor. Tacitus has, in fact, tried to say two things at once, viz. ' Nero gave largess for the people to spend ', and ' the decent folk spent it because they had to, the vicious as if they were proud of it '. The ablatives *necessitate* and *gloria* may be either modal or causal, i.e. ' under compulsion ' or ' because they were compelled ', ' vaingloriously ' or ' out of vainglory '.

§ 3. **nec ulla** sc. *colluuies*, anticipated from below. ' Thence came the increase of crime and scandal, nor did any gathering import more vicious practices into social manners long ago corrupt than did the scum that gathered there .'

artibus honestis. *Artes* = ' acquired accomplishments ' as opposed to natural powers, but is often used of the pursuits themselves in which the skill is acquired. So here ' honourable pursuits '. The abl. may be instr., but is more likely of att. circs., since it is parallel to *inter certamina*.

nedum . . . reseruaretur. *Ne-dum* strictly = ' in order that . . . not at all ', and is accordingly followed by the subj., e.g. Ter. *Heaut.* 452, *satrapa nunquam sufferre sumptus queat, nedum tu possis*, ' a Persian satrap could not bear the expense, so that (naturally) you may not ', which = ' much less can you '. When there is an ellipse of the verb, *nedum* is best trans. ' much less ', or sometimes, after an affirmative statement, ' much more '. Cf. c. 35, 2, *ne strepitum quidem . . . nedum impetus et manus perlaturos* (' much less '); *Ann.* XIII, 38, *cuicunque mortalium, nedum ueteri et prouido duci, barbarae astutiae patuissent* (' much more '). Trans. ' It is difficult to keep a sense of shame amidst honourable pursuits, still less could chastity or decency or any uprightness of character be kept alive amidst rivalries in vice .'

scaenam incedit. The acc. depends on the prep. contained in the verb. Class. Latin would repeat the prep.

temptans . . . praemeditans, ' tuning his lyre and trying out his voice.'.

maerens Burrus ac laudans. Notice the inimitable literary skill with which Tacitus, by means of these two epithets attached to Burrus, a decent man, manages to characterize Nero and his times in such a way that there is no more to be said. The effect is spoilt if we trans. *ac* by an adversative conj.

§ 4. **Augustianorum,** not elsewhere mentioned by Tacitus. Suetonius mentions them (*Ner.* 25) as *plausores*. Dio calls them Αὐγούστειοι.

deum uocabulis, i.e. they praised his beauty by calling him ' Apollo ' ' Hercules ', and the like.

quasi . . . agere, ' they lived as distinguished and honoured men, as if they owed it to their virtue '. *agere* here = *esse* or *uiuere*, rather than *se gerere*. Cf. c. 44, 2. *tuti . . . non inulti . . . agere.*

16. § 1. **ludicrae artes,** see on c. 14, 1.

adfectauit. This verb is used both in the sense of ' to lay false claim to ', ' to pretend to ', and ' to aim at something seriously '. Thus this sentence might = ' he *affected* a zeal for poetry ', or ' he adopted (seriously) the pursuit of poetry '. The general tone of the chapter suggests that Tacitus meant the former, though the latter was the actual truth.

contractis quibus, &c., i.e. *contractis iis* (abl. abs.) *quibus* (dat.), ' gathering together those who had some skill in versification, but had not yet made a name thereby. These used to sit down together, after dinner . . .'. The text is that of Halm. M reads *contractis quibus aliqua pangendi facultas. necdum insignis aetatis nati considere. . . .* The text given accounts for *nati*, but it seems rather bold to rule out *aetatis*, since a more direct reference to the youthful age of these poets is not out of place. It is probably now impossible to recover what Tacitus wrote, but it is tempting to suggest *necdum insignis aetatis erant. ii considere.* . . . Lucan was one of the young poets referred to. In spite of his youth, he soon began to put Nero in the shade to such an extent that the latter forbade him to give any more public recitations.

adlatos uel ibidem repertos. Does this mean 'verses brought by them to Nero or invented by them on the spot', or 'verses put before them by Nero or invented by him on the spot'? One would naturally expect the agent with *adlatos*, when not expressed, to be the same as the subject of *considere . . . conectere.* Editors and translators are divided. It is unlikely, however, that *adlatos uersus* are Nero's, since *ipsius uerba* are mentioned separately, and Tacitus is being as unkind to Nero in this chapter as he can. He is making out that very few of the verses published under Nero's name were his own. Suetonius (*Ner.* 52) thought otherwise, nor is real artistic ability inconsistent in one of Nero's temperament.

quoquo modo prolata, 'just as they fell from his mouth', i.e., if Nero thought of a good phrase or half-line, they would supplement it and work it into a respectable line of verse.

non impetu . . . fluens, 'for they do not flow with force and inspiration, nor with uniformity of style'. Notice that the epithet *fluens* has been transferred to *species*, though logically it should be *fluentium*, in agreement with *carminum.* Such transference of epithet is more common in poetry than prose.

§ 2. utque . . . frueretur. If -*que* is right, it can only be explained as joining the *ut*-clause closely to, and explaining the phrase *post epulas*, which is placed after its verb for that purpose, i.e. Nero used to give some of his time to professors of philosophy, not, however, out of thirst for knowledge, but as an after-dinner entertainment, and from a vulgar desire to enjoy their quarrels.

nec deerant qui . . . cuperent There were Stoic philosophers of the baser sort who were glad of a chance to parade their pretended austerity amid the delights of the court, even if they could only get there at the price of being mocked.

17. § 1. Nucerinos, the people of Nūceria Alfaterna, a few miles east of Pompeii.

Liuineius Regulus, not elsewhere mentioned by Tacitus. His expulsion from the Senate must have been related in the lost portion of the Annals.

oppidana lasciuia, 'with the unruliness usual in provincial towns', where police precautions were not as efficient as in Rome.

incessentes, sc. *se*, which is easily understood with a phr. like *in uicem.* Distinguish this verb from *incedo*, which would require a dat. after it. (L. & S. quote many of the same exx. for both verbs!)

probra . . . saxa . . . ferrum, all taken by zeugma as objects of *sumpsere*, though in an Eng. rendering a different verb will be required for each.

in urbem, 'to Town', 'to Rome', i.e. as evidence to support complaints against the Pompeians. Beware of trans. 'to Nuceria', for which *urbs* would not be used.

trunco . . . corpore, abl. of accompaniment, or of att. circs., ' carried to Rome with their bodies mutilated '.

plerique, ' very many ', as usually in Tacitus. Cf. c. 53, 4 *plerumque* = ' very often '; 55, 4, *plerique . . . plura tenuerunt,* where the class. sense of ' most ', or ' the majority ' is quite impossible.

§ 2. **rursus re relata,** i.e. the Senate had commissioned the consuls to hold an enquiry, the result of which was in due course put before the Senate, which then proceeded to decide punishments. Under the so-called ' dyarchy ' set up by Augustus, the Senate was allowed to retain many of its republican functions, including its authority in the affairs of Italy. It also became a permanent court of justice. These rights were confirmed by Nero at the beginning of his reign (see *Ann.* XIII, 4). That is why a riot in an Italian town was dealt with by the Senate and consuls.

prohibiti publice . . . *not,* ' the Pompeians were publicly forbidden . . .', but ' were forbidden *as a community* ', i.e. the municipality was forbidden to sanction such shows. For this sense of *publice,* cf. *Ann.* IV, 36, *obiecta publice Cyzicenis incuria,* ' the people of Cyzicus, as a community, were charged with neglect ', i.e. the charge was brought against their government. It may sometimes be trans. ' officially ' or ' with state sanction ', e.g. *Germ.* 15, 10, *(dona) non modo a singulis sed et publice mittuntur.*

collegia. The term *collegium* was used of any sort of association from political clubs to poor people's burial societies. Other terms were *sodālitas* and *sodālicium,* the former being used particularly of religious brotherhoods. Towards the end of the Republic, the political *collegia sodālicia* were instruments of terrorism and corruption, as in large American cities recently. In 47 B.C. Julius Caesar, having been himself a successful gangster, suppressed by edict all the *collegia* except the ancient corporations. Henceforward no society could be formed in Rome or in the provinces without authorisation by the Senate or by the emperor. *Collegia inlicita* (i.e. *quae contra leges instituerant*) were severely punished, but as the attitude was less strict towards *collegia funeraticia* (burial societies), doubtless many questionable societies were formed under cover of this purpose.

18. § 1. **Pedius Blaesus.** He was restored by Otho ten years later, see *Hist.* I, 77.

Cyrenensibus, the people of Cyrene in N. Africa. The Cyrenaica had been made a Roman province in 74 B.C. It remained a senatorial province under the Empire.

uiolatum ab eo thesaurum, sc. *esse.* The acc. and infin. after *accuso* is very rare and unclassical. The ground of accusation is normally given in a subj. *quod-*clause.

pretio et ambitione corruptum, i.e. he had accepted bribes and yielded to unlawful pressure in exempting people from service. Trans. ' he was accused by the people of Cyrene of having plundered the treasury of Aesculapius (i.e. in the temple of the god of Healing) and of having accepted bribes and exercised favouritism in the conduct of a military levy '.

Acilium Strabonem, not elsewhere mentioned by Tacitus.

praetoria potestate usum. It is impossible to decide whether

Tacitus means ' an ex-praetor ', for which the normal phrase is *praetura functus* or *praetorius*, or whether it means that he had been given temporary praetorian power during his commission.

disceptatorem . . . agrorum, ' as an arbitrator with regard to territories . . .'. The gen. is obj.

regis Apionis, Ptolemaeus Apion, last king of Cyrene, who died in 96 B.C., leaving his kingdom to Rome.

proximus quisque possessor, ' all the neighbouring occupiers '. Notice that *quisque* may be followed by a plur. verb by *constructio ad sensum*.

diutinaque . . . nitebantur. *licentia et iniuria* is hendiadys for ' wrong-doing that has been allowed, or overlooked '. Trans. ' they rested their case on the fact that their wrong-doing had been overlooked for so long, as if that constituted right and justice .'

§ 2. **subuenire . . . concedere.** For the tense, see on c. 14, 3.

usurpata. In class. Latin *usurpare* = ' to make use of ', ' employ ', ' take possession of ', without any idea of wrongfulness, unless there are other words to indicate it. So often in Tacitus, e.g. *Ann.* III, 60, *quod falso usurpauerant sponte omisere.* In post-Aug. Latin, however, it is often used in the sense of ' to usurp ', i.e. wrongfully. Cf. *Ann.* IV, 15, *si uim praectoris usurpasset . . . spreta in eo mandata sua.* In c. 55, 2, *usurpare otium*, it is used in its class. sense.

19. § 1. **Domitii Afri.** Cn. Domitius Afer was a famous informer (*delator*). He is described in *Ann.* IV, 52 as a man of humble origin, talented, but unprincipled (cf. *morum diuersus* below).

M. Seruilii, M. Servilius Nonianus, consul in A.D. 35, a famous pleader and historian. Quintilian (X, 1, 102) says of him, ' Servilius, whom I myself have heard, is remarkable for the force of his intellect, and is full of general reflections, but is less restrained than the dignity of history demands '. The period covered by his histories is unknown, but he may have been one of Tacitus' authorities.

orando causas . . . tradendis rebus . . . The variation between the gerund and gerundive constr. is obviously studied.

clariorem, i.e. than that of Afer, because, though equal in other respects, he was upright, while Afer was not.

par ingenio . . . morum diuersus, another intentional variation. For the gen., see Introd. III, 2, (i).

20. § 1. **Nerone . . . consulibus,** ' In the year in which Nero was consul for the fourth time, with Cornelius Cossus as his colleague ', i.e. A.D. 60, the sixth year of Nero's reign. This Cossus was son of the Cornelius Cossus who was consul in A.D. 25.

quinquennale ludicrum, a five-yearly festival referred to in *Ann.* XVI, 4 as *lustrale certamen*, because it was intended that it should be held at the end of each *lustrum* (five-year period). Nero called it the *Neronia*, ' Neronian Games ' (Suet. *Ner.* 12). The innovation consisted in the combination of three types of contest: chariot-races, gymnastic, and musical.

uaria fama, abl. of att. circs. with the verb *institutum est*, though the abl. is so loosely attached as to be almost abs. But, if it is construed absolutely, the nom. *cuncta noua* will have no construction. As it is, the adv. phrase *uaria fama* leads us to understand the verb for it. The full expression would be *ludicrum* . . . *institutum est* . . . *uaria fama, ut cuncta ferme noua* (*instituuntur*). Trans. ' a five-yearly festival was instituted on the model of a Greek contest, the opinions expressed about it being varied, as usually happens with innovations '.

incusatum, ' censured '.

mansuram, ' permanent '. The use of the fut. part. as an adj. is unclassical. Pompey's theatre was built in 55 B.C. near the Campus Martius.

§ 2. **nam antea,** &c. The rest of the chapter is in o.o., reporting the adverse opinions expressed. The sequence of tenses in sub. clauses varies between primary and historic.

stantem populum. Before 145 B.C. the place for the spectators was a space surrounded by a wooden barrier, within which the public stood and looked on in a promiscuous mass. In 154 B.C. an attempt was made to build a theatre with fixed seats, but it was pulled down by order of the Senate. But see article by W. Beare, *Class. Rev.* May 1939, p. 51.

ne, si consideret . . . **continuaret,** ' in case, if they sat down in the theatre, they might spend whole days on end in idleness '. By the Ciceronian age, the *Ludi Romani* actually went on for fifteen days. *theatro,* for omission of *in,* see Introd. III, 4, (i). *ignauia,* modal abl.

spectaculorum . . . **certandi.** The criticisms in the previous sentence deplore the increasing importance attached to theatrical shows and the time devoted to them. The critics now turn to the character of the shows themselves and express a plea that the shows exhibited by the praetors at the regular festivals, at any rate, should keep their Roman character unimpaired, the performances, of whatever kind, being left to professionals. There is an obvious reference to cc. 14 and 15. Nero has so far restricted his innovations to private shows of his own, in which he has forced Roman citizens to take part. He has now made a more ambitious attempt by instituting a *public* exhibition intended to be repeated regularly at the public expense. Anxiety is now felt that he may try to alter the character of the regular State spectacles supervised by the praetors. In republican times the public games were supervised by the aediles, the duty being transferred to the praetors under Augustus. These new ' Neronia ' were supervised by men of consular rank chosen by lot (Suet. *Ner.* 12). Trans. ' the ancient character of the shows at least, when regularly given by the praetors, must be preserved, and no Roman citizen must be compelled to take part .'

§ 3. **ceterum,** 'However ', ' All the same ', here grants a concession and = *tamen.* Cf. 14, 3; 49, 2.

accitam, ' imported ', i.e. from Greece, *ut* . . . *uisatur :* both Nipperdey and Furneaux take this as a final clause denoting the intention of the importers, i.e. the *ut*-clause depends on *accitam.* This would require the order *euerti per lasciuiam accitam ut* . . ., and is most unlikely. The clause is consec. Trans. ' All the same, native Roman manners, which had been gradually undermined, were being completely overthrown by imported immorality, so that anything in any sphere which could be abused or cause corruption was to be seen in the city .'

gymnasia . . . **exercendo.** Often the abl. of the gerund is merely equivalent to a pres. part. agreeing with the subject, see Introd. III, 4, (iv). But here the abl. is plainly as much instr. as *studiis externis*. *gymnasia* is joined with *otia* and *amores* as its obj. by zeugma. Trans. ' through frequenting gymnasia and practising loafing and immorality '.

§ 4. **quid superesse**, &c., a rhet. qu. So far nobles had only been forced to take part in musical or literary contests, though in c. 14, 4 we are told that Nero got them to promise to take part in the more vulgar contests of the amphitheatre. Though the Greek contests, in which free-born citizens took part, included boxing-matches, a Roman would consider such contests as equivalent to gladiatorial fights and wild-beast hunting, the performers in which were trained slaves. The only sort of physical contests in which the Roman thought it dignified to take part, were those included in the curriculum of military training.

caestus. The ancient boxing-gloves were not made to soften blows, but consisted of leather thongs studded with metal.

decurias equitum, ' jury-panels of knights '. The list of jurymen was divided into classes called *decuriae*. Though the word originally meant ' a group of ten ' (cf. *centuria*), it was now used in a general sense of ' class ' or ' division '. Actually each class contained 300. In 122 B.C. C. Gracchus transferred the right of serving as *iudices* from the Senate to the knights. In 70 B.C. a compromise between the orders was effected, but Augustus excluded senators altogether. Under him there were four *decuriae* of *iudices*. Caligula added a fifth.

expleturos. The part. is made masc. instead of agreeing with *decurias*, because Tacitus is thinking of the knights who composed the *decuriae*. This is known as *constructio ad sensum*, and is very common.

fractos sonos et dulcedinem uocum, ' quavering notes and musical voices '. Cf. Quint. I, 10, 31, *musice . . . effeminata et impudicis modis fracta*.

perite audissent, ' listened with an expert ear to . . .'.

ne quod . . . sed . . . audeat, ' that decency might not have a moment left, but that all the worst elements might, in the confused gathering, dare to satisfy in the darkness the lusts they had conceived during the day '. *ut* is understood after *sed* out of the preceding *ne*.

21. § 1. **Pluribus,** ' the majority ', as in c. 42, 2. *Plures* and *plura* have three senses in Tacitus: (1) the true comp. sense of ' more than ', cf. c. 58, 1; (2) ' the majority ' or ' the greater number '; (3) ' a number ', ' several ', = *complures*, cf. c. 49, 3; 51, 1.

nomina, not ' excuses ', ' pretexts ', as Nipperdey and Furneaux, for cp. c. 39, 3, *honestum pacis nomen segni otio imposuit ;* also *Ann.* II, 33, *sub nominibus honestis confessio uitiorum*. Most people favoured the new institution simply because of the very (*ipsa*) relaxation of convention which it involved, but they did not call it *licentia*, they called it *laetitia*, *uoluptates concessae*, &c.

pro fortuna . . ., ' in proportion to the resources of the time '.

a Tuscis accitos histriones. The *locus classicus* on the history of dramatic performances in Rome is Livy VII, 2, where we are told that in 361 B.C., on the occasion of a plague, among other attempts to placate the divine anger, Etruscan actors were summoned to perform in Rome. The Etruscan name for an actor was *hister*, and when play-acting caught on in Rome, native players were called *histriones*.

a Thuriis. Thurii was a Greek colony in Bruttium founded in the time of Pericles on the site of the earlier city of Sybaris. Class. Lat. usually does not use a prep. with the name of a town, unless it means ' from the neighbourhood of '.

possessa Achaia Asiaque. Greece came under Roman rule after the defeat of the Achaean League and the destruction of Corinth by L. Mummius in 146 B.C. The province of Asia was organized in 126 B.C. out of the dominions bequeathed to Rome by Attalus III, last king of Pergamum.

curatius, ' more sumptuously '.

ad theatrales artes degenerauisse, ' stooped to adopt a theatrical profession '. Individual Romans had taken part as amateurs from time to time long before Nero forced citizens to do so.

ducentis iam annis, abl. of ' time within which ', ' during the 200 years which had now elapsed since . . .'. Though it is possible to take the phrase as abl. abs., ' it being now 200 years since . . .'.

id genus spectaculi, i.e. Greek plays, referring to *theatrales artes*.

§ 2. **potius quam . . . consurgeret.** After *potius quam*, ' rather than ', two constructions are possible, according to the sense. (1) Where two alternatives are given between which a deliberate choice is exercised, so that one is chosen and the other deliberately rejected, the subj. is used, e.g. Cic., *T. D.* 2, 52, *perpessus est omnia potius quam conscios indicaret*, ' he suffered all things rather than give away his accomplices '. (2) When *potius quam* is used to compare two statements of fact, one of which is more exact than the other, the same mood is used after *potius quam* as before it. Hence *fugit potius quam pugnauit* = ' his action was a flight rather than a fight ', whereas *pugnaret* would mean ' he fled rather than fight '. N.b. *ut* is *not* understood with this subj., though it is sometimes inserted, particularly by Livy. Cf. c. 1, 2, *ubi audiret potius quam uiseret*, though there the final subj. is required in any case.

rem exhausturos. The fact that the responsible magistrate had to provide the money for popular entertainments out of his own purse had been a source of great corruption under the Republic. The aedile who aspired to higher office had to ruin himself in order to win votes. He reimbursed himself later from the wretched province that he was sent to govern. Under the Empire, when this was no longer possible, the office (now the praetorship) which entailed this duty of giving shows became a burden and not a prize.

efflagitandi . . . causam. This sentence contains an answer to the objection that no new shows were needed. It is implied that the people had been in the habit of demanding the inclusion of Greek contests as an additional turn in the regular shows.

§ 3. **graue,** ' serious ', i.e. a serious misdemeanour. The adj. is also used in the sense of ' burdensome ' or ' offensive '.

tanta luce, either abl. of cause, of att. circs., or local.

§ 4. **quamquam,** with *redditi* alone. For the postponement, cf. *Ann.* V, 9 *uanescente quamquam plebis ira* ; VI, 30 *haec, mira quamquam* . . .

pantomimi. Both the *pantomimus* and the *mimus* relied on dancing and gesticulation without words. *Mimi* are probably meant to be included here, as they acted scenes from low life, whereas the *pantomimus* acted scenes from tragedies as a rule, and aimed at sensual charm rather than sheer buffoonery. However, Tacitus seems to use the terms *histrio*, *mimus*, and *pantomimus* as interchangeable. The indecency of the mimes was outrageous, partisanship in the audience ran high and often ended in free fights. Several attempts were made to banish *histriones* from Italy on account of the riots they caused. See *Ann.* I, 54; IV, 14; XIII, 25.

certaminibus sacris. The Greek contests were held at religious festivals in honour of a god. Accordingly the Neronia, held in imitation of them, were ostensibly religious also.

primas, sc. *partes,* which here = 'first prize', though usually *primae partes* = 'chief rôle', 'star part'.

oxoleuerunt, 'went out of fashion'.

22. § 1. sidus cometes. Though *cometes* is a Greek adj. (κομήτης) = 'long-haired', the word is normally used as a noun, of a comet, so that here it must be in apposition to *sidus*. Seneca says that this comet was visible for six months, and that no particular evil accompanied it.

tamquam, see Introd. III, 6, ii (*e*).

regis, in the general sense of 'ruler'.

Rubellius Plautus, son of Rubellius Blandus and Julia, the grand-daughter of Tiberius. See *Ann.* XIII, 19 sqq., where Agrippina is accused of plotting to make him emperor. For his murder, see cc. 58 sqq.

placita maiorum, 'old-fashioned ideas'.

habitu seuero, casta domo, abl. of quality, the pres. part. of the verb 'to be' being understood in agreement with *ipse*. It is not impossible, however, to take the ablatives as modal with *colebat,* though the former is preferable, since the nominatives *occultior* and *adeptus* are parallel to them. Trans. 'He himself cultivated old-fashioned habits, being of austere bearing, with a chaste and secluded home, and the more he avoided publicity through fear, the greater the reputation which he acquired.'

§ 2. Simbruina stagna, three lakes formed by the river Anio. The villa was called *Sublaqueum* as 'lying below the lakes'.

Tiburtum, adj. *Tiburs, -urtis,* 'of or belonging to Tibur'.

hunc illum . . . destinari, short for *hunc illum esse qui destinaretur,* 'this was he who was marked out . . .' Cf. Virg., *Aen.* vii, 255, *hunc illum fatis . . . portendi,* which Tacitus doubtless had in mind.

ambitio = 'a striving to secure favour', i.e. 'method of securing advancement'. Trans. 'and he began to be courted by many whose greedy and usually unreliable method of securing advancement is to pay premature court to new and doubtful fortunes'.

§ 3. consuleret . . . subtraheret, subj. of ind. command depending on a verb of commanding understood from *componit litteras.* Notice that when a command is reported amongst indir. statements and is not introduced by an actual verb of commanding, the sub. conj. is usually omitted.

praua diffamantibus. *diffamare* is also used with a personal obj. in the sense of 'to defame'. Here *praua* is its 'internal obj.', 'spreading base reports'.

frueretur, final subj. The letter said '*sunt tibi agri, in quibus . . . fruaris*'.

§ 4. **nimia luxus cupido,** ' his excessive thirst after extravagance '. *luxus* is often translated ' wantonness ', but it is not the sort of impish wantonness that gratuitously outrages people's feelings, but the sort of extravagance that bathes in champagne. The *aqua Marcia*, an aqueduct constructed by the praetor L. Marcius Rex in 149 B.C., which led from the Sabine hills, brought Rome its purest drinking-water. Nero had obviously decided that he must have the very best water to bathe in, in spite of the fact that a religious sanctity attached to the headwaters of rivers.

nando, see note on c. 7, 1 and 4, 3.

incesserat. For the bare acc. after this verb, see c. 15, 3.

23. § 1. At Corbulo, &c. For the circumstances of the war in Armenia, see Introd. ch. V. The narrative is here resumed from Bk. XIII, 41.

post deleta Artaxata, cf. c. 14, 3, *euulgatus pudor*.

utendum recenti terrore. Notice that though the verbs *utor*, *fruor*, &c., have a pass. gerundive adj., it is not used predicatively, i.e. one can say *his rebus utendis hostes uicit*, but not *hae res utendae sunt*. For the latter, the gerund must be used, followed by the abl.

quibus excisis . . . adipisceretur, a final rel. clause equivalent to: *ut eis excisis . . . intenderet, uel, si (eis) pepercisset . . . adipisceretur,* ' in order that, by destroying it, he might increase the enemy's fear, or, if he spared it, acquire a reputation for clemency '. With *si pepercisset* it is rather *ut eis* (dat.) which is understood from *quibus excisis* than the repetition of the relative in the dat. *pepercisset,* of course, stands for *pepercero* of Corbulo's direct thought.

non infenso exercitu, i.e. the army did not advance ravaging and destroying.

facilem mutatu, ' prone to change of front '. The Supine *mutatu* is used only by Tacitus, and only twice by him (cf. *Hist.* II, 63).

ut segnem . . . ita infidam . . ., ' though reluctant to face danger, yet treacherous when advantage offered '.

§ 2. **pro ingenio quisque,** sc. *egerunt; alii . . . quidam,* in apposition to *barbari*. Notice Tacitus' variation for the usual *alii . . . alii*.

diuersis artibus . . . immitis. Editors generally seem to take *diuersis artibus* as a strange use of the abl. of quality. Actually it must be an instr. abl. It cannot be abl. of qual., because it is parallel to and is amplified by *misericordia* and *celeritate*, which are obviously instr. or modal. The verb which these ablatives qualify is grammatically *exurit*, but logically some verb denoting action in general is understood. Cf. the previous sentence, where the verb of which *quisque* is the subject has to be understood out of *offerre . . . deserere*. We have here another case of anacoluthon, or variation of construction, similar to that in c. 4, 3 (see note *ad loc.*). Tacitus starts off with *adverbial* ablatives describing Corbulo's method of procedure against the various natives, but instead of saying, e.g. *crudelitate aduersus eos qui latebras insederant*, he substitutes the adj. *immitis* agreeing with the subject (cf. *adductus* in c. 4, 3). This does not mean that *diuersis artibus* must therefore be adjectival. Having substituted this adj. describing Corbulo in the one action only, Tacitus does not now put in a verb of general significance, e.g. *egit*, for the ablatives to qualify, but they are left grammatically qualifying the one verb *exurit*, to which they do not logically belong. It is, however, just possible that *usus* has dropped out after *artib-us*, by haplography, which would simplify the constr. somewhat. Trans. ' Accordingly the Roman general adopted different tactics, leniency towards the suppliants and speedy pursuit when dealing with fugitives. Acting with harshness against those who had ensconced themselves in hiding-places, he filled up the entrances and exits to the caves with brushwood and branches and burned them out .'

§ 3. **praegredientem**, not here = ' going before ', but ' passing in front of ', ' passing by ' = *praetergredientem*.

Mardi, a robber tribe who lived in the vicinity of Lake Van, the ancestors of the modern Kurds.

Hiberis, (*Iberi*) a tribe that lived between Mt. Caucasus and the Araxes, from whose neighbourhood Corbulo began his march. They would be present in the Roman army as auxiliaries.

24. § 1. **fatiscebant**, lit. ' gaped with chinks ', ' were cracking to pieces ', i.e. ' were worn out '.

carne pecudum. It was a great hardship to a Roman to have to make meat his chief article of diet.

propulsare . . . adacti, see Introd. III, 5, (ii).

gregario milite. The use of the abl. of comparison here for *plura quam gregarius miles* (sc. *tolerauit*) is irregular. The abl. can normally only be substituted when the word after *quam* would be in the same case as the comparative, if that would be nom. or acc. (i.e. when both compared things are subjects or objects in the sentence). Most exceptions to this rule are in poetry. M reads *eadem plura quam gregario milite toleranti*, which possibly has not been correctly emended.

§ 2. **Tauraunitium.** The *Tauraunites* are not elsewhere mentioned, but the name indicates that they must have lived in the neighbourhood of the Antitaurus range, to the west of Lake Van.

non ignobilis barbarus, ' a native of some standing '.

ordinem, ' a detailed (orderly) account ', a frequent meaning of the word.

seque auctorem, sc. *esse*. The acc. and infin. phrase is joined by zeugma with the other objects of *edidit*.

§ 3. **Tigranocerta,** abl., ' from Tigranocerta '. In c. 23, 1 above, the name is treated as neut. plur. Similar inconsistency is found in the treatment of the name *Artaxata*.

intentos popularis ad iussa, ' that their compatriots were eager to submit '. Notice this meaning of *popularis*, in addition to ' of or belonging to the people ', ' democratic '.

nec quicquam urbi detractum, ' no loss was inflicted on the city '.

integri, equivalent to a conditional, or, perhaps, a causal clause: ' in order that, if they suffered no loss (*or* ' being left in possession of their property '), they might the more readily retain their allegianc e'.

25. § 1. **praesidium Legerda,** corrected from *legerat* of M, in accordance with the mention by Ptolemy of a place Legerda in this district. It has been identified with the modern Lidja, a town on the higher slopes of Taurus, commanding the pass to the plain in which Tigranocerta lay. Notice that, after sending the envoys, the *facilis mutatu gens* had changed its mind, before Corbulo actually reached Tigranocerta.

Hyrcano bello, see Introd. ch. V.

§ 2. Vologesen, see Introd. ch. V.

maris rubri. If this reading were right, it would refer to the shore of the Persian Gulf (*mare Erythraeum*), but how any route could be found from the shore of the Persian Gulf to the southern shore of the Caspian, without crossing the very centre of the Parthian power, is a mystery. The *Camb. Anc. Hist.* talks vaguely of a route ' probably by way of the kingdom of Persis and its dependancy Carmania ', both of which were effectively separated from Hyrcania by Parthia itself. Are we to suppose that the ambassadors sailed still farther east to the Indus and skirted the mountains of Afghanistan? The idea is absurd. If they could not cross Mesopotamia and Media, their obvious course was to go north to the Araxes by the way which Corbulo had come and which their escort would know. They could then reach the Caspian by skirting Parthian territory to the west. Lipsius was probably right in reading *maris sui*.

26. § 1. Quin et . . . subegit, ' Nay, further, he also compelled . . .' Nipperdey is obviously right in referring *Quin et* back to *quae facilius proueniebant*. . . . Because the attention of the Parthians was distracted, Corbulo was enabled not only to reduce Legerda without interruption, but even to make Tiridates' invasion abortive. *Quin* points to a further benefit derived by the Romans from the Hyrcanian revolt.

praemisso Verulano . . . atque ipse . . . ' by sending on Verulanus the legate, with the auxiliaries, and by following in person by forced marches '. *ipse legionibus citis* is parallel to *praemisso Verulano* as showing the means by which Corbulo compelled Tiridates to retire; but as *ipse* refers to the subject of *subegit*, it is naturally nom. In translating, it is necessary to understand *sequendo* or *secutus*. For the infin. with *subegit*, see Introd. III, 5, (ii). Verulanus Severus is mentioned again in Bk. XV. 3.

possessionem . . . usurpabat, ' was taking possession of . . .'. This does not mean that the Roman government had yet decided on annexation. A temporary military occupation was a necessity. For the government's changes of policy, see Introd. ch. V.

Tigranes, nephew of Tigranes IV and a great-grandson of both Herod the Great and of Archelaus, the last King of Cappadocia. Tacitus seems to be using *nepos* loosely for *pronepos*.

§ 2. durante . . . Arsacidarum, i.e. they preferred a Parthian to a Roman nominee. Tigranes was only very distantly connected with the Parthian royal family.

pars . . . iussae sunt. *Pars* is understood to be repeated with each dat., i.e. *pars Pharasmani, pars Polemoni*, &c., so that the verb is naturally plural.

Pharasmani, &c. Pharasmanes was King of Iberia, Polemo of Pontus, Aristobulus of Armenia Minor, Antiochus of Commagene. This partition of Armenia was intended to reward these client kings for the part they had played in the war as much as to make Tigranes' task easier. It was not likely to endear him to his people.

Vmmidii, Ummidius Quadratus, governor of Syria. For his relations with Corbulo, see Introd. ch. V.

sibi permissam. As Corbulo remained in charge of Syria, *sibi* obviously refers to him. The explanation of *sibi* for *ei* must be that Tacitus is looking at things through Corbulo's eyes.

27. § 1. Laodicea, in Phrygia, near the river Maeander. Earthquakes were very frequent in Asia Minor, and contributions from the imperial exchequer were often necessary to repair the damage.

oppidum Puteoli . . . apiscuntur. With geographical place-names, it is usually the common noun in apposition which decides the inflexion of the verb, e.g. Livy II, 33, 8, *Corioli oppidum captum. apiscuntur* is therefore an exception. Notice Tacitus' fondness for simple as opposed to compound verbs. *apiscor* for *adipiscor* is classical but rare. As a colony of Roman citizens had been planted at Puteoli as early as 194 B.C., and Augustus had settled new colonists there, it seems difficult to account for Tacitus' statement, unless we suppose with Lipsius, who is followed by Nipperdey and Furneaux, that the colonists had existed as a separate community within the place, and that Nero now gave colonial status to the rest of the inhabitants.

cognomentum, i.e. Colonia Claudia Augusta Neronensis.

Tarentum et Antium, acc. of goal of motion without prep., because *adscripti* is practically equivalent to *missi. adscribere* is the regular word for enrolling colonists. Tarentum became a colony in 122 B.C. and Antium was a colony of still longer standing.

pluribus, ' the majority '.

stipendia expleuerant, From meaning ' military pay ', *stipendium* came to mean a campaign, or a year's service, so that *explere* is used as with *annos* in the sense of completing a period of time. At this time twenty years was the usual period of military service. The usual way of providing for time-expired veterans was to settle them in colonies with grants of land. Such colonies settled in this period were Colchester and Cologne. Settlements in Italy were unpopular, since the soldiers formed close ties with the inhabitants of the provinces where they served. Marriage was not permitted during service and there were no married, quarters in the legionary camps, but soldiers often formed unions with provincial women which were legalized on their discharge.

§ 2. non enim, &c. ' For not now, as formerly, were entire legions settled in colonies, with their tribunes and centurions and the soldiers all in their own companies . . . ' The mass settlement of veterans from the same legion in one district had been found by Augustus a cheap method of garrisoning frontier provinces (cf. the settlement of veterans at Camulodunum, c. 31). Such colonists would know how to unite together to defend themselves. But since such bodies of men retained their loyalty to the families of the generals under whom they had served, the planting of them in Italy or near might prove dangerous, when the emperor no longer led his troops in person. A rebel might be able to raise an army of loyal followers at a stroke. Probably this is why the custom had been dropped, and the veterans split up amongst different colonies. **sui cuiusque ordinis,** for (*cum*) *sui quoque ordinis. Quisque* is frequently attracted to the gender, number, and case of *suus*, so as to form, in effect, a compound adj. = ' their several '; e.g. cp. Cato, *R. R.* 68 *omnia in suo quidque loco ponito* with Varro, *R. R.* I, 22, 6 *omnia certo* *suo quoque loco posita.* The gen. is a type of gen. of quality and corresponds to *diuersis manipulis* ('from different maniples') below.

sed ignoti, &c. The verb is again *deducebantur* understood, so that *collecti* is the participle, not a main verb with *sunt* understood.

numerus, 'multitude', 'rabble'. Cf. Hist. IV. 15, *nomen magis exercitus quam robur*: *quippe . . . Vitellius . . . segnem numerum armis onerauerat.*

28. § 1. comitia praetorum. Under Augustus the number of praetors had been raised to twelve, four of whom the emperor selected for appointment *sine repulsa et ambitu* (Tac., *Ann.* I, 15), the rest being elected by the popular *comitia*, as before. Tiberius, on his accession, transferred the elections from the people to the Senate.

quod acriore ambitu exarserant, 'because they had given rise to unusually keen competition'. On one occasion, under Augustus, there had been sixteen candidates for the twelve places, and Augustus had allowed them all to act. On this occasion there were fifteen, and to the three extra ones (*qui supra numerum petebant*) Nero gave the office of *legatus legionis* as a consolation prize. *Legati legionum* at this time had usually already held the praetorship, though under Tiberius they were normally ex-quaestors (*Ann.* II, 36). As a number of provinces were governed by ex-praetors, it was obviously necessary for the governor to have military experience before his appointment, and the twelve candidates who were appointed to the praetorship would have to serve as *legati legionum* after their year of office, so that they really secured no advantage over the disappointed candidates.

qui . . . appellarent. *facerent* and *appellarent* do not both represent the same tense (or mood) of o.r. The decree said: *qui . . . prouocauerint, eiusdem pecuniae periculum facient* (or *faciant,* 'are to . . .'), *cuius* (*periculum faciunt) si qui imperatorem appellant.* Trans. ' He raised the dignity of the Senate by decreeing that people who appealed from civil tribunals to the Senate should risk the same forfeit as any who appealed to the emperor.' By *priuati iudices* is meant the ordinary praetors' courts, in which the juries were composed of knights (see on c. 20, 4). The Senate came to be used as a High Court of Justice some time during the rule of Augustus, but it only tried important cases, and, as we see here, cases of appeal from the lower courts. The raising of its dignity by this action of Nero lay in the fact that it would no longer have its time wasted by frivolous appeals. Caution-money to the value of one-third of the sum involved in the action had to be laid down, and was lost, if the original judgement was confirmed.

§ 2. Vibius Secundus, mentioned by Tacitus only here and in *Hist.* II, 10, where his brother is said to have brought to trial Annius Faustus, who had attacked him on some other occasion. Claudius had divided Mauretania into two provinces under imperial procurators of equestrian rank. Accusations of extortion were now laid before the Senate instead of before the venal *Quaestio repetundarum* of the Republic, but it looks as if the senatorial court was accessible to influence.

ne . . . afficeretur, negative final clause. After *enitor =* 'struggle out of', 'exert oneself', 'strive', one might expect a consecutive *ut non* clause, but after many verbs a consecutive or a final clause is often optional, according to whether the result was accidental or intended. Cf. Sall., *Jug.* 13, 8, *nitebantur ne grauius in eum consuleretur.*

Vibius Crispus, a more famous man than his brother. In *Hist.* II, 10 Tacitus describes him as *pecunia, potentia, ingenio inter claros magis quam inter bonos.*

29. § 1. Caesennio Paeto et Petronio Turpiliano coss., i.e. in A.D. 61. Paetus later disgraced himself in Armenia. The latter, who succeeded Suetonius Paulinus in Britain later the same year, is also depreciated by Tacitus (c. 39), but see Introd. ch. VI.

Britannia. For a short account of the Romans in Britain up to thi time, see Introd. ch. VI.

ut memoraui, i.e. in *Ann.* XII, 40. Didius was an old man when he succeeded Ostorius as governor in A.D. 50. This accounts for his inactivity.

Veranius, consul in A.D. 48. He probably succeeded Didius in A.D. 58, but died before he had been in the province a year (*Agr.* 14).

Siluras. The Silures inhabited South Wales and Herefordshire. Their swarthy complexions and curly hair made Tacitus think they had come from Spain (see *Agr.* 11).

quin proferret. The use of *quin* as a subordinating conj. after a verb of hindering or preventing that is not negatived is very rare indeed. This seems to be the only ex. found in a good author.

magna . . . fama. abl. of quality, ' a man of great reputation for austerity during his lifetime '.

supremis testamenti uerbis. Most edd. seem to take *testamenti* to be the defining or ' appositional ' type of gen., i.e. ' in his last words, viz. his will ', cf. c. 4, 2, *gestamine sellae.* The verb *addidit,* in the next sentence, which indicates an additional note at the end, shows that the more obvious meaning, ' in the last words (i.e. the last part) of his will ', is the right one.

ambitionis. The words *multa adulatione,* in the next sentence, would lead one to think that *ambitio* is used in the sense of ' seeking after favour ', ' toadyism '. However, Veranius' boast partakes rather of the nature of ' vainglory ', and *ambitio* is also used in this sense. Veranius' object was surely to make people think what a great general he was, rather than to curry favour with Nero. Gen. as with verbs of accusing and condemning, see Introd. III, 2, (ii).

multa adulatione. If *ambitionis* does not mean ' toadyism ' or ' servility ', and if the boast is not referred to this quality, these ablatives can scarcely be abl. of manner, but must be loose abl. of att. circs., referring to other things that Veranius said in his will. Trans. ' amid a great deal of flattery towards Nero, he added that he would have subdued the province for him, if he had lived for the next two years '.

biennio proximo, see Introd. III, 4, (v.)

§ 2. Paulinus Suetonius, one of the best known names in connexion with Roman Britain. Of his previous history we learn nothing from Tacitus, but we know that he had had experience of fighting as *legatus* of Mauretania in A.D. 41. He was consul in A.D. 66, but as he was ex-praetor in A.D. 41, it is hardly likely that he had not been at least *consul suffectus* before that. He subsequently supported Otho in the civil war of A.D. 69.

obtinebat. Notice that this verb does not mean ' obtain ', but rather ' retain ', ' maintain ', ' keep under control '.

concertator, a new word coined by Tacitus, = *aemulus*.

receptae Armeniae decus, cf. Introd. III, 7, (i).

perduellibus, an archaic word = *hostibus*, used only here by Tacitus.

Monam, Anglesey.

plano alueo, ' flat-bottomed ', lit. ' with flat hull '.

aduersus breue et incertum, ' to contend with the shallows and quicksands ', cf. *Ann.* I, 70 *neque discerni poterant incerta ab solidis, breuia a profundis*.

sic pedes, sc. *tramisit*.

uado secuti. *Pedites* must be understood as obj. of *secuti*, ' the cavalry came after them through the shoal-water, or swimming beside their horses, where the water was deeper '. Possibly *aut* signifies that the cavalry was divided into two divisions which crossed at different places.

30. § 1. Stabat pro litore diuersa acies. Notice the emphatic position of the verb at the beginning. *pro litore*, here not ' in front of ', but ' on the front part of ', ' forward on ', as in the expressions *pro tribunali, pro rostris*. *diuersa* = ' opposite ', ' opposing ', as often. Trans. ' There stood the opposing battle-line on the foreshore.'

diras, sc. *res*, ' ill-boding things ', ' curses '.

§ 2. cohortationibus, instr. abl. of cause, ' under the exhortations of their leader . . .'

fanaticum, lit. ' of or pertaining to a temple (*fanum*) ', hence ' divinely inspired ', and so ' furious ', ' mad ', ' fanatical '.

pauescerent. For this trans. use, see Introd. III, 1, (i).

igni suo, ' enveloped them in the'fire of their own torches '. Normally the reflexive *suo* should refer to the subject of *inuoluunt*, but there are many instances where the reflexive refers to the subject that is uppermost in the writer's mind, instead of to the grammatical subject, e.g. *Hannibalem sui ciues eiecerunt* would be legitimate and unambiguous. So here *suo* could hardly refer to the Romans.

saeuis superstitionibus sacri, dat., ' consecrated to cruel rites '.

adolere aras. The meaning of *adoleo* is doubtful and its derivation obscure, but it seems to be connected with *alo*, as *candeo* with *ac-cendo*. Its meaning would then be ' to display the effect of nourishment ', ' to rise up ', ' increase in size ', cf. *adolesco*. However, it seems to have been used only in connexion with sacrificial language, and as a trans. verb, with either the altar or the sacrifice as obj. In the first case it would mean ' to make to smoke ', cf. Virg., *Aen.* I, 704, *flammis adolere penates*; in the second ' to sacrifice'. *cruore* will then be instr. abl. Trans. ' to make their altars smoke with the blood of captives '.

fibris, poet. and post-Aug. for *extis*, ' internal organs '. **Consulere deos**, ' consult their gods ', i.e. obtain responses, referring to divination by examining the entrails of victims.

prouinciae, i.e. the south and east of England, already conquered.

31. § 1. Rex Icenorum Prasutagus, see Introd. ch. VI.

longa opulentia clarus, ' distinguished by long-continued prosperity '.

quod contra uertit, ' but it turned out to the contrary '.

centuriones . . . seruos. The centurions were the agents of the military governor, the slaves were public slaves attached to the staff of the imperial procurator, who supervised taxation, was appointed independently of the *legatus*, and was often at loggerheads with him. Cf. c. 38, 3; also *Agr.* 15, *singulos sibi olim reges fuisse, nunc binos imponi, e quibus legatus in sanguinem, procurator in bona saeuiret . . . alterius manus centuriones, alterius seruos uim et contumelias miscere*.

praecipui quique Icenorum. As *praecipuus*, 'chief', 'foremost', is equivalent in sense to a superlative, it may be used in combination with *quisque*. The plur. *quique*, when referring to persons, is exceedingly rare (unless, of course, 'each party' is meant).

quasi . . . accepissent, sc. *illi*, i.e. *centuriones et serui*. The change of grammatical subject is rather harsh, but note that there is no change of logical subject. The centurions and slaves are the agents throughout. It used to be thought (cf. Nipperdey, and Furneaux *ad loc.*) that the words were an interpolation, or else that the subject had dropped out. But recent research has shown that the passage conforms to Tacitean usage. See Sörbom, *Variatio Sermonis Tacitei*, p. 141.

auitis bonis, abl. of separation, as with *priuare*.

inter mancipia habebantur, 'were treated like slaves'.

§ 2. **contumelia . . . metu,** causal abl.

quando, = *quoniam*, cf. c. 4, 1, a sense in which it is found occasionally even in classical authors.

in formam pr. cesserant, 'since they (i.e. their client-kingdom) had been reduced to the status of a Roman province'. *cedere in*, with acc., = 'be changed into'. The connexion with the ordinary meaning of 'yield' is the idea of one thing or state 'giving place to' another. Cf. c. 54, 3, *hoc quoque in tuam gloriam cedet* = 'will turn out to be a glory to you'.

rebellationem, unusual form for *rebellionem*.

Trinouantibus, the neighbours of the Iceni to the south. Their capital was Camulodunum.

resumere . . . pepigerant, see Introd. III, 5, (ii).

recens deducti, under Claudius, in A.D. 50.

appellando, see on c. 4, 3.

impotentiam, 'lack of self-control', 'lawlessness'.

§ 3. **quasi arx . . . aspiciebatur,** not quite the same as *uidebatur esse . . .,* 'was looked upon as . . .', but = 'the temple set up to the deified Claudius was planted before their gaze as the citadel of masters who intended to rule them for ever'. Cf. note on c. 62, 2 *quasi exprobrantes aspiciuntur*.

omnes fortunas. The words *specie religionis*, 'in the name of religion', 'on the plea of offering sacrifices', do not suggest that only the fortunes of the priests themselves are intended. The priests were chosen from among leading natives, in the hope that the honour of holding office would attach them to Rome. Such offices undoubtedly proved costly to their holders, but the context here suggests that the priests were levying excessive contributions for sacrifices from among their fellows. It is best, therefore, to take *omnis fortunas* = *omnium fortunas*, rather than *omnis suas fortunas*.

ducibus nostris, dat. of agent.

amoenitati. The words *amoenus* and *amoenitas* are used chiefly with reference to pleasant landscapes.

32. § 1. palam, as being an adv., should strictly qualify the adj.

nulla, ' for apparently no reason ', but its position makes it equivalent to an adj., e.g. *manifesta.* Cf. *Ann.* XV, 7, *nulla palam causa turbatus eques.*

   delapsum . . . conuersum, sc. *est,* ' fell down and turned backwards '. This does not suggest a very clear picture, but probably the statue fell from its pedestal and then turned on its face.

   externos, ' foreign ', i.e. barbarian. The shouting of British warriors is meant.

   in curia eorum, i.e. *colonorum Camulodunensium,* the Council House of the Roman colony.

   uisamque speciem, &c., ' and that an image of the colony in ruins had been seen in the estuary of the Thames '. Colchester is too far up the coast to justify describing it as lying on the estuary of the Thames, but such a vague indication of its position might pass muster. It is difficult to conceive what can have been the natural phenomenon which this story represents. In any case, the text is doubtful. M apparently reads *tam esae,* but *tam* is so blotted as to be almost illegible, and over it, in a later hand, is written *notam.*

   iam, here = ' then, too . . .', ' and what is more . . .'.

   Oceanus cruento aspectu . . . effigies relictae, = *quod Oceanus cruento aspectu erat . . . quod effigies relictae sunt.* For the noun with an epithet in agreement standing for a substantival clause, see Introd. III, 7, (i). *cruento aspectu* is abl. of qual. and therefore equivalent to an adj. Trans. ' then, too, the fact that the sea had assumed a bloodred appearance, and that, when the tide went out, images of human corpses were left behind, were things upon which the Britons put a hopeful interpretation, and the veterans a fearful one '.

   Britannis . . . ueteranis, see Introd. III, 3, (ii). *trahere ad* or *in,* ' to draw in such and such a direction ' is often used in the sense of ' interpreting in a certain way ', ' putting such and such a construction on something '. Cf. *Ann.* III, 22, *quod alii ciuile rebantur . . . , quidam ad saeuitiam trahebant;* XIII, 47, *socors ingenium eius in contrarium trahens callidumque et simulatorem interpretando.*

   § 2. Cato Deciano, the master of the slaves mentioned in c. 31. Little more is known of him than is told here.

   iustis, ' regular ', ' proper '. Cf. *iustus exercitus,* ' a regular army '.

   praeduxerunt, lit. ' drew up in front '.

   neque motis . . . restitit. *neque* does not belong only to the abl. abs., but negatives the whole clause of which *motis . . . feminis* is part : ' nor were the old men and the women removed and the young fighting-men alone left behind '.

   § 3. impetu, ' at a rush ', i.e. ' at the first onset '.

   biduo. The abl. here seems to answer both the questions ' when ? ' and ' how long ? ' ' The temple . . . was besieged for two days and stormed.' See Introd. III, 4, (v).

   Petilio Cereali, a distinguished officer who later fought on Vespasian's side in the civil war, put down the revolt of Civilis in Germany, and later became governor of Britain.

   quod peditum, sc. *erat,* ' what infantry there was ', ' all the infantry '. For the part. gen. after *quod,* cf. c. 38, 2, *quodque nationum . . . fuerat.*

   clade . . . odiis, causal abl., ' on account of . . .', with *trepidus.*

33. § 1. medios inter hostes, i.e. the disaffection had now spread westwards, and Suetonius' column of march was liable to be attacked at any moment as he hurried down Watling Street.

Londinium. This is the earliest extant mention of London. It had leapt into prominence as a commercial centre from the very beginning of the Roman occupation. Whether it was founded on the site of an earlier British community is not certain. At all events, it had not been a great tribal centre like Camulodunum. It remained unwalled until the third century.

coloniae, defining gen., ' not distinguished by the title "colonia".'

commeatuum, ' stores ', ' merchandise '.

illam sedem. Notice the attraction of the pronoun to the gender of the predicated noun. ' Whether he should choose that (i.e. *Londinium*) as his base of operations '.

satisque . . . coercitam, sc. *esse.* The verb of thinking to which this acc. and infin. phrase is obj. is understood from *circumspecta infrequentia,* which = *cum circumspexisset.* Trans. ' taking into account the inadequacy of his forces and the fact that the rashness of Petilius had received a sufficiently severe lesson '. The point is that London was not fortified and Suetonius had not sufficient forces with him to meet the Britons in the open. It was necessary to effect a junction with the IInd. and IXth legions, which he had presumably summoned to join him and of whose fate he did not know. This meant leaving London to its fate, but it was better than being shut up helpless while the rest of the province was destroyed.

et comitantis . . . acciperet. The meaning of some restrictive word such as *tantum,* ' only ', ' merely ', has to be supplied in translating. They could not turn him ' from giving the order for departure and (merely) admitting into part of his column of march those who could accompany him '.

§ 2. municipio Verulamio. The fact that Verulamium was a *municipium* shows that it was a centre of civilian population, like London.

praesidiisque militarium, ' garrisons of the military ', a variation of c. 45, 2, *militaribus praesidiis. militaris* is used substantivally in *Ann.* III, 1. Madvig read *militare horreum,* an alteration of M which is quite gratuitous.

aliorum segnes, ' slothful with regard to other things '. For the gen., see Introd. III, 2, (i).

sociorum. Probably loyal Romanized Britons are meant, as well as merchants from Gaul.

neque enim capere, &c. It is difficult to decide whether *capere . . . uenundare . . . commercium* should be taken by zeugma as objects of *festinabant* along with *caedes,* &c., or whether the infins. are hist., and *esse* or *exercere* to be supplied with *commercium.* Syntactically either is possible, but logically the former presents the greater difficulty, for the sense should be ' they did not *stop* to take prisoners, &c. . . . ' rather than ' *hurry,* to do so. For the transitive use of *festinare,* cf. *Ann.* I, 6, *caedem festinauisse.* So also *properare, maturare.* Except when the obj. is a neut. pron. or adj., which could be explained as internal obj., the use is mostly poetic and post-Aug.

tamquam, &c. represents the thoughts or motives of the barbarians, i.e. ' as being about to pay retribution ' = ' knowing well that they would pay . . .' at praerepta . . . If *at* and not *ac* is right, *praerepta ultione* is probably not adverbial with *festinabant*, but with *reddituri*. Trans. 'There was no taking of prisoners or selling them as slaves, nor any other traffic of war, but they hastened to murder, gibbet, burn, and crucify, well knowing that they would pay retribution, though having in the meantime snatched their vengeance first .'

34. § 1. Iam. We are to understand that Suetonius, in his retreat along Watling Street, has now gathered in whatever auxiliaries from the scattered posts could join him. Where Boudicca caught up with him, Tacitus gives no indication, but it was probably in the Midlands, perhaps between Towcester and Atherstone. He then turned to meet his pursuers. That he was pursued, we can gather from the fact that he was able to choose the site for the battle.

quarta decima legio . . . uicesimanis. For the legions serving in Britain, see Introd. ch. VI.

uexillariis, not necessarily 'veteran reservists', the most frequent meaning of the term, but probably simply ' detachments '. Auxiliaries, cavalry, and detachments from the main body of a legion served under a *uexillum* ' ensign ', not under a legionary ' standard ' (*signum*). Veteran reservists, who were kept for a time with the colours, were not incorporated in a legion, but formed a separate detachment. Hence both they and the members of any other detached portion of a legion were called *uexillarii*.

artis faucibus, i.e. a place where the road ran out of a plain into a cleft between hills, with woods rising up on either side, so that he would be safe from any but a frontal attack.

apertam, pred., ' that the plain was open '.

§ 2. frequens ordinibus, 'in close formation', lit. 'thick with ranks '. The abl. is instr., but is not used with *frequens* in class. prose. Cf. Livy I, 9, 9, *frequentem urbem tectis*.

quanta non alias . . ., 'in greater numbers than ever before ', for (*tanta*) *quanta non alias* (*fuerat*).

35. § 1. ut quamque . . . accesserat, ' as she approached each tribe '. There are four other exx. of the bare acc. after *accedo* in Tac. Class. Latin normally repeats the prep. *ad* which is contained in the verb. Cf. Introd. III, 1, (i).

feminarum ductu, cf. *Agr.* 16, *neque enim sexum in imperiis discernunt.*

tunc, for the *nunc* of o. r., ' now, on this occasion '.

non ut . . . ulcisci, 'but on this occasion, it was not as a queen descended from mighty ancestors seeking to avenge the loss of kingdom and wealth, but as one of the common people that she sought to avenge the scourging of her body and the violation of her daughters' chastity '. For the omission of *se* with the acc. and infin. *ortam . . . ulcisci,* cf. c. 29, 1, *addidit subiecturum . . . fuisse.* *regnum et opes ulcisci* by itself would mean ' avenge the loss of . . .', or ' avenge injury to . . .', since *ulciscor* may take the acc. of the person or thing to which injury has been done. Notice that the pres. tense may have a conative sense, so that *ulciscor* may mean ' I am trying to, setting out to avenge .'

§ 2. adesse . . . uindictae, ' the gods were present to help them exact a just vengeance '. *uindictae*, dat., because *adesse* is equivalent to *fauere* or *subuenire*.

cecidisse legionem, i.e. the IXth, under Petilius Cerealis.

ceteros . . . occultari, ' the rest were skulking in their camps ', i.e. the IInd probably at Gloucester, the rest of the XXth, which had evidently been left to guard the base camp in the north-west, and the remnants of the IXth at Lincoln. The XIVth and the rest present with Suetonius are those who are ' looking round for a way of escape '.

nedum, ' much less ', see on c. 15, 3.

impetus et manus, ' their charge and the (subsequent) hand-to-hand conflict '.

si expenderent, ' if they considered ', ' reflected upon '. Notice the change from vivid primary (*relinquant . . . ausa sit*) to historic sequence.

uincendum esse, sc. *eos intellecturos esse,* ' they would see that they must either conquer on that field, or fall '. The considerations which led to this conclusion were that they would never again be able to gather in such numbers, and, if they failed now, they would have to submit for ever to the sort of oppression which had driven them to rebel.

uel here seems to be a complete substitute for *aut*, though the latter is the normal conjunction where two mutually exclusive alternatives are denoted. See on c. 61, 4.

id mulieri destinatum, sc. *esse,* ' that was a woman's resolve ', lit. ' that was (the end) marked out for '.

36. § 1. ne . . . quidem, here used in the sense of ' neither ',— ' neither was Suetonius silent '. Cf. Caes., *B. C.* II, 33, *Curio milites in acie collocat*: *ne Varus quidem dubitat copias producere,* ' . . . *neither* is Varus reluctant to lead out his troops '. The usual sense ' not even ' would have no point here.

quamquam confideret, see Introd. III, 6, ii (d).

sonores, a poetic word for *sonitus.*

inermes, ' poorly armed '.

cessuros . . . agnouissent, ' having been routed so often, they would give way at once, when they recognized the steel and courage of those who always defeated them '. *uincentium* is used substantively, = ' conquerors ', but the sense of the pres. part. has to be rendered; perhaps ' their habitual conquerors ' (Furneaux). Notice the rhetorical device whereby *uincentium* and *totiens fusi* are placed in juxtaposition.

§ 2. etiam in multis, &c., ' even in armies consisting of many legions, it was only a few who decided the issue of a battle ', i.e. advantage of position may make up for the absence of numbers, who might be inactive in any case. *profligare*, with *bellum* or *proelium* as obj. = ' all but finish ', ' give the decisive impulse to '.

gloriaeque, &c., lit. ' to their glory would be added the fact that . . .'. o.r. *accedet quod . . . adipiscemini.*

continuarent, ' let them keep up without interruption ', i.e. there must be no hanging back after the discharge of javelins, but they must close the gap immediately and press the enemy back with their shield-bosses. It was for this close work that the short *gladius* was specially suitable. Notice that *et* joins *conferti* with all that follows, and not simply to *pilis emissis. post,* adv., = ' later ', ' presently ', ' next '.

§ 3. multa . . . experientia, abl. of quality.

certus euentūs, ' sure of the result '. An obj. gen. with *certus* is poetic and post-Aug. After *certior* it is classical, though rare, the usual constr. being *certior de*. For the extended use of the gen. with adj. in Silver Latin, see Introd. III, 2, (i).

37. § 1. gradu immota, 'not moving from its position'. However, the participles had best be trans. by main verbs.

certo iactu, ' with sure aim ', ' with deadly effect '.

uelut cuneo, ' as in wedge-shaped formation '.

difficili effugio, loose abl. of att. circs. again, or abl. abs., the participle of the verb ' to be ' being understood.

saepserant . . . temperabat . . . auxerant. Notice the reasons for the use of these tenses. The vehicles *had* blocked the exits, even before the battle began. After the Britons had broken in flight, the soldiers *proceeded to* slaughter even the women, but even before this, the pile of bodies was high enough, for the baggage-animals *had already been* killed by missiles and added to the heap.

neci temperabat. *Temperare* (= *moderari*) with dat. = ' be sparing towards (a person or thing) '; so here, ' they did not spare the slaughter of . . .' This is equivalent to ' refrain from ', and so we also find *temperare ab aliqua re*. With the acc., *temperare* = ' govern ', or ' control '.

§ 2. antiquis uictoriis par, short for (*laudi*) *antiquarum uictoriarum*. For this abbreviated method of comparison (*comparatio compendiaria*), cf. Hor. *Od.* II, 6, 14 sqq., *ubi non Hymetto/mella decedunt uiridique certat/baca Venafro* (for *mellibus Hymetti, bacis Venafri*).

sunt qui . . . tradant. This implication of uncertainty suggests that Tacitus did not consult the memoirs of Suetonius Paulinus himself who would surely have stated the numbers of slain from certain knowledge. Doubtless one of T.'s authorities for these events was his father-in-law Agricola, who served as a young officer in this campaign, see Introd. ch. I. On Tacitus' sources in general, see Introd. ch. II.

nec multo amplius, sc. *quam quadringentis*.

Poenius Postumus, not otherwise known. As no *legatus legionis* is mentioned, he was evidently in temporary command. For another view of his conduct, see Introd. ch. VI.

ritum, ' military regulation ', ' usage ', ' convention '.

38. § 1. sub pellibus, lit. ' under skins ' i.e. under tents of skin, or, as we should say, ' under canvas '.

octo auxiliarium cohortibus. These were apparently attached to the XIVth legion, not to the IXth, for eight Batavian cohorts are mentioned in *Hist.* I, 59 as belonging to the XIVth.

nonani, the remnant of the IXth legion, cut up under Petilius Cerealis, see c. 32. Nipperdey's note on that passage implies that he thinks the 2,000 legionaries here sent to supplement it were a detachment from it, which had thus escaped and was now sent back. This is most unlikely, since 2,000 men were less than half a legion, and if the other half had been all but destroyed, 2,000 men would not have brought it up to strength. Probably only about half the legion had been destroyed, the other half having been left to defend Lincoln.

§ 2. cohortes alaeque, the auxiliaries and cavalry referred to above.

nouis hibernaculis. For the locatival abl. without *in*, see Introd. III, 4, (i).

quodque nationum, part. gen. See on c. 32, 3.

uastatur. This is the reading of M, which most edd. alter to *uastatum,* to conform to the aorist *locatae (sunt).* For exx. of variation between aorist and hist. pres., see Sörbom, *Var. Serm. Tac.,* p. 101.

aeque quam. *quam* instead of *atque* as a conjunction in expressions of comparison denoting likeness or unlikeness is classical with *alius* and *aliter,* but not with *aeque.* With the latter it is found in Plautus and class. poetry, and comes into prose with Livy.

serendis frugibus incuriosos. It is difficult to decide whether this is an example of dat. of purpose (Introd. III, 3, (iv)) or abl. of respect. Tacitus most often uses the gen. of reference with this word. For other constructions used with *curiosus* and *incuriosus,* cf. Cic., *ad Fam.* 4, 13, 5, *sum ad inuestigandum curiosior ; de Dom.* 39, *non sum in exquirendo curiosus.* As *ad* with the acc. is very common with these words, and as they approach the meaning of *studiosus* and its opposite, *serendis frugibus* here and *melioribus incuriosos* in *Hist.* II, 17 are more likely to be dat.

dum . . . destinant. As there is no new main verb for *et* to intro-duce, it must be joining *serendis . . . incuriosos* and *omni . . . uersa* as two parallel reasons for the prevalence of famine (*gentes-que* adds a third, see below). The adj. *incuriosos,* however, must describe a general characteristic of the Britons rather than their behaviour on this particular occasion. The *dum-*clause, therefore, is an afterthought, referring to *omni uersa* only. Trans. ' But nothing afflicted them so much as famine, careless as they were in the matter of sowing corn, and their menfolk young and old, having taken up arms, while marking down the Roman provisions for their own use; &c.'.

§ 3. **gentesque,** &c. *-que* here causes editors needless difficulty, because they fail to see that Tacitus is merely continuing his account of the causes of famine. He is not saying ' The Britons were suffering severely from famine, *but in spite of that* were reluctant to make peace .' He is saying ' But famine caused more distress than the vengeance of the Romans, because the Britons were careless about sowing crops, all the menfolk had gone to war, *and* the fierce tribes were reluctant to return to peaceful conditions (which might have afforded some relief), because . . .'. Not understanding this, Nipperdey marked a lacuna after *destinant,* supposing *tamen* or its equivalent to have been among the words lost. Furneaux followed Jacob in attributing the required adversative force to *-que.* It is true that sometimes two contradictory statements are joined merely by *et* or *-que* (cf. ' he refused to stay, and went out ', for ' but '). But here *-que* has its normal force.

disperseratque, sc. *rumorem.*

consulturum, ' who would consult the interests of . . .' Tacitus often uses a participle where class. Latin would use a *qui-*clause.

mandabat . . . expectarent, o.o. for *ne expectaueritis, nisi succedetur.*

prauitati, ' perverseness ', ' incompetence '. For the variation between the dat. and *ad.* see Introd. III, p. 11.

39. § 1. **e libertis Polyclitus,** ' P., one of the imperial freedmen '. For the power and wealth of the emperor's freedmen, cf. *Ann.* XIII, 14, (*Pallas*) *uelut arbitrium regni agebat.* Also c. 65 below. Any wealthy Roman might employ a slave or freedman as farm-bailiff, curator of his estates, private secretary, &c., but when, as in the case of the emperor, the estates comprised important provinces of the Roman Empire, as well as extensive ' Crown Lands ', such posts became of national importance.

Under Claudius, freedmen of the imperial household became heads of a regular Civil Service. The most important posts were *ab epistulis* (Secretary-General), *a rationibus* (Financial Secretary), and *a libellis* (Secretary for Petitions). It is not known what post Polyclitus held. His wealth and avarice are referred to in *Hist.* I, 37; II, 95.

magna . . . spe, abl. of att. circs., 'with high hopes on the part of Nero that . . .'.

posse . . . gigni . . . componi. Notice the frequent use of *possum* with pres. Infin. to provide a passive equivalent of e.g. *auctoritatem eius . . . genituram . . . composituram esse*, or to replace the periphrastic *fore ut*, &c.

barbarum, gen. plur. This form of the 2nd declension gen. plur. is not, of course, a shortening of *-orum*, but is the original archaic form.

pace, modal abl. = an adv., ' peacefully '.

§ 2. nec defuit . . . quominus. Besides the usual verbs of hindering or preventing, a subordinate clause introduced by *quominus* may follow almost any expression into which a similar idea may be read. Cf. Cic. *Inv.* 2, 130, *scriptori neque ingenium neque operam . . . defuisse quominus. . . .* Except in a few expressions, *quominus* is far commoner than *quin*, even when the governing verb is negatived. Nipperdey and Furneaux, therefore, are hardly right in saying that *quominus* here stands for *quin*. A better example of irregularity is c. 29, 1, where *quin* is used for *quominus*.

ingenti agmine . . . grauis. The adj. is here equivalent to a past part. act., ' having been burdensome to Italy and Gaul with his immense suite '.

terribilis, ' an object of dread '.

flagrante. The metaphor in this word may be kept in trans. ' the flame of liberty still burned '.

quod . . . oboedirent. The subj. is that of virtual o. o., giving the Britons' reasons for astonishment, not the author's. Other constructions possible with *miror* are the acc. and infin. (by far the commonest in Cic.), a *si*-clause, and an ind. quest.

seruitiis, abstr. for concrete, = ' a slave '.

§ 3. in mollius, ' in a more favourable light ', i.e. than the report of Classicianus.

detentusque rebus gerundis, dat. of purpose, not abl. of sep., i.e. ' kept for carrying on affairs ' or ' retained as governor '. For this sense of *detinere*, cf. *Agr.* 9, *minus triennium in ea legatione detentus*.

postea. M reads *past*, but the *s t* seem to have been written over an erasure by a later hand. Koestermann omits, thinking that *pa* was written by dittography in front of *paucas*.

tamquam durante bello, ' on the ground that ', ' on the excuse that a state of war continued '. For *tamquam* with a participial phrase, cf. c. 41, 1 *tamquam . . . gnarum*.

Petronio Turpiliano, see c. 29. Notice that under the Empire the consulship did not last the whole year. Augustus introduced the fashion of replacing the two consuls who entered on office in January by two *consules suffecti* at the end of six months. Later on even shorter terms were sometimes instituted. By this means the ambition of a greater number was satisfied.

40. § 1. **senatoris . . . seruili . . . audacia,** a good example of
Tacitus' fondness for variety, the instr. abl. replacing the possessive (or
subjective) gen. The term *senator* is used loosely for *homo senatorii ordinis,*
for Fabianus had apparently not yet taken an office which would have
qualified him to enter the Senate.

Domitius Balbus, not otherwise known. The name may be corrupt,
for no others of the Domitii seem to have had the cognomen Balbus.

simul . . . simul, 'whose advanced old age, childlessness, and
wealth alike rendered him a potential victim of fraud'. The ablatives
are causal. Notice that *obnoxius* = 'liable to be hurt by'.

§ 2. **subdidit,** 'forged'. *subdere* derives this meaning from the idea
of 'stealthily replacing something', i.e. 'substituting falsely'. Seven
witnesses were required to sign a Roman's will; hence the number of
accomplices required.

Antonium Primum. He recovered his senatorial rank during the
troubles of the civil war, and was placed by Galba in command of
the VIIth legion in Pannonia. Later on, his accession to the side of
Vespasian was a decisive factor in the latter's victory.

Asinium Marcellum, consul in A.D. 54, see *Ann.* XII, 64.

audacia promptus, lit. 'ready in boldness', 'a man of ready effron-
tery'.

Asinio Pollione, instr. abl. 'rendered distinguished by'. Trans.
'had the distinction of being descended from Asinius Pollio'. This
was the famous Pollio, partisan of Julius Caesar, negotiator of the treaty
of Brundisium between Antony and Octavian, patron of Virgil and
Horace. To him Virgil's Fourth Eclogue is addressed.

morum spernendus, see Introd. III, 2, (i).

§ 3. **ascitis.** M reads *iis,* which might stand as an instr. abl. (by
means of', i.e. 'with the help of'). *ascitis* is a better correction than
sociis (Nipperdey), as its corruption can be explained by haplography.

conuictum, 'proved', 'brought home'.

lege Cornelia, i.e. the law of Cornelius Sulla which established the
Quaestiones perpetuae in 80 B.C., one of which dealt with fraud and forgery
(*de falsis*). Here only the penalties imposed by this law are meant, for
the case was tried in the Senate, not before a praetor presiding over a
quaestio. See n. on next ch.

poenae . . . infamiae exemere, see Introd. III, p. 13, also section
3, (i).

41. § 1. **iuuenem quaestorium.** Ex-quaestors were *ex officio* members of the Senate.

tamquam . . . gnarum, 'on the charge that he was cognisant
of . . .'.

eique . . . interdictum est. The dat. of the person and the abl.
of separation of the thing is the normal constr. of *interdicere.*

quod reos . . . elusurus, 'because he had lodged information
against the accused before the praetor, in order to prevent the case being
tried by the City Prefect, his intention being to postpone their punishment for the time being by this legal subterfuge, and later to get them
off by collusion'. The explanation of this is that the office of Prefect
of the City was a comparatively new institution as a permanent office,
and its position in relation to the praetorship was not yet clearly defined.

The *Praefectus Vrbi* was appointed by Augustus to keep order in the city, and was therefore allowed summary jurisdiction in dealing with minor criminal activities. He was not hindered by the lengthy processes and legal red tape which bound the praetor's court. In course of time he took cognisance of more important cases, and so encroached on the function of the praetor and the *quaestiones perpetuae*. His jurisdiction was summary and not accessible to the same corrupt influences as the praetor's court with its panel of jurymen. Appeal from him lay to the emperor, as he was an imperial official. Possibly the *reos* referred to were only the *minus inlustres* of c. 40, 3, but whether the more important culprits were included or not, they were all as good as done for, if they were brought up before the Prefect. Consequently they put up Valerius Ponticus to stage a sham trial before the praetor. It would be some time before the trial came on, and in the meantime evidence might be faked, and the sham accuser could arrange with the defending counsel how best to hoodwink or bribe the jury. When a sham accuser forestalled action by a real accuser and colluded with the defence, he was said *praeuaricari*. Cf. Cicero's preliminary action against the *praeuaricator* Caecilius in the trial of Verres, to decide which of them should conduct the prosecution. It was probably news of this collusion, coupled with the fact that some of the defendants were of senatorial rank, which caused the case to be taken straight to the higher senatorial court.

elusurus. See Introd. III, 7, (ii). Notice that, when used to express purpose, the fut. part. is nearly always placed as last word of the sentence or phrase.

consulto, probably dat. ' a rider was added to the senatorial decree to the effect that . . . '. In this case the *senatus consultum* will probably be that which fixed the punishment of Pompeius Aelianus and Valerius Ponticus, though not necessarily so. If *consulto* is abl. (i.e. instr., ' an additional precaution was taken by means of a senatorial decree '), then a new *s. c.* was passed. Furneaux' statement that the term *senatus consultum* is not elsewhere used of a judicial sentence is incorrect. See *Hist.* IV, 44; *Ann.* I, 6; III, 24; XVI, 9.

qui . . . emptitasset . . . teneretur, indir. for (*is*) *qui emptitauerit . . . tenebitur* (or *teneatur*).

calumniae, legal gen., ' condemned for calumny '. *Calumnia*, as a technical term, is the opposite of *praeuaricatio*, i.e. an attempt to get some one condemned unjustly, as the latter is an attempt to secure unjust acquittal. In the case of criminal charges, the penalty for false accusation varied. In the earliest times the calumniator was branded on the forehead with the letter K (for *Kalumniator*). In later times the offence was punished with exile, relegation, or at least loss of rank, and the guilty person was prohibited from ever again appearing as a prosecutor.

42. § 1. **Pedanium Secundum,** not elsewhere mentioned by Tacitus. For the office of Prefect of the City, see n. on c. 41, 1 above.

negata . . . pepigerat, ' either because his master had denied him his liberty, after settling on the price for it . . . '. A decent master allowed his slave to save up his pocket-money (*peculium*) and buy himself, but, as the slave's belongings, as well as himself, belonged to the master, the latter was not legally bound by any agreement.

ceterum, see on c. 58, 2.

uetere ex more. We can gather from Cic. *ad Fam.* 4, 12 that under the Republic slaves were liable to be tortured or put to death, if their master was murdered. Such laws are inseparable from the custom of slavery. Under the Empire, when slave establishments increased in size, the danger in which Romans stood from their slaves was very real, and repressive laws became more stringent as time went on. Characteristically enough, the worst masters seem to have been freedmen who had got on in the world. Pliny, *Ep.* III, 14, describing how Largius Macedo, ' an arrogant and cruel master, who forgot, or rather remembered too well that his own father had been a slave ', was thrashed and left for dead by his own slaves, goes on to say : ' You see to what insults and outrages we are exposed, nor can any one feel safe because he is a gentle and kind master, for masters are murdered by the criminality, not by the just deliberation of their slaves '. However, the great proportion of freedmen in Rome (see *Ann.* XIII, 27) testifies to the fact that relations between masters and slaves were, on the whole, good, and that the lot of the slave, at any rate of the household slave, was not so hopeless and abject as is sometimes implied.

familiam. Notice that *familia* = ' household ', i.e. slaves, domestic staff. The Latin for ' family ' is *gens*.

senatu quoque in ipso . . ., ' Even in the Senate itself there was a party which strenuously opposed extreme severity, though the majority were of opinion that no change should be made.' M here reads *senatusque in quo ipso . . .*, which might be construed by taking *senatus* as partitive gen. with *pluribus*, ' owing to a gathering of the people . . . a disturbance amounting to a riot was caused, and owing to a majority of the Senate . . . moving that no change should be made '. It would be quite in the Tacitean manner to refuse to balance *uentum est* by another main verb, but the constr. is so awkward that edd. generally emend the text. Lipsius, followed by many, read *senatuque in ipso ;* F. Jacob *senatusque obsessus* (sc. *est*) *;* Heraeus *uocatus ;* Koestermann *ideo uocatus.* For *quoque* in this position cf. *Agr.* 2, *memoriam quoque ipsam ;* Germ. 26, *annum quoque ipsum ;* and *Ann.* XIV, 11, 12, 62.

sententiae loco, ' in his turn for giving his opinion ', not ' instead of . . .', a meaning which *loco* often has. Cf. *Ann.* I, 74, *Piso* ' *quo*' ' *inquit* ' *loco censebis, Caesar ?* ' *;* Ann. II. 38, 6, *a maioribus concessum est egredi aliquando relationem et quod in commune conducat loco sententiae proferre.*

C. Cassius, consul suffectus in A.D. 30, predecessor of Ummidius Quadratus as governor of Syria. He was a famous lawyer. See *Ann.* XII, 12, *Ea tempestate Cassius ceteros praeminebat peritia legum.* For his severity, cf. *Ann.* XIII, 48.

43. § 1. non quia dubitarem. The subj. is regular with *non quia . . . sed . . .*, of the rejected reason.

super. See on c. 9, 2.

prouisum, sc. *esse.* An acc. and infin. phrase, instead of the classical *quin*-clause with the subj. is the regular constr. in Tacitus after *non dubito* = ' do not doubt that '. See Introd. III, 5, (ii).

ad deterius. M omits the prep. Most edd. insert *in. ad* (Koestermann) is better, as there is an obvious reason for its omission.

sed ne . . . uiderer, ' but for fear my excessive fondness for ancient usage might make me seem to be advertising my profession ', i.e. he was afraid of seeming to show off the knowledge of ancient precedent which his profession of jurisprudence required, and of seeming to exaggerate the importance (*extollere*) of that profession.

§ 2. **quicquid hoc . . . est** = *quicquid auctoritatis hoc est quod in nobis est*, ' whatever extent of influence this is which I wield '. As Furneaux points out, the part. gen. with *hoc* makes the expression more modest for *haec auctoritas*. Trans. ' At the same time I felt that I ought not to undermine whatever influence I have by speaking in opposition too often, so that I might wield it unimpaired, if ever the State was in need of my guidance .' *eguisset* is indir. (dep. on *existimabam*) for *eguerit* (fut. perf.).

uenit = *euenit.*

senatus consulto. There is a reference in *Ann.* XIII, 32 to a senatorial decree passed in A.D. 57 : *Factum et senatus consultum ultioni iuxta et securitati, ut si quis a suis seruis interfectus esset, ii quoque qui testamento manu missi sub eodem tecto mansissent inter seruos supplicia penderent.* This was only four years before, whereas the words *nondum concusso* suggest that the reference is to some much older decree which might have been attacked on the ground that it was out of date.

§ 3. **decernite . . . profuerit,** ' Vote for their impunity, by heaven! so that whom can his rank defend, when it did not defend the Prefect of the City? ' *defendat* is the subj. of a deliberative question of the type which expresses sarcasm or indignation, but it is made to depend on a consecutive *ut*. Cf. Livy 40, 13, ' *parricidium . . . uolutabam in animo : ut quibus . . . sacris . . . contaminatam omni scelere mentem expiarem ? ' . . .* ' so that with what sacrifices could I have expiated . . .? ' Livy 44, 39, *Sine ulla sede uagi dimicassemus : ut quo uictores nos reciperemus ?* When the *ut* is final, the interr. word usually comes first, e.g. *quid ut faciatis uenistis ?*

M here reads *ut quem . . . defendat, cui praefectus urbis non profuit ; quem . . . tuebitur . . . cui familia opem ferat . . . .* There is obviously some error in the words *cui praefectus . . . profuit,* but there is no need to alter *ut . . . defendat* to *at . . . defendet,* or *tuebitur* to *tueatur,* as some edd. do. For the variation of moods, see Sörbom, *Var. Serm. Tac.* pp. 105 ff., where this passage is dealt with. *cui* can scarcely stand, but even if it is altered to *cum,* it is not absolutely necessary to change *profuit* to *profuerit.* An explanatory *cum,* = ' since ', sometimes has the indic. in class. Latin, cf. Cic., *Fam.* 9, 14, 3, *gratulor tibi, cum tantum uales ;* ibid. 13, 24, 2, *tibi maximas gratias ago, cum tantum litterae meae potuerunt. praefectus* must be changed either to *praefecto* or *praefectura.*

numerus seruorum, ' a host of slaves '.

aduertit = *animaduertit,* ' takes notice of '. Cf. *Ann.* IV, 54, *donec aduertit Tiberius.* Also in the sense of *animaduertere* ' to punish ', *Ann.* IV, 35, *si quis aduertit, dictis dicta ultus est.* ' To draw attention upon oneself ', *Ann.* II, 17, *octo aquilae . . . imperatorem aduertere.* Tacitus is fond of using a simple verb for a more usual compound verb.

§ 4. **quia de paterna,** &c. An ironical reference to the motives suggested for the murder at the beginning of c. 42. If the slave thought himself robbed by his master, it was of his *peculium,* which legally belonged to his master. A slave could not in law be robbed of anything, because he possessed nothing.

ultro, ' freely ', ' without more ado '.

44. § 1. libet . . . ? 'are you wantonly desirous of searching out arguments in a matter which has been maturely considered by wiser men than you?'

sapientioribus, dat. of agent (cf. dat. ' of person judging ').

si . . . statuendum haberemus, 'if we had it now to decide for the first time '. Strangely enough, classical Latin normally uses the infin. with *habeo* in this sense, e.g. Cic. *Balb.* 33, *Quid habes igitur dicere de Gaditano foedere ? Att.* 2, 22, 6, *nihil habeo ad te scribere ;* or else cf. *Cael.* 104, *haec habui . . . quae dicerem.* The infin. with *habeo* later came to be used as a periphrasis for the fut. tense (hence *j' aimerai = amare habeo*).

interficiendi domini animum sumpsisse, 'raised the courage to kill his master '. For the gen. see Introd. III, 2 (v).

ut . . . nihil . . . proloqueretur, 'without rashly saying anything aloud '.

sane, here = *at enim,* ' to be sure ', or ' granted, he concealed his design . . .'. Such concessions for the sake of argument are usually expressed by the subj. The indic., as indicating a fact, is more rhetorical and makes a more generous concession.

excubias, ' sentinels ', i.e. slaves on night duty at the entrance to the bed-chamber. The word strictly = ' a lying out (on outpost duty) ', but it is often used concretely of the persons. Cf. *uigiliae, insidiae.*

transire . . . poterat, ' could he have passed, &c.?' *poterat* is an editorial addition. M reads *transiret . . . recluderet . . . inferret . . . patraret,* which would mean the same. But M originally read the infin. and the imperf. subj. is a not very clear alteration by another hand.

§ 2. serui si prodant, &c. In this sentence clarity of argument has been sacrificed to brevity. The real point is that the death penalty for the whole *familia* must be retained, but this is left to be inferred from the statement of the advantages to be gained, if slaves reveal the criminal intentions of their fellows. It goes without saying that they will not do this without having the fear of death in them (*anxios*). The one infin. *agere* (= ' to live ', or ' to be ', cf. c. 15, 4) serves, by zeugma, for the three phrases *singuli inter plures, tuti inter anxios, non inulti inter nocentes.* Trans., ' Many indications of a coming crime precede it. If our slaves reveal them, we can live isolated amongst their numbers, safe while they are in fear of death, and in the end, if we must be murdered, we can die not unavenged amidst their guilt .'

suspecta . . . fuerunt, ' were objects of suspicion to . . .'. This renders the real sense of the dat. better than ' were suspected by '.

cum . . . nascerentur. The Latin word for a slave born in the house and not purchased from abroad is *uerna,* whence the adj. *uernaculus,* ' belonging to such a slave ', or ' native-born ', ' indigenous ', and Eng. ' vernacular '.

caritatemque . . . acciperent, ' and conceived an affection for their masters from the start ', i.e. the gen. is objective, not subjective. It is just possible that the meaning is ' and experienced the affection of their masters ', but it is hardly likely, in view of the fact that, of the nine instances of the gen. with *caritas* in Tacitus, only one is subjective, viz. *Ann.* IV. 11, *caritate in eum Caesaris,* where the object is expressed by the prepositional phrase.

§ 3. **nationes.** The word is suggestive of their numbers as well as their foreign origin. Trans. ' tribes of heathen '.

ritus, elsewhere often interchangeable with *sacra*, ' religious rites ' or ' religious usage ', is here obviously used in the sense of ' usage ', ' behaviour ', without special reference to religion: ' who have different ways from ours, and foreign religions, or none at all '.

coercueris. For this use of the perf. subj., see Introd. III, 6, (i).

at, here introduces a supposed objection, ' But, you may say . . .'. Cf. also *at enim*.

nam admits the validity of the objection and palliates it by quoting another example: ' Yes! and when a routed army is decimated, the brave too draw lots .'

habet . . . rependitur, ' Every case of severe exemplary punishment involves some injustice, but this injustice done to individuals is counterbalanced by the advantage to the common weal .'

45. § 1. **nemo unus,** ' no one alone ', ' no single individual ', i.e. no one cared to stand forth as the spokesman of the contrary opinion, but the speech of Cassius evoked replies from all over the House in the shape of expressions of pity for the intended victims .

decernebat. Notice the conative force of the imperf., ' the party which *was for decreeing* '. This has been called the ' imperfect of endeavour '.

obtemperari, impersonal and absolute: ' obedience was impossible ', i.e. ' the decree could not be carried into effect '.

§ 2. **edicto increpuit,** ' censured the populace in an edict '. The emperor, as a magistrate, was empowered to issue edicts which had the force of laws, primarily to regulate special cases, as here, but often with general application.

Cingonius Varro, mentioned in *Hist.* I, 6 as consul designate in A.D. 68, and put to death by Galba as an accomplice of Nymphidius.

Italia. For the abl. without prep., see Introd. III, 4, (i).

intenderetur, for this sense, ' to strain ', cf. c. 23, 1.

46. § 1. **Tarquitius Priscus.** For his false accusation of Statilius Taurus, proconsul of Africa, at the instigation of Agrippina, see Ann. XII, 59.

repetundarum, to be taken both with *damnatus* and *interrogantibus*.

interrogantibus. *Interrogare*, ' to cross-examine ', as a legal term, has reference to the questions put by the accuser to the accused, and so comes to mean ' to prosecute '. It may therefore be followed by the legal gen., on which see Introd. III, 2. Cf. *Ann.* XIII, 14, *sane pepigerat Pallas ne cuius facti in praeteritum interrogaretur.*

magno patrum gaudio. N.b. that though this may be trans. ' *to* the great joy of the Senate ', the case is abl. of att. circs., cf. n. on c. 11, 2, and cf. 14, 2; 20, 1; 20, 2; 59, 4.

pro consule ipsius. Although *proconsul*, as a declinable noun, was already in use by Cicero's time, the prepositional phrase *pro consule* still continues to be used as if it were an indeclinable noun, when in apposition to another noun.

§ 2. **census . . . acti sunt.** *censum agere* or *habere*, ' to hold a census ', meant not only to count heads, but to register and assess property for the purpose of taxation and tribute.

Gallias, plur. because there were four provinces of Gaul, viz. Narbonensis, Aquitania, Lugudunensis, and Belgica.

Q. Volusio, consul in A.D. 56.

Sextio Africano, referred to in *Ann.* XIII, 19 as *nobilem iuuenem*.

Trebellio Maximo, consul in A.D. 58. In A.D. 64 he succeeded Petronius Turpilianus as governor of Britain, where he bore an evil character. See *Hist.* I, 60.

Trebellium . . . tulere, ' their common disdain of Trebellius rendered his authority superior to theirs ', i.e. their jealousy of each other caused them to thwart each other's authority. Meanwhile Trebellius, unhindered because considered beneath jealousy, became the most important member of the commission.

47. § 1. Memmius Regulus, consul suffectus in A.D. 31, when he was instrumental in securing the condemnation of Sejanus. He succeeded Poppaeus Sabinus as governor of Moesia, Macedonia and Achaea. He married Lollia Paulina (c. 12, 4), whom the emperor Gaius forced him to divorce.

in quantum . . . datur, ' so far as is possible under the emperor's overshadowing eminence '.

adeo ut . . . responderit, cf. n. on c. 12, 2 *continuauerit*.

si quid . . . pateretur, o.o. for *si quid patiaris;* a euphemism for *si fatum obiret*.

§ 2. tamen, i.e. in spite of having been thus stamped as a potential rival.

noua . . . claritudine . . . opibus, ablatives of quality.

praebitumque oleum, for anointing themselves, before taking part in the exercises.

facilitate, ' bountifulness ', ' liberality '. The word contains a sneer. Oil was provided free of charge in Greek gymnasia. Nero was trying to Grecize Rome, and the providing of public oil for the wealthy upper-class participants was a hint that they were expected to set an example in patronizing the gymnastic contests.

48. § 1. P. Mario L. Afinio. Neither is elsewhere mentioned by Tacitus. The year is A.D. 62.

Antistius. For his turbulence as tribune, see *Ann.* XIII, 28, where he is said to have obstructed the praetor Vibullius in the execution of his duty. See also *Ann.* XVI, 14; 21; *Hist.* IV, 44.

Ostorium Scapulam, distinguished for bravery in Britain during the governorship of his father, P. Ostorius, see *Ann.* XII, 31. His attempt to shield Antistius was ill repaid by the latter, who attempted to gain remission of his exile by trumping up a charge against him. Ostorius was forced to commit suicide. See *Ann.* XVI, 14-15.

Cossutiano Capitone, a notorious informer. The occasion of his expulsion from the Senate was in A.D. 57, when he was condemned for extortion and corrupt practices in Cilicia (*Ann.* XIII, 33). The Cilician plaintiffs were supported by Thrasea, so that the feud between him and Cossutianus was of long standing. We hear nothing more of Cossutianus after his accusation of Thrasea in A.D. 66 (*Ann.* XVI, 28).

Tigellini. This is the first mention in Tacitus of Ofonius Tigellinus, who, with Faenius Rufus as his colleague, succeeded Burrus as Praetorian Prefect. For his character, see cc. 51, 57, 60, also *Hist.* I, 72, where his death under Otho is described. After pandering to Nero's vices and helping to make his master even more infamous than he was, he finally deserted him and managed to secure impunity under Galba. Otho's order for his death caused great public rejoicing.

maiestatis, Introd. III, 2, (ii).

§ 2. **tum primum reuocata ea lex.** The law against high treason (*maiestatem minuere* or *laedere*) was not an imperial invention. It was a republican crime, which Cicero defines as follows (*de Inv.* II, 53): *maiestatem minuere est de dignitate aut amplitudine aut potestate populi aut eorum quibus populus potestatem dedit, aliquid derogare.* It would cover cowardice in the field, breaches of faith on the part of a magistrate which would impair the credit of the State, &c. Julius Caesar had defined and restricted the scope of the law. Augustus extended it as a potential weapon against opponents, but refrained from enforcing it. Tiberius, who had not the prestige of Augustus, resorted to the law of *maiestas* to protect himself, and extended it to include offences against the person of the emperor, who was thus claimed to embody the State. This let loose a horde of informers, and accounts for the black character which Tacitus gives Tiberius. Such odium was aroused that, under Claudius, the law was left in abeyance, to be revived on the present occasion.

credebaturque . . . eximeret, ' it was thought that the object was not so much the death of Antistius as the glorification of the emperor, that he might grant him a reprieve by the exercise of his tribunician veto, after he had been condemned by the Senate '. **intercessione tribunicia :** the right to protect citizens against summary jurisdiction (*ius auxilii*) was the original prerogative of the tribunate, which later expanded into a power to interfere with legislation. Hence the *tribunicia potestas* was an important element in the authority of the emperor. For the dat. *morti*, see Introd. III, 3, (i).

more maiorum, i.e. by scourging him to death.

§ 3. **Paetus Thrasea,** see on c. 12, 1.

§ 4. **carnificem . . . abolita,** ' the hangman and the noose were things that had long gone out of fashion '. The reference is to the usual method of executing criminals, by strangling in the Tullianum. This punishment was rarely carried out against Roman citizens under the Republic. Under the Empire, a citizen, if condemned to death, usually committed suicide. The point is that, if criminals are no longer strangled, the more ancient and barbarous punishments are still more out of date. N.b. that, since *carnifex* and *laqueus* are both masc., the part. *abolita* is being used substantivally = ' *things* that have gone out of fashion '.

poenas. Outlawry was usually considered sufficient punishment.

quibus . . . decernerentur, a rel. final clause.

priuatim . . . publicae clementiae. There seems to be an attempt to secure a strained point by opposing *priuatim* to *publicae.* The State could claim to have shown clemency, while, in effect the individual would suffer more. Trans. ' the more wretched would he be personally, while affording an excellent example of clemency on the part of the State '.

49. § 1. **postquam . . . permiserat,** ' after the consul had allowed a division '. The presiding consul could refuse to put a motion or any part of a motion which displeased him. After he had put forward a matter for discussion (*rem referre, relatio*), he asked senators, in order of seniority, for their opinion (*rogare sententiam, rogatio*). When asked, senators could stand up and make a speech, or remain sitting and indicate agreement with a speech already made. When no more opinions were forthcoming, senators were asked *pedibus ire in sententiam* (= *discessio*), which meant that they got up and gathered in groups round the senator whose opinion they favoured. The groups were then counted and a simple majority decided. A small committee was then formed to formulate the required *senatus consultum*. It was even within the discretion of the presiding consul to refuse to appoint the latter committee, so as not to give effect to the decree (*perficere decretum* below). However, undue obstruction by a consul was not possible, as tribunes had the right to convene the Senate and put motions.

A. Vitellius, the future emperor.

lacessens . . . reticens. This use of the participle as an epithet of general application, independent of the time of the main verb, is classical, though not common in prose, but is very common in Silver Latin poetry. Cf. Cic. *Phil.* 11, 28, *est . . . lex . . . recta ratio, imperans honesta, prohibens contraria* (for *quae imperat,* &c.). The earliest instance seems to be Cat. 64, 8 *diua quibus retinens* (= *quae retinet*) *in summis urbibus arces | ipsa leui fecit uolitantem flamine currum.* Trans. 'A. Vitellius, *a man who provoked* all decent people with his abuse, but was silent in face of a rejoinder, as cowards usually are.'

§ 2. **pro magnitudine delicti,** 'in proportion to the magnitude of the offence'.

par fuisse, 'it *would have been* just'. But *fuisse* does not stand for *futurum fuisse,* because Nero did not say *par fuisset,* but *par fuit.* In expressions to denote what is or was the right or suitable thing to do, Latin used the indic., and not the subj. as we do, e.g. *par, iustum, melius, satius erat, fuit* = 'it would have been fair, just, better, &c.'. Cf. also *longum est, erat,* 'it would be, would have been tedious'. The reason for the indic. is probably that the Roman mind realized that the rightness of an action was an absolute fact, independent of any condition. In a somewhat similar way *hoc facturus eram, fui,* 'I was intending or was about to do this' = *hoc fecissem,* 'I should have done it (under certain conditions)'. Cf. next note.

impediturus fuerit. Nero's words were: *ego, qui seueritatem . . . impediuissem, moderationem non prohibeo.* But Latin disliked to make a subj. form do double duty. Accordingly, instead of merely changing *impediuissem* to *impediuisset* in o. o., recourse is had to the alternative *impediturus eram* or *fui,* mentioned in the preceding note. The change of *eram* or *fui* to *fuerit* thus marks the obliqueness, while the 'potentiality' is marked by other means. This method of dealing with the apodosis of a conditional sentence, whether it occurs in o. o., or in a clause of which the verb should be for other reasons subj., e.g. in a *cum*-clause, after consec. *ut,* or in an indir. quest., is regular and classical. Cf. Livy 9, 33, 7, *dic quidnam facturus fueris, si eo tempore censor fuisses.* The only other remark that need be made is that in the use of the perf. subj. *fuerit,* the sequence of tenses is often neglected, as in *impediturus fuerit* above, where the governing verb *rescripsit* is past.

statuerent ut uellent, 'they might decide as they wished', i.e. *ut = quo modo,* 'in what way', and is the rel. adverb, not the subordinating conj. 'that' (i.e. in function, for they are both the same word etymologically).

§ 3. **non ideo . . . deseruere,** 'for all that neither did the consuls change the form of the motion, nor Thrasea retreat from his opinion or the rest cancel their votes'. For *relationem . . . sententia,* see note on § 1 above. The point of *mutauere relationem* is that the consuls might have put the motion in the form ' Does Antistius deserve punishment?', taking the traditional form of punishment for granted. In that case, senators would have had to vote in the affirmative. As it was, they evidently asked ' Shall he be punished as Junius Marullus proposes?', which takes the punishment for granted, but not its form.

ne . . . uiderentur, ' in case they might be thought to have exposed the emperor to odium', i.e. any alteration in their decision would have been an obvious concession to the emperor's vindictiveness, and they knew that he would blame them for his consequent unpopularity.

plures = *maior pars,* cf. n. on c. 21, 1.

sueta firmitudine, abl. of cause, ' with, *or* out of his usual courage of mind'. Notice how Tacitus varies his methods in giving the various reasons for the actions of the various parties. A clause of neg. purpose is followed by a nom. participial phrase (for a part. has to be understood with *tuti,* ' the majority being safe because of their numbers', i.e. ' because they felt that there was safety in numbers'); and lastly comes a causal abl. joined with another clause of neg. purpose.

ne gloria intercideret, ' in case his reputation might suffer'. The suggestion of vanity which Tacitus attributes to Thrasea in these words is, perhaps, not without foundation. Continual opposition to the Empire had become a pose with some of the die-hards.

50. § 1. **Fabricius Veiento,** infamous as an informer in the reign of Domitian. Juvenal mentions him several times, and in IV, 113 calls him *prudens Veiento,* an epithet justified by the fact that he remained in favour even under the good Nerva. Hence *conflictatus* here = ' harassed' rather than ' ruined'.

quibus nomen codicillorum dederat, ' which he had entitled " My Will " '. *codicilli* (lit. ' little tablets ') means the same as Eng. ' codicil '. The word is used of an appendix to a will, giving supplementary directions to the executors or making comments on any matter which the testator wished to leave on record. Under a system of government where free speech was dangerous, it often happened that a wronged and embittered man gave expression to his feelings in a supplement to his will. Hence Veiento's satires were obviously a skit on such bitter attacks. The defining or appositional gen. *codicillorum* is not classical. With *nomen alicui est,* Cicero uses either the dat. (by attraction) or the nom. of the name, e.g. *Rosc. Am.* 17, *duo sunt Roscii, quorum alteri Capitoni cognomen est ; Verr.* IV, 118 *fons cui nomen Arethusa est.* The gen. occurs first in post-Aug. authors, e.g. Val. Max. 1, 8, *Ext.* 8 *cui nomen erat Equi ;* Tac., *Hist.* IV, 18, *castra quibus Veterum nomen est.* Tacitus, however, more often uses the nom. with proper names, cf. c. 22, 2, *cui Sublaqueum nomen est.*

uenditata . . . ius, ' that he had carried on a traffic in the emperor's

favours and the right of nomination to office ', i.e. he had taken money
from people in return for using his influence with the emperor to
secure them advancement. *adipiscendorum ius* is a reference to the
emperor's right of *commendatio*, whereby he nominated a certain number
of candidates (*candidati Caesaris*) who were elected as a matter of course.
Notice that the grammar-book rule about avoiding the gen. plur. of
the gerundive has no foundation in fact. It is rarely observed by
Cicero, and not always by Caesar.

§ 2. **suscipiendi iudicii.** Whether this means that Nero took the
case cut of the hands of the Senate and tried it in the emperor's private
court, or merely that he presided over the senatorial High Court of
Justice, is uncertain. The emperor could pass judgement without a
jury, though he usually called in the aid of assessors (*consilium*). As
Nero is the subject of *depulit* and *iussit*, it is more likely that he tried
the case privately.

conquisitos lectitatosque. N. b. this does not mean that he ordered
them to be burned ' *after* they had been sought out and read . . .', as
it would in classical Latin, but the past part. makes a subsequent
statement, as in c. 24, 1; i.e. ' but they were sought out and eagerly
read, so long as it was dangerous to procure them '. For this loose
' timeless ' use of the past part., see Introd. III, 7, (i). For the observa-
tion of human weakness here noted, cf. *Ann.* IV, 34, *carmina Bibaculi
et Catulli referta contumeliis Caesarum leguntur : sed ipse diuus Iulius, ipse
diuus Augustus et tulere ista et reliquere . . . namque spreta exolescunt : si
irascare, adgnita uidentur.*

51. § 1. grauescentibus. *grauesco*, ' grow heavy ', ' grow worse ', is
poet. and post-Aug.

concessitque . . ., ' for Burrus passed away '. The -*que* is explanatory, as often. Cf. c. 38, 3 *disperseratque*.

in se, ' internally ', though it is possible that *se* is acc., in which case
the sense would be that ' the walls of his throat swelled and *came
together* '.

plures, ' the greater number ', ' the majority ' = *maior pars*, cf. 49, 3;
60, 2. This passage gives a good example of Tacitus' historical method.
He gives all the facts known to him, but colours them. Without
passing judgement on the two versions, by giving one of them at greater
length, he suggests which is the more likely. Suet., *Ner.* 35, says
outright, *Burro praefecto remedium ad fauces pollicitus, toxicum misit.*

aspectum eius auersatum, ' shunning the sight of him ', ' turning
his back on him '.

hactenus, lit. ' thus far ', i.e. ' only this '.

ego me bene habeo, ' *I* am all right'. Burrus' supposed reply has
reference to his state of mind, not his bodily health. He means that
he has an easy conscience, while Nero has not.

§ 2. **segnem innocentiam,** ' good but ineffective character ', i.e. he
was not vicious, but was not a power for good, as Burrus had been.

imposuerat. The pluperf. tense does not, of course, indicate priority
to the time of Burrus' death, but to the time when the community
began to realize what a loss it had suffered.

Faenium Rufum. He was appointed to the *praefectura annonae* in
A.D. 55, in deference to the wishes of Agrippina (*Ann.* XIII, 22). For

the fact that he had been a partisan of Agrippina, see c. 57. The enmity of Tigellinus later drove him to join the ill-starred conspiracy of Piso (XV, 50), on the discovery of which his conduct was not very laudable.

Ofonium Tigellinum. See c. 48, 1. Such is the form of his name in the MSS. of Tacitus. Most edd. take the form *Sofonius* from Dio. Son of an Agrigentine, poor, but handsome, he was brought up in the households of M. Vinicius and L. Domitius, the husbands of Agrippina and Julia, the sisters of Caligula. Suspected of adultery with these ladies, he was banished in A.D. 39, and lived as a fisherman in Achaea until he inherited a fortune. Allowed to return, probably in A.D. 41, he bought estates in Calabria and Apulia, and bred race-horses. This is probably how he became acquainted with Nero, whom he infected with a passion for the circus. He seems to have been Nero's evil genius from beginning to end.

ueterem . . . secutus, ' attracted by his ingrained shamelessness and notoriety '. The reference of *ueterem impudicitiam* will be clear from the previous note.

§ 3. **pro cognitis moribus fuere,** lit. ' they were (existed) according to their known characters ', i.e. ' their subsequent history tallied with what was known of their characters, Tigellinus having the greater influence over the mind of the emperor and being associated with him in his most private debauches, while Rufus enjoyed popularity with the people and soldiers, a fact which he found to count against him with Nero '.

prospera . . . fama, abl. of quality, the pres. part. of the verb ' to be ' being understood in agreement with *Rufus*.

52. § 1. **nec . . . et** = ' not only . . . but also '.

idem uirium. The part. gen. with pronouns expressing quantity is regular and classical. See Introd. III, 2 (iv).

tamquam . . . augeret, quodque . . . uerteret . . . quasi . . . supergrederetur. For these different methods of quoting the ground of accusation, i.e. for making what amounts to an ind. statement, see Introd. III, 6, ii (e) and (f).

priuatum modum euectas. Although one would expect verbs compounded with *ex*, such as *egredi, euadere, euehi*, to be qualified by an abl. of source, they are often used in the transitive sense of ' passing beyond something ', ' escaping something ', and consequently govern an acc. E.g. Caes. *B. C.* 3,52,2, *Germani munitiones nostras egressi . . .*, ' *passing by* our fortifications '; Liv. 2,61,4, *modum egredi*. But cf. Liv. 8,38,5, *castris egredi*, ' to come *out of* . . . '. In class. Latin the bare acc. with these verbs is very rare, but is extended from Livy on.

studia . . . uerteret, ' that he was attracting to himself the loyalty of the citizens ', an obvious reference to the *coetus salutantium* mentioned in c. 56 below. That such court was paid to him suggested that he was regarded as the power behind the throne.

§ 2. **laudem,** here = ' merit ', as often.

quotiens caneret, ' whenever he sang '. This would have been a good ex. of the ' frequentative subj.', were it not obscured by the fact that the clause is in o. o. (Introd. III, 6, ii (b).)

quem ad finem, lit. ' up to what limit ? ', i.e. ' for how long ? ' Trans.

'How long would there be nothing of note in the State, but Seneca must be credited with its invention?'

satis . . . amplis . . . suis, 'equipped as he was with sufficiently illustrious teachers in his ancestors'. But although *amplus* as applied to a person (cf. *uir amplissimus*) means no more than 'illustrious' in a vague and general sense, Nipperdey is probably right in understanding it here as 'many-sided', 'broad'. For all activities in which he engaged, Nero would find good models among his ancestors.

53. § 1. quibus aliqua honesti cura, 'those who had any regard for decency'.

quartus . . . obtines, 'It is thirteen years since I became connected with your hopes, seven since you came to the throne.' Seneca had been appointed tutor to Nero in A.D. 49, and Claudius died in A.D. 54. As Seneca does not call A.D. 62 the 'ninth' year of Nero's reign, obviously the anniversary of his accession has not yet arrived, but the anniversary of Seneca's appointment is past. *spei tuae admotus,* 'attached to your hopes', i.e. 'put in charge of the career opening before you'.

ex quo . . . admotus sum, octauus ut . . . obtines. Notice the different tenses = 'since I *was attached* (once and for all) . . . ' and 'the eighth year since you *have been holding* power'. Latin, having no tense to denote action 'complete but continued', has to use the pres. and the imperf., which are tenses of incomplete action; thus *multos annos hoc facio, faciebam* = 'I have been, had been doing this for many years'. Notice that *ut* is here a temporal conj. = *cum* or *in quo* or *ex quo*. The use of *ut* = *ubi, postquam, simul ac,* is common enough, but its use to denote 'time since when' (= *cum, ex quo*) is comparatively rare. Cf. Cic. *Att.* 1,15,2, *ut Brundisium profectus es, nullae mihi abs te sunt redditae litterae,* '*since* you left Brundisium, I have received no letter from you'. The only other two exx. noted of its use with the idiomatic pres. indic. of the type indicated above are in Plautus and Ovid.

medio temporis, 'in the meantime'.

moderatio eius. Since *moderor,* according as it governs the acc. or dat. = either 'keep under control' or 'act with moderation towards' (i.e. 'control oneself in respect of something'), so *moderatio* can partake of either or both of these meanings. Thus it can mean either 'control', or 'self-control', 'moderation', 'modesty'. Here it = 'wise control', and the gen. is objective. Cf. *Ann.* XII, 37, *si quanta nobilitas mihi fuit, tanta rerum prosperarum moderatio fuisset.* Trans. 'so that nothing is wanting to my good fortune but the ability to make the right use of it'.

§ 2. abauus, 'great-great-grandfather'. On the female side, Nero was descended in a direct line from Augustus, being the son of Agrippina the Younger, daughter of Agrippina the Elder, daughter of Julia, daughter of Augustus. As his grandfather Germanicus had been adopted by Tiberius and the latter by Augustus, legally he was descended from Augustus on the male side also.

Mytilenense secretum, 'retirement at Mytilene'. The real reason for Agrippa's retirement to Mytilene in Lesbos was probably less honourable. Augustus was trying to found a dynasty by marrying his daughter Julia to his sister's son Marcellus. During an illness in 23 B.C., Augustus, feeling that Marcellus was yet too young for responsibility, gave his signet-ring to Agrippa. This raised Agrippa's hopes and càused jealousy between him and Marcellus. When Augustus recovered, he had to separate them by removing Agrippa, on an honourable pretext, to the East. Instead of fulfilling in person the mission assigned to him, Agrippa sulked at Mytilene.

pluribus = *compluribus* or *multis*. See on c. 21, 1.

pro . . . meritis, 'in proportion to the greatness of their services'.

§ 3. ego quid aliud, &c., 'But in my case, what else could I urge upon your bounty except my studies, pursued, so to speak, in the cloister, and which have gained distinction because I am thought to have aided the early instruction of your youth, itself a bountiful reward for such a service?' *adhibere* with *ad* or dat. generally means to apply something to something, or to employ something for a purpose, e.g. it would be used of 'applying ointment to a wound'. Here the sense is 'to bring to bear upon', i.e. 'to influence by means of'. Seneca means that, while Agrippa and Maecenas could establish a claim on Augustus' bounty by means of great and tangible services, he, Seneca, on the other hand (hence emphatic *ego*), had only his knowledge of literature and philosophy with which to establish a claim on Nero's bounty. Such accomplishments, acquired *in umbra*, i.e. not outside in the world of affairs, were not adapted to such service as could lay an emperor under obligation.

ut sic dixerim, see Introd. III, 6, (i).

educata, agreeing with *studia*, though the verb is usually applied to a person, who is 'educated', not to the studies which are the means of his education.

grande huius rei pretium, acc. in apposition to the sentence, see Introd. III, 1, (iii). The very distinction arising from being the emperor's tutor was an ample reward.

§ 4. gratiam . . . circumdedisti, sc. *mihi*. The alternative constr. would be the acc. of the person and the instr. abl. of the thing.

plerumque, 'very often'. Cf. c. 17, 1 *plerique*, also c. 55, 4 below.

longa decora praeferentes, 'displaying a long series of honours'. Notice that *praefero* is here used in its literal sense of 'bearing before', as e.g. a banner in a procession. The reference will be to the long series of *imagines* of office-holders which were kept in the atrium and carried in procession at funerals.

nouitas, the quality of being a *nouus homo,* the first of a family to hold high office. Perhaps with the metaphor *enituit,* one might trans. 'has my newly-risen star shone out . . . ?'

incedit. *animus* is continued as the subject. Notice that *incedo* always has the sense of 'walking proudly', 'stalking', 'strutting'. Cf. Virg., *Aen.* 1, 46, *ast ego quae diuom incedo regina.* The point is that this material splendour is inconsistent with Seneca's profession of Stoic philosophy.

tam lato faenore, 'such widely extended investments'. *Faenus* is strictly the 'interest' on capital invested. Seneca is supposed to have had a great deal of money invested in Britain, where the exaction of his interest helped to aggravate the distress and unrest.

obniti non debui, 'it was not my duty to resist'. The more usual auxiliary sense of *debui* with pres. infin. ('ought not to have . . . ') would be wrong here, since it would imply that he had resisted. Cf. the modal use of *possum.*

54. § 1. mensuram impleuimus, 'have filled our measure (i.e. reached the limit), you of what an emperor could bestow on a friend, I of what a friend could accept from his emperor'. *quantum* stands for (*tanti*) *quantum*, 'the measure of that amount which . . .' *posset,* generic subj. The amount is one 'such that . . .'.

cetera, 'all the rest', i.e. 'all above that limit'.

infra . . . iacet, 'lies beneath your greatness', in the sense that the emperor is too powerful to be assailed or hurt by envy.

incumbit, 'bears down upon', 'weighs heavily on'.

§ 2. procuratores. The *procuratores Augusti* were financial officers, usually of equestrian rank, who administered the taxes in the imperial provinces or imperial domains in Italy itself. They corresponded to the republican quaestors, but differed from the latter in that they were not state officials with a legally defined *potestas*, being merely servants of the emperor.

§ 3. quod temporis . . . reuocabo, 'I shall resume for spiritual contemplation the time which is set aside for the care of my parks and villas'.

superest tibi . . . regimen. The MS. is possibly corrupt here. *summi* is omitted, while Tacitus rarely uses *fastigium* in the sense of 'station' or 'high station' without an epithet. The sentence is usually taken to mean 'You have strength in abundance, and the administration of supreme power has been watched by you (i.e. you have learned how to do it from watching others) through so many years'. This means that *est tibi* with *uisum* is understood out of *superest tibi.* Nero has learned enough from the study of the history of imperial administration and from the regency of Seneca and Burrus to be able now to rule by himself. This fits the long period of time suggested by *tot per annos,* and means that Seneca is repeating the argument of his detractors in c. 52, 2, *exueret . . . maioribus suis.* However, Nero has now been on the throne nearly eight years, a period long enough to justify the phrase *tot per annos,* and it is unlikely that Seneca would imply that during this time he has not stood on his own feet. It is far better to understand the agent with *uisum* to be, not Nero, but the rest of mankind. Trans. 'You have in abundance the vigour of youth, and for many years men have seen you wielding supreme power.' *uisum* is almost used in the sense of *spectatum,* 'proved', i.e. 'you have proved to mankind your ability to rule'.

reposcere, 'ask as our due'. Cf. also *reddere,* which besides 'to give *back*', can also mean 'render what is due'.

cedet. For *cedere in* with acc. = 'to be counted as', 'to be interpreted as', 'to pass for', cf. *Germ.* 36, *Chattis uictoribus fortuna in sapientiam cessit,* 'when the Chatti were victorious, their luck passed for wisdom'. So here, 'This also will be counted to your credit, that . . .' Cf. c. 31, 2 and note.

55. § 1. quod . . . habeo, 'The fact that I can counter your studied speech on the spot is, to begin with, a gift which I hold at your hands.' *occurram* is 'potential' subj., which often has the sense of 'can' or 'may' as well as likelihood. See Introd. III, 6, (i). *tui muneris* is a type of gen. usually placed in grammars under the heading 'partitive'. Cf. Suet., *Claud.* 23, 2, *commeatus a senatu peti solitos beneficii sui fecit,*

'. . . made them part of his own benefactions'; Hor., *Od.* 4, 3, 21, *totum muneris hoc tui est,* ' this is entirely your gift' or ' lies in your dispensation '.

§ 2. **usurpare.** For the infin., see Introd. III, 5, (ii).

concessit, emphatic, as being equivalent to a concessive clause: ' he did allow them to retire, to be sure, but . . .'

sed in ea ipse, &c., ' but he himself had reached an age which gave him sufficient prestige to stand by the privilege, if privilege it was, which he had granted '. The point of this is explained in the next chapter by the words *non tua moderatio . . . uersabitur.* Nero knew quite well that people would attribute Seneca's retirement and surrender of his wealth to Nero's greed and cruelty. Augustus' power and character, on the other hand, were so well established that no one would accuse him of ' throwing the pilot overboard ', if he relieved Agrippa and Maecenas of their responsibilities. His age and power had *such* prestige *as to* ' protect ' his action (i.e. from misrepresentation). *tueretur* is generic, i.e. consec. subj., and *tribuisset* is subj. by attraction. *quicquid illud et qualecumque* stands for *illud, quicquid . . . esset, quod . . .*

ac tamen, i.e. in spite of his being in a position to do so with impunity.

datis . . . praemiis, abl. of separation.

bello . . . meruerant. Nero anticipates an objection from Seneca that Agrippa and Maecenas were allowed to retain their wealth because they had earned it in more active service than he had. To this Nero replies that this was only owing to the accidental circumstances of Augustus' youth. In their place Seneca would have done as much.

obnoxia, cf. note on c. 40, 1.

§ 4. **plerique,** ' very many ', cf. 17, 1; 53, 4.

libertinos, e.g. Narcissus and Pallas, freedmen of Claudius, the latter of whom was still alive. The thought of the wealth acquired by these men anticipates the reference to Claudius at the beginning of the next chapter, and explains it.

antecellis. In class. Latin *antecello* is normally constr. with the dat. of the person or thing excelled, cf. *praestare;* it has become transitive.

56. § 1. **Verum . . . ingredimur.** Nipperdey places this sentence after *nisi . . . potest,* thinking that it serves better to anticipate the appeal *quin . . . regis?* However, the words *prima imperii spatia ingredimur,* ' I am only entering on the first lap of my reign ', do not mean that Nero is still a novice who needs further guidance, but that he has plenty of time before him in which to make up deficiencies in Seneca's fortune, while Seneca is still not too old to repay his bounty with service to the State. The words *nisi . . . potest* fit on to this quite well, and mean: ' unless, of course, you think yourself incapable of serving me as long as Vitellius served Claudius, and think me less generous in rewarding my servants than Claudius was, and that an emperor cannot give a minister as much as a private subject can acquire for himself '.

rebusque et fructui rerum sufficiens, ' capable of undertaking (state-) business and enjoying the rewards of it '.

Vitellio. L. Vitellius was consul first in A.D. 34 (*Ann.* VI, 28) and afterwards proconsul of Syria in A.D. 35. He was one of the foremost courtiers of Claudius, under whom he obtained two more consulships and the censorship. He was the father of A. Vitellius who became emperor.

Volusio. L. Volusius died in A.D. 56 at the age of 93, having accumulated a vast fortune. See *Ann.* XIII, 30.

quin . . . reuocas . . . regis? An interrogative *quin?* (lit. 'why not?') with the indic. is equivalent to a command, or, in the first person, to exhortation or deliberation. Cf. Sall., *Cat.* 20, 14, *Quin igitur expergiscimini?* 'Why not wake up?' Livy 1, 57, 7, *Quin conscendimus equos?* 'Why do we not mount our horses?', i.e. 'Let us mount . . .'.

lubricum adulescentiae, 'the instability of my youth', 'my youthful instability'. For the part. gen. with a neut. adj., see Introd. III, 2, (iv).

ornatumque . . . regis? 'Why not enhance my youthful vigour with your support, and guide me all the more zealously?' In spite of the order, *subsidio* must go with *ornatum*. Nero is referring to Seneca's words in c. 54, 3, *superest tibi robur*. Nero may now be in the vigour of manhood, but, he says, his vigour will be all the better for being tempered with Seneca's wisdom.

§ 2. **non tua . . . uersabitur.** Tacitus cynically makes Nero reveal his real reasons for refraining from taking Seneca at his word. Strangely enough, Nero was very sensitive to public opinion.

fuerit, Introd. III, 6, (i).

paret, consec. subj., 'to win glory for himself from such a source as to bring unpopularity on his friend'.

§ 3. **factus . . . exercitus uelare.** For the explanatory infin. with adjectives, see Introd. III, 5, (i).

qui finis, sc. *est*. The sentence itself is the antecedent to the relative, cf. the parenthetic *id quod* clause. Though a sentence is regarded as a neut. 'thing', notice that the relative is attracted to the gender of the predicated noun *finis*.

coetus salutantium . . . comitantis. The former refers to the crowd of 'morning-callers' who thronged the ante-rooms to pay their respects to their *patronus*, the latter to the retinue of *clientes* who escorted him on visits to the city.

quasi . . . attineretur, 'under pretence that . . .', 'on the excuse that . . .' See Introd. III, 6, ii (*e*).

57, § 1. **promptum . . . criminantibus,** 'it was an easy matter to undermine the position of Faenius Rufus by making a charge in his case of friendship with Agrippina'. *criminari* may have an acc. of either the person or the thing complained of. *criminantibus* is more likely to be dat. with *promptum fuit* than abl. abs., so that the constr. is 'the undermining of the position of Faenius Rufus was easy for people charging him . . .'. For Faenius Rufus, see note on c. 51, 2.

malas . . . artes obstringeret, 'thinking that his wicked ways, on which alone his power rested, would gain a greater hold over the emperor, if he laid him under obligation by becoming his partner in crime . . .'. The commonest meaning of *obstringere*, lit. 'to tie up', is 'to bind some one by putting him under an obligation'. With *gratiores* understand *fore*. The source of Tigellinus' influence with Nero was his skill in pandering to his vices (= *malas artes*).

metus eius rimatur, ' he probed (the sources of) his fears '.
comperto. See Introd. III, 4, (ii).

Plautum et Sullam. For Rubellius Plautus, see on c. 22, 1.
Faustus Cornelius Sulla Felix was consul in A.D. 51. He was allied to
the family of the Caesars by having married Antonia, daughter of
Claudius. His character and exile to Massilia are described in *Ann.*
XIII, 47.

nobilitatem eorum et propinquos . . . exercitus. It is doubtful whether one should understand *esse* with *propinquos*, since, by the idiom
described in Introd. III, 7, (i), *propinquos exercitus* can stand for *propin-
quitatem exercituum*, the emphasis being on the adj. Notice that the
armies of the East were near to Plautus (*huic*), those of Germany to
Sulla (*illi*), so that the usual reference of *hic—ille* is reversed.

§ 2. **diuersas spes,** lit. ' opposite hopes ', i.e. ' hopes from opposite
quarters '. The point is that Burrus owed his appointment to Agrippina
(see *Ann.* XII, 42), and was therefore only half-hearted in taking
Nero's side against her. A further insidious suggestion is involved in
this comparison with the former Prefect. In A.D. 55 Agrippina had
been accused of plotting to make this same Rubellius Plautus emperor
(*Ann.* XIII, 19). It was Burrus who prevailed on Nero to give her a
hearing, and so saved her life and that of Plautus. Tigellinus' words
would remind Nero of this and suggest that he now had a Pretorian
Prefect who was willing to act against Plautus.

cui caueri . . . praesenti opera, ' for which precautions against
conspiracies in the city were being taken, in one way or another, by
his activity on the spot '. Notice that the constr. of *cauere*, ' to take
precautions ' is *alicui*, ' on some one's behalf ', *ab aliquo* or *aliqua re*,
' against some one, or something '. *utcumque* is really a relative adverb
= ' in what way soever ' (cf. *quicumque*, ' whosoever '), but owing to
ellipse of the subordinate verb (e.g. here *fieri potest*), it has come to be
treated as an indefinite adv. = ' somehow or other '. Cf. the similar
use of *quicumque* = ' some or other '. Both these indefinite uses became
common from Livy on.

longinquos . . . posse? acc. and infin. because the qu. is
rhet.

erectas, &c., ' The provinces of Gaul were all agog at the name
of the dictator Sulla, and the peoples of Asia were no less excited by
the famous name of (Plautus') grandfather Drusus.' The name of
the dictator Sulla can scarcely have been a name to conjure with after
nearly a century and a half. Plautus, on the other hand, had he been
really meditating rebellion, might possibly have made capital out of
the fact that Tiberius' son Drusus was his maternal grandfather.

§ 3. **unde praecipuam audaciam,** ' the source of the worst attempts
at revolution '.

dum . . . reperiret. The subj. is final, standing for *dum . . .
reperiat,* ' until he can find . . .', of the o. r.

magnis opibus, abl. of qual. When attached directly to a proper
name, instead of qualifying a common noun (e.g. *uirum*) in apposition,
this abl. is more like a loose abl. of att. circs.(from which, of course,
the abl. of qual. is derived), i.e. the nearest Eng. equivalent would be:
' Plautus, *with his great wealth*, did not even pretend . . .'.

praeferre, ' ostentatiously displayed '. *imitamenta* suggests that Plautus' austerity, like Sulla's sloth, was also a pretence.

Stoicorum adrogantia sectaque. Hendiadys for ' the arrogant creed of the Stoics '.

quae turbidos, &c., ' which made men turbulent and eager to take part in affairs '. Stoicism did not, like Epicureanism, advocate passive resistance. Stoics were not debarred by their creed from taking an active part in the affairs of this world. *negotiorum* here means ' political activity '. Cf. Seneca, *de Otio*, III, 2, *Epicurus ait : Non accedet ad rem p. sapiens nisi si quid interuenerit : Ẓenon ait : Accedet ad rem p. nisi si quid impedierit.* The Stoics were the backbone of the republican opposition under the Empire. Cf. note on Thrasea, c. 12, 1.

§ 4. **peruectis . . . percussoribus.** Beware of taking this as abl. of the *agent.* It is probably instr., the assassins being the instruments in the hands of another. Alternatively, though less probably, it may be construed as absolute.

tamquam, ' as being ' or ' on the ground that it was . . .'. Cf. 39, 3, *tamquam durante bello ;* 41, 1, *tamquam . . . gnarum.*

58. § 1. **pluribus . . . curabatur,** ' was being cared for by more people ', sc. than the safety of Sulla was. *pluribus* is dat. of ag., but even here it can be seen that the dat. was really the case of ' the person concerned '.

spatium itineris ac maris, ' the distance by land and sea '. *tempus interiectum,* i.e. the time that had to elapse between the decision and the perpetration of the crime.

petitum ab eo Corbulonem, ' that he had sought refuge with Corbulo '.

clari . . . interficerentur, part of the reported rumour, which said *clari . . . si interficiuntur.*

praecipuum ad pericula. Though Tacitus usually applies *praecipuus* to a ' chief mover ' rather than ' sufferer ' (cf. *Ann.* VI, 7, *praecipuos ad scelera ;* XVI, 14, *opes . . . praecipuas ad eliciendam cupidinem*), it is difficult to take this to mean anything but ' especially endangered '.

nequiuerint, perf. subj., as if the governing verb were hist. pres. *fingunt,* instead of *fingebant.*

§ 2. **uana haec . . . augebantur,** ' these unfounded reports, after the manner of rumours, were exaggerated by the idle and credulous '. Lit. ' by the idleness of people believing them '. The reference in *otio* is not to the fact that people were too lazy to sift the true from the false (as Furneaux), but to people who had nothing better to do than bandy gossip. Such people accept anything, and believe more than they hear, i.e. the phr. really = *credulitate otiosorum.*

ceterum. Notice that this conj. normally means ' However that may be . . .', i.e. ' whatever the truth of the foregoing, the following is a fact '. Cf. c. 42, 2, *ceterum cum uetere ex more . . .* Besides this more strongly adversative sense, *ceterum* is often used when resuming after a digression, cf. c. 12, 3.

centurionem, the officer in charge of the executioners.

L. Antistii. L. Antistius Vetus had been consul in A.D. 55 and Legatus of Upper Germany in A.D. 58. He did not long survive his son-in-law, being put to death in A.D. 65 along with his daughter, Plautus'.widow, Pollitta. See *Ann.* XVI, 10.

effugeret, ind. jussive, depending on verb of advising understood from *mandata attulit*.

dum suffugium esset, a conjecture which most modern edd. adopt for the MS. *otium suffugium et*. Trans., ' He must shun a tame death, so long as there was a remedy. By pity for his great name he would find loyal followers and rally bold spirits round him .'

§ 3. **dum refertur . . . permeat.** The retention of the pres. indic. with *dum* in o. o. is very common from Livy on, but rare in class. Latin. It is by no means an invariable rule, even in Tacitus, for cf. *Ann.* I, 46, *ciuitas incusare Tiberium quod, dum patres et plebem . . . ludificetur, dissideat miles.* The usual explanation of the retention of the indic. in a subord. clause in o. o. is that it is merely parenthetic.

multa secutura . . . eualescerent, ' many results would follow, which might strengthen into civil war '. *eualesco* is a poetic and post-Aug. word. *adusque* for *usque ad* is also poetic. For the tense of the subj., see Introd. III, 6, ii (*c*).

quaeri. For the tense, cf. 14, 3, *molliri* ; 18, 2, *subuenire.*

aut nihil grauius . . ., ' or he would have to suffer nothing worse through being bold than by tamely submitting '.

59. § 1. **siue . . . seu . . . an.** Occasionally, even in classical Latin, *an* is used to make an alternative suggestion in parenthesis, and in such cases it does not essentially differ in meaning from *aut*, *uel*, or *siue*. Cf. Cic. *Fin.* 2, 104, *cum ei Simonides an quis . . . alius . . . polliceretur*, ' when Simonides (or was it some one else?) promised him . . .'. In the present passage, *siue . . . seu* give two alternative reasons for Plautus' tame submission, while *an* hints at a third possibility by introducing, as it were, a parenthetic question, of which, ostensibly, less notice is to be taken: ' . . . whether because he saw no prospect of aid, unarmed and an exile as he was, or else (he remained unmoved) through weariness at the uncertainty (or was it through love of his wife and children, . . .?) '. So Tacitus, with his usual skill, manages in a mere aside to show Nero in the character of an imperial gangster.

turbatum. The part. is equivalent to a *si*-clause.

alios . . . nuntios . . . tamquam, ' another message to the effect that . . .'. See Introd. III, 6, ii (*e*).

Coeranum . . . Musonium. Of the former little is known. The latter was C. Musonius Rufus, a Roman knight, a famous Stoic philosopher, friend of the younger Pliny, and teacher of Epictetus.

constantiam opperiendae mortis, ' firmness in awaiting death '. See Introd. II, 2, (v).

§ 2. **nudus exercitando corpori**, ' stripped for taking physical exercise '. Dat. of purpose, see Introd. III, 3, (iv).

talem, ' in such a guise ', i.e. just as he was, in his gymnastic garb.

quasi satellitibus ministrum regium, ' like a royal vizier in command of his bodyguard '. *satelles* has a sinister connotation, being the word used of a tyrant's bodyguard or a master-criminal's henchman. Pelago was sent to make sure that the centurion carried out his orders. Cf. *Ann.* XI, 37, where Euodus is sent to supervise the execution of Messalina. For the importance of freedmen, see on c. 39, 1.

§ 3. **cur, inquit, Nero,** &c. The words between *Nero* and *et posito metu* are lost from the MS. It seems quite likely, however, that Nero would make some beastly and puerile jest about the man's looks, just as he did in the case of Sulla (c. 57, 4), and Dio, 62, 14, 1, actually tells us that he said ' I did not know that he had a big nose ', as if he would have spared him, had he known. *Cur, inquit, Nero, hominem nasutum timuisti ?* is Halm's conjecture.

maturare, ' to hurry on ', tr.

amoliri, ' to put away ', ' remove ', i.e. ' divorce '.

quamuis modeste ageret, to be taken with what follows: ' In spite of her unassuming behaviour, she was obnoxious to him on account of her father's name and her popularity with the people '. Octavia was the daughter of Claudius and Messalina, and was thus a true Claudian, while Nero had only been adopted. She thus enjoyed great prestige in the minds of the people, quite apart from popularity derived from her likeable character. The very presence of such a partner made Nero feel that he was an outsider who had only come to power through his mother's intrigues.

§ 4. **haud confessus,** i.e. Nero was still too much afraid of public opinion to admit his guilt openly, but pretended that the two men were still alive, and that they were a danger to the State. In this way he hoped to make the Senate his accomplices after the fact.

sibi . . . magna cura haberi, ' that the safety of the State was being upheld by him with great care '. Notice that *magna cura* is either instr. or modal abl., and does not mean the same as the pred. dat. *magnae curae* would. In the latter case the meaning would be ' was considered by him a great responsibility ' or ' was very near to his heart '. The former expression does actually contain a hint that measures are being or have been taken. For the dat. of the agent *sibi,* see Introd. III, 3, (ii).

eo nomine, ' on that account ', ' on that pretext '.

grauioribus iam ludibriis quam malis, ' the mockery being even more revolting than the crimes '. For *iam = etiam,* cf. *Germ.* 44, 1, *trans Lugios Gotones regnantur, paulo iam adductius quam ceterae . . .* M reads *tam,* but *iam,* an easy correction adopted by most modern edd., is better, since Tacitus seems to be referring only to this particular incident. *tam* would mean that the expression stands for *tam ludibria graviora fiebant quam mala,* and would be a general reflection on the times, e.g. ' the growth of mockery was keeping pace with Nero's tyranny '. Cf. the thought in c. 51, 1 *Sed grauescentibus in dies publicis malis subsidia minuebantur.*

60. § 1. cuncta scelerum. For this unclassical use of the partit. gen., see Introd. III, 2, (iv).

diu paelex. Her connexion with Nero began in A.D. 58, see *Ann.* XIII, 46.

impulit obicere. See Introd. III, 5, (ii).

§ 2. **destinaturque . . . Eucaerus,** ' a man named Eucaerus was marked out as defendant '.

canere per tibias doctus, ' skilled at playing on the flute '. Most edd. change *per tibias* of M to *tibiis.* The change is unnecessary, since Tacitus is fond of substituting prepositional phrases for bare cases, and *per* with acc. is equivalent in sense to the instr. case.   See Sörbom, *Var. Serm. Tac.* p. 68.

uictis quibusdam.   The abl. abs. is equivalent to a concessive clause: ' although some were coerced by the severity of the torture into bearing witness to falsehoods . . . '.

perstitere . . . tueri, ' held out in maintaining . . . '.   It is impossible to know, in the perf. tenses, whether the verb is *persto* or *persisto.*   In either case the usual constr. is *in aliqua re.*   There is one ex. of the infin. in Cicero, and cf. *Ann.* IV, 38, *perstititque . . . aspernari.*

§ 3. **ciuilis discidii specie,** ' under pretence of a legal divorce ', i.e. as the charge of unfaithfulness, which in the case of the emperor's wife, would have amounted to a charge of treason, could not be substantiated, Nero could only get rid of her on less serious grounds. Instead of being put to death, she actually received alimony (*dona*).

his . . . tamquam Nero.   M reads here *his quamquam Nero . . . reuocauit.*   It is quite clear that some words are missing, and that of those remaining, *reuocauit* at least is corrupt.   The sense of the passage must have been something like, ' out of this a false rumour arose to the effect that Nero, in repentance of his crime, had recalled Octavia to be his wife ', e.g. *His* (causal Abl.) ⟨*uana fama oritur*⟩ *tamquam Nero . . . reuocarit Octauiam.*

61. § 1. **deosque tandem uenerantur,** ' praised Heaven at last '. The point of *tandem* is that there had been nothing for which to praise the gods for so long.

proruunt.   *Ruo* and most of its compounds may be either tr. or intr.

foroque ac templis.   On the poetic use of the locatival Abl. without *in,* see Introd. III, 4, (i).

itur . . . uenerantium, ' a noisy cheering crowd even set out to give the emperor an ovation '.   More lit. ' a movement was made to praise the emperor with the noise of acclaiming people '.   *strepitu* is Andresen's conjecture for the meaningless *repetitum* of M.   No noun *repetitus* is elsewhere found.

et Palatium, i.e. they began to crowd on to Mt. Palatine, where the emperor's residence was, *as well as* on to the Capitol.   *multitudine et clamoribus,* hendiadys for ' in a shouting mob '.

§ 2. **mutataque . . . uerterant,** ' The changes they had made in the disorder were reversed .'   The reference is, of course, to the substitution of Octavia's statues for Poppaea's.

quae . . . genibus eius.   Possibly *prouoluta* (sc. *est*) is the main verb of this sentence, but it is more likely that it is a participle and that the main verb is the verb of speaking which has to be understood, on which the following acc. and infins. depend.   *ne . . . ingrueret . . . mutaretur* is a clause of fearing, depending on *metu,* and not a clause of neg. purpose.   Trans. ' She, always savage in her hatred and now wild with fear lest more serious mob-violence should threaten, or Nero be influenced by the popular will, flung herself at his knees and (cried) . . . '.

prouoluta genibus.   Cf. *Ann.* XI, 30, *Calpurnia . . . genibus Caesaris prouoluta . . . exclamat;* XII, 18, *genibus eius prouolutus . . . inquit.*   Tacitus nowhere says *prouolui ad genua,* as Livy and class. writers usually do.

non eo loci res suas agi, ' Her affairs were not in such a position that . . . '.   The partit. gen. after the adv. *eo* is parallel to that in *id temporis*.   See on c. 2, 1.

quamquam . . . potius, ' though that desire was dearer to her than life '.

a clientelis et seruitiis, abstr. for concrete, ' by the dependants and slaves '.

quae . . . indiderint, ' who had dubbed themselves "the people" ', or ' who claimed to be the people '.   As the gen. *plebis*, however, does not represent a proper name, it may simply be a possessive gen., ' had taken on themselves the people's name ', instead of being the defining gen. discussed in note on c. 50, 1.

ausi, masc. by ' construction according to the sense ', since *clientelae et seruitia* really = *clientes et serui*.

euenirent.   According to Silver Latin usage (see Introd. III, 6, ii (c)), this might stand for either *eueniunt, eueniant,* or *euenient* of o. r. Probably it stands for *eueniant,* ' things which would scarcely happen in a state of war '.   On the other hand, *reperiretur* below probably stands for *reperietur* of o. r.   Notice the change of sequence, once more, between *indiderint* and *euenirent*.

§ 3. **arma illa contra principem sumpta,** &c., ' That rising had been against the emperor .'   Poppaea is trying to hide the fact that the popular outburst had been spontaneous and due to her own unpopularity, and to frighten Nero into believing that it was evidence of a conspiracy by Octavia to bring about a change of emperors.   The present rising had ended lamely because a suitable candidate had not been found, but if Octavia appeared in Rome in person, her influence would be strong enough to cause serious trouble, and any stick would be seized on with which to beat Nero.

omitteret modo, &c., the type of jussive subj. which states a hypothesis: ' let her only leave Campania and proceed to Rome in person '. This serves as a protasis to *qui facile reperiretur*.   Poppaea said: *dux tantum defuit, qui . . . facile reperietur, omittat modo Campaniam. . . . qui* here is not really subordinate, but connective (= *sed is*), so that in o. o. one would have expected *quem . . . repertum iri, omitteret modo* . . . Tacitus, however, reports it as if it introduced a mere adjectival clause qualifying *dux*.

ad cuius . . . cierentur, ' she, at whose nod, even in her absence, rebellions were raised '.   o. o. obscures the fact that Poppaea probably used the generic or causal subj. *cieantur*.

§ 4. **quod alioquin suum delictum ?** sc. *esse*.   A rhet. question. ' What, otherwise, was her crime?   What offence had she given to any one?'   By *alioquin,* ' otherwise ', is meant ' if the outbreak was *not* directed against the emperor, but simply against Poppaea '.   The argument is that, if the outbreak had been spontaneous and directed against Poppaea, she must have done something to deserve such unpopularity.   But she had offended no one; unless it was an offence that any offspring she had by Nero would be legitimate, etc.   **cuiusquam,** ' any one ', is used because the question is equivalent to a negative statement, *nullam cuiusquam offensionem esse*.

malle . . . ?   For the omission of the interrogative particle, Nipperdey compares *Ann.* II, 15, *aliud sibi reliquum* . . . ?; *Ann.* XIII, 21, *uiuere ego . . . poteram?*

tibicinis Aegyptii, a reference to Eucaerus, see c. 60, 2.

imperatorio fastigio induci, 'to be introduced into the imperial family ', ' thrust into high estate ', ' born into the purple '. For the dat., see Introd. III, 3, (iii).

libens quam coactus, 'voluntarily *rather* than under compulsion'. The ellipse of the comparative is quite frequent in Tac., cf. *Ann*. I, 58, *pacem quam bellum*; III, 17, *miseratio quam inuidia augebatur*; and often.

uel consuleret securitati iusta ultione. Editors are divided as to how this sentence should be punctuated. Some, including Furneaux, and Fisher (*O. T.*), put the stop after *securitati*. The punctuation given in the text has the merit of placing the interpretation beyond doubt, for ' to consult his safety by exacting a just vengeance ' can only refer to the execution of Octavia. *uel*, therefore, must stand for *aut*, as in c. 35, 2, *uincendum illa acie uel cadendum esse*; 62, 3, *praemia . . . promittit, uel, si negauisset, necem intentat*; since it disjoins incompatible alternatives. The sense will then be: ' Finally, if such an event was expedient in the circumstances, let him voluntarily rather than under compulsion summon Octavia to lord it over him, or else consult his safety by exacting a just punishment ' (i.e. by putting Octavia to death).

et modicis remediis, &c., ' Even mild measures had been enough to allay the first outbreak '. This is a supposed objection, which is immediately answered by pointing out that the people had not yet been deprived of hope of Octavia's return. The reference is merely to the dispersal of the crowd by the soldiers. This could not be called an *ultio*, which is further evidence that *iusta ultione* belongs to the previous sentence.

62. § 1. uarius sermo. The point of *uarius* is that Poppaea switched alternately from frightening to exasperating Nero.

in seruo, i.e. ' in the case of Eucaerus '.

cui . . . crimen affingeretur, a rel. final clause: ' some one against whom a charge of rebellion might also be trumped up '.

§ 2. patrator, ' perpetrator ', a noun not elsewhere found. For Anicetus, see c. 3. 3.

leui . . . gratia . . . grauiore odio, abl. of quality: ' he had enjoyed little favour after the commission of the crime, and had afterwards come to be more and more hated '.

quasi exprobrantes aspiciuntur, not quite ' are looked upon as reproaching us ', for the expression = *cum aspiciuntur, quasi exprobrare uidentur*, i.e. *aspiciuntur* is doing double duty, both as an autonomous verb ' are before our eyes ' and as a link verb ' seem to be '. Cf. c. 31, 3, *quasi arx . . . aspiciebatur*. Trans. ' because the sight of the agents of our evil deeds acts as a standing reproach to us '.

§ 3. operae prioris admonet. The gen. with *admonere* is classical and regular, as after other verbs of remembering and reminding, cf. *in mentem uenit alicuius rei.*

instare si . . . depelleret, for *instat si . . . depelles* of o. r.

manu aut telo, ' violence or bloodshed '.

si negauisset, sc. *se facturum*, for *si negaueris* of o. r.

§ 4. uaecordia, ' senseless malice '.

facilitate priorum flagitiorum, 'with the readiness he had displayed in his former crimes '. The gen. is an ordinary one of possession, 'the readiness of his former crimes', though used in a rather unusual way.

uelut consilio, 'as if for a meeting of the emperor's private court of justice'. On this imperial *consilium*, see on c. 50, 2, and cf. *Ann.* III, 10, where Tiberius is asked to take cognisance of the case of Piso, and hears the evidence *paucis familiarium adhibitis.*

fato obiit. N.b. that this does not mean the same as *fatum obiit,* which would be quite normal Latin for 'to meet one's death'. Here *fato* is instr. abl., and *obiit* is used absolutely, i.e. 'he died by the ordinary course of fate', or 'died a natural death'.

63. § 1. in spem sociandae classis corruptum. For *in* with acc. denoting either purpose or result, see on c. 8, 4. *In* with the acc. must under all circumstances signify movement towards a goal, whether concrete or abstract. These words therefore mean lit. 'seduced into the hope of winning over the fleet'; in other words, Nero said 'that the Prefect had been seduced (by Octavia) into hoping that he might win over the fleet to her'. Editors, however, generally take the words to mean 'that the Prefect had been corrupted with hope in view (i.e. Octavia's hope) of winning over the fleet', i.e. as if *spe* and not *in spem* had been written. Cf. c. 15, 4, *procaces . . . in spem potentiae,* 'with a shamelessness that *aimed at* hopes of power'. Here, however, *in spem,* with the passive *corruptum* would more naturally refer to the result of the influence brought to bear on Anicetus. Cf. *Hist.* III, 47, *corrupto in spem rapinarum egentissimo quoque,* 'all the most needy having been seduced into hoping for plunder'.

incusatae . . . oblitus. The ref. is to c. 60, 1. For the idiom whereby the participle *incusatae,* in agreement with *Octauiae* understood, takes the place of a substantival clause or phrase, e.g. *eam incusatam esse,* cf. Introd. III. 7, (i). Cf. also *meminerant Agrippinae . . . pulsae* below.

abactos . . . libidinum, 'that she had practised abortion to hide her guilty lust'.

§ 2. Agrippinae . . . Iuliae. The former was the wife of Germanicus and grandmother of Nero. She was banished to Pandateria in A.D. 33. The latter was her daughter, banished by the intrigues of Messalina in A.D. 41.

primum, 'to begin with', anticipating *tum . . . postremo* below.

deductae, dat. with *huic.* The part. is equivalent to a causal clause: 'her wedding day had been as good as the day of her death, since she had been married into a house where she was to have nothing but grief'. *haberet* may be either final or consec. subj. The former is more likely, as if it were the purpose of Fate to marry her into a house 'in which she might have . . .'.

erepto . . . patre . . . fratre. Claudius and Britannicus died *after* Octavia's marriage. For this 'timeless' use of the past part., see Introd. III, 7, (i).

tum ancilla . . . grauius. To complete the syntax of this sentence it is necessary to understand *huic . . . fuit* from above: 'there existed to her sorrow', or 'she had to endure . . .' Trans. 'Secondly, she had to put up with a female slave being more influential than the mistress, and with Poppaea, whose marriage (with Nero) could only result in the death of his (former) wife; and, lastly, a charge had been brought against her more grievous than any death.' The *ancilla* was Acte, see c. 2, 1.

64. § 1. uicesimo aetatis anno. The figure is undoubtedly wrong, since we know from Suetonius that Octavia was older than her brother, would would have been 21, had he lived to A.D. 62. Octavia must therefore have been at least 22. The mistake is so obvious that it seems improbable that Tacitus made it.

praesagio . . . exempta, ' though her foreknowledge of doom placed her no longer amongst the living '.

nondum . . . acquiescebat, ' she still did not yet find rest in the grave '. The point is that the poor young woman was kept lingering in terror and suspense for several days, though it was obvious what the end would be. *morte* may be either locatival (= *in morte*) or instr. (did not find rest by means of . . .).

cum . . . testaretur . . . cieret. *Cum* is here adversative: ' in spite of her protestations that she was not now his wife, but only his sister, and although she appealed to their common kinship with the Germanici, and lastly to the name of Agrippina . . .'. **sororem,** because Nero had been adopted by her father Claudius. **Germanicos:** her grandfather Drusus (brother of Tiberius), and her uncle Germanicus Caesar (son of Drusus, adopted son of Tiberius, and brother of Claudius) are meant. Germanicus Caesar was Nero's maternal grandfather.

pertulisset, subj. of o. o., since this is still part of what Octavia said.

§ 2. tardius, ' too slowly '.

praeferuidi . . . enecatur, ' death was brought on by the heat of a very hot bath '. This does not mean that she was put in the water, but in a heated chamber.

additurque, &c., ' a yet more savage piece of cruelty was added, in that . . .'. The atrocity consisted in Poppaea's being allowed to gloat over the head of her rival.

§ 3. quem ad finem. *Finis* might here be used either of ' limit ' (in time) or of ' aim ' (purpose). In the former case the meaning would be ' how long shall I go on relating? ', in the latter, ' what is the point of my continuing to relate? ' The former is preferable, cf. c. 52, 2, *quem ad finem nihil . . . fore . . .?*

nobis uel aliis auctoribus, abl. abs., ' in my pages or those of other authors '.

praesumptum habeant, jussive subj., ' let them take it for granted that . . .', or ' may take it for granted that . . .'. Notice that this does not mean quite the same as *praesumant*, but rather ' let them keep the assumption in mind '. *habere* with the past part., although the form of the perf. act. in Romance languages is descended from it, is not simply an auxiliary verb in Latin, e.g. *domitas habere libidines* (Cic.) does not mean ' to have tamed one's passions ', but ' to have one's passions tamed '.

quotiens . . . iussit, indic. because the clause is not considered as dependent on *praesumptum habeant.*

quaeque . . . olim, sc. *fuerunt* (or *fuerint*, if really dep., see above). **insignia,** ' tokens.'

neque tamen silebimus, &c., ' Nevertheless, I shall not remain silent about any senatorial decree that marked a new advance in flattery or descended to the lowest depths of servile endurance.' *adulatione, patientia* are abl. of respect, i.e. ' new in respect of flattery ', ' last word in respect of endurance '.

65. § 1. **potissimos,** 'most prominent'. The word is not used of persons in class. Latin.

creditus est. The personal constr. (nom. with infin.) is used with *credor* by Sallust and Livy, but not by Caesar and Cicero. Cf. c. 52, 2 *quod non . . . reperiri credatur.*

Doryphorum, not elsewhere mentioned by Tacitus. He had probably succeeded Callistus as secretary *a libellis.*

quasi aduersatum, 'as having opposed', 'on the ground that he had opposed '. See on c. 8, 1.

Pallantem. Pallas had been secretary *a rationibus,* i.e. Treasurer, under Claudius.

quod . . . detineret, ' because, by living to such an old age, he was keeping immense wealth from him '. The exact sense of *detineo* here may be either that Pallas was ' retaining ' his money too long, or ' keeping it from Nero '. The point is that, when a rich freedman died, leaving less than three children to inherit, a portion of his wealth reverted by law to his former master. Either sense of *detineo* here will result in the same interpretation, but the interpretation of *detentus* in c. 39, 3 is more important.

§ 2. **Romanus,** probably the name of another freedman. The absence of *praenomen* and gentile name means that he must have been mentioned before in a part of Tacitus that is now lost.

ut C. Pisonis socium, ' as being an associate of C. Piso '. C. Calpurnius Piso was of noble birth, tall and handsome in person, and of great popularity. His famous conspiracy against Nero, the failure of which caused the deaths of many prominent people, including Seneca and the poet Lucan, took place in A.D. 65. The context of this passage shows that he was not yet a traitor, so that it is not clear why the word *socius,* which implies ' partnership in some enterprise ', is used, nor why association with him should get any one into trouble. Probably any prominent and popular noble was a dangerous man to associate with at this time. The fact that his name could be used to ruin any one (*perculsus est*) evidently made Piso realize his own extreme peril, and was the source of the conspiracy.

INDEX TO NOTES

ablative:
  causal, 5, 3; of comparison, irregular use, 24, 1; of separation, 31, 1;
    55, 2; of source, without preposition, 10, 2; 45, 2.
  instrumental: of attendant circumstances, 11, 2; 14, 2; 17, 1; 20,
    1, n.; 29, 1; 37, 1; with *comitatus*, 8, 3: of quality, 11, 3; 22, 1;
    29, 1; attached to proper name, 57, 3; 62, 2.
  locatival: without preposition, 10, 2; 14, 2; 20, 2; 61, 1; of
    ' time throughout which ', 10, 1; 21, 1; 29, 1; 32, 3.
  absolute: = causal clause, 3, 2; 5, 2; = concessive clause, 60, 2;
    joined with nom. pt. 1, 1; impers. use, 7, 4; 57, 1; instead of
    agreement of pt., 10, 1.
  quasi-instr. of gerund (see gerund).
abstract nouns, concrete meaning in pl., 4, 1; 39, 2; 44, 1; 61, 2.
accusative:
  with infin., see ' infinitive '.
  goal of motion, without prep., 27, 1; 35, 1.
  in apposition to sentence, 53, 3.
actors, social position of, 14, 3; 21, 1.
adjective, equivalent to participial phrase, 39, 2.
aeque quam, 38, 2.
agreement, of vb. with noun in apposition to subject, 27, 1.
anacoluthon (variation of constr.), 4, 3; 23, 2.
anastrophe, of preposition, 9, 1.
attraction, of pron. to gender of predicate noun, 33, 1.
Augustiani, 15, 4.

commendatio, 50, 1.
comparatio compendiaria (abbreviated comparison), 37, 2.
conditions: in o.o., or otherwise dependant, 49, 2.
constructio ad sensum, 18, 1; 20, 4; 61, 2.

dative:
  denoting goal of motion, 5, 3; for *ad* with acc., 61, 2; for *in* with acc.,
    61, 4: of agent, 14, 1; 32, 1; 58, 1.
  of advantage and disadvantage, with vbs. of ' depriving ', 40, 3;
    64, 1 etc.
  with nouns, 15, 2.
  predicative, 15, 1.
  of purpose, 3, 3; 4, 2; 15, 2; 39, 3; 59, 2.
debeo, as autonomous vb. *v.* its auxiliary use, 53, 4.
dramatic performances, 21, 1; 21, 4.
dum-clauses: tenses in, 9, 1; with final subj., 57, 3; with pres. indic.
    retained in o.o., 58, 3.

edictum, ' imperial edict ', 45, 2.
ellipse: of verb, 8, 2; of verb of speaking, 8, 3; of comparative with
quam, 61, 4.
epigrams, 15, 3.
epithet, transference of, 16, 1.
et or *-que*, with adversative force, 38, 3.

freedmen, importance of, 39, 1.

Gaul, provinces of, 46, 2.
genitive:
    after adjectives denoting ' fulness ' and the reverse, 10, 1.
    defining or appositional, 4, 2; 6, 1; 15, 1; 29, 2; 61, 2; with
        nomen est etc., 50, 1.
    ' legal gen.' after vbs. of ' accusing ' etc., 29, 1; 46, 1.
    objective, 1, 2; 8, 2; 18, 1; representing ' internal ' object, 13, 2;
        representing ' indirect ' object, Introd., p. 18.
    gen. of personal pronoun as objective, 6, 1; 9, 2; 13, 1.
    partitive: with neut. adj., 2, 1; 56, 1; with neut. pl. adj., 60, 1;
        with positive adj., 8, 2; with neut. pron., 32, 3; 38, 2; 52, 1.
    gen. pl., archaic form in 2nd decl., 39, 1.
    of reference or respect, 2, 1; implying purpose, 7, 1; 19, 1; 33, 2;
        40, 2; 44, 1; 59, 1.
gerund and gerundive:
    abl. = pres. participle, 4, 3; 7, 1; 20, 3; 22, 4; 31, 2.
    of *utor, fruor* etc., 23, 1.
    gen. pl. of, not avoided, 50, 1.

habeo, with gerundive or infin., 44, 1.
hendiadys, 10, 1.

imperfect tense, denoting ' endeavour ', 45, 1.
in, with acc. expressing purpose or result, 8, 4; 63, 1.
incertum an, 7, 2.
indefinite clauses, clauses of repeated action, 5, 3; 35, 1.
indicative, instead of subj. in expressions like *par, melius, satius fuit*, 49, 2.
infinitive:
    after verbs of ' asking ', 13, 1.
    with acc., after *accuso*, 18, 1; *se* omitted, 6, 1; 29, 1; 35, 1.
    explaining adjectives, 56, 3; explaining a verbal noun, 14, 1.
    present for future, 14, 3; 18, 2; 58, 3.
    after *adigo*, 24, 1; *concedo*, 55, 2; *non dubito*, instead of *quin*, 43, 1;
        impello, 60, 1; *pango* or *paciscor*, 31, 2; *permitto*, 12, 4; *subigo*,
        14, 4; 26, 1.
    historic, in *cum*-clause, 5, 1; in rel. clause, 1, 1.
iurare in verba alicuius, 11, 1.

jurymen, 20, 4.

legatus legionis, 28, 1.

maiestas, ' high-treason ', 48, 2.

sources of Tacitus, 37, 2; Introd. II.
Stoic philosophy and the Republican opposition, 12, 1; 57, 3.
subjunctive:
    deliberative, dep. on *ut*-clause, 43, 3; indirect delib., 13, 1; with
      donec etc., 8, 2; in final relative clauses, 15, 2; 23, 1; final clause,
      after *enitor*, 28, 2; indirect jussive, with governing vb. understood,
      22, 3; 58, 2; = protasis of cond., 61, 3; potential, 11, 2; 44, 3;
      55, 1; 56, 2; of repeated action, 13, 2; 14, 2; 52, 2; tenses of, in
      consec. clauses, 12, 2, *n.*; 47, 1; simple tense for periphrastic, 13, 1;
      58, 3; 61, 3; in virtual o.o., 10, 1; 11, 3; *ut dixerim*, 53, 3.

tamquam = ' to the effect that ', ' on ground that ', 22, 1; 52, 1; 59, 1:
    with participial or adj. phr., 39, 3; 41, 1; 57, 4.
tribunicia potestas, 48, 2.

variation of construction:
    abl. with gen. of respect, 19, 1; abl. with prep. phrase, 1, 1; 5, 2;
    different methods of expressing cause, 49, 3; dat. with *ad.* + acc.,
    38, 3; gerund and gerundive, 19, 1; subjective gen. and instr.
    abl., 40, 1; variation between primary and historic sequence, see
    sequence of tenses.
uel = *aut*, 35, 2; 61, 4.
verbs, simple for compound, 27, 1; 43, 3.
uerna, 44, 2.
ut, introducing clauses of comparison, 14, 2; = *quo modo*, 49, 2; as a
    temporal conj., 53, 1.
utcumque, as indef. adv., 57, 2.
uterque, use of pl., 14, 2.

INDEX OF PROPER NAMES

VOCABULARY

Diphthongs are long, unless marked. Other long vowels, including many ' hidden ' quantities, are marked. Short vowels are occasionally marked in words liable to be mispronounced or wrongly identified. When principal parts of a verb are not given, they are regular. Hyphens are for convenience of abbreviation and have not necessarily any phonetic or etymological significance.

abau-us, -ī (m.), *great-great-grand-father*

ab-dō, -didī, -ditum, 3 (tr.), *put away, hide*

ab-horreō, -horruī, (no sup.), 2 (intr. w. ab and abl.), *shrink from*

ab-iciō, -iēcī, -iectum, 3 (tr.), *throw away, cast off, cast down*

abit-us, -ūs (m.), *way out*

ab-iūdicō, 1 (tr.), *take away by a judicial decision*

ab-nuo, -nuī, -nuitum or nūtum, 3 (intr. and tr.), *dissent, deny, refuse*

ab-oleō, -olēuī, -olitum, 2 (tr.), *abolish, get rid of*

ab-ripiō, -ripuī, -reptum, 3 (tr.), *carry off by force, seize*

abs-cēdō, -cessi, -cessum, 3 (intr.), *go away, depart*

ab-soluō, -soluī, -solūtum, 3 (tr.), *absolve, acquit*

ac-cendo, -cendī, -cēnsum, 3 (tr.), *set on fire, inflame, rouse*

ac-cidō, -cidī (no sup.), 3, *happen, occur*

ac-ciō, -cīuī, -cītum, 4 (tr.), *summon*

ac-cipiō, -cēpī, -ceptum, 3 (tr.), *receive*

accommodō, 1 (tr.), *suit, adapt, adjust*

accūsō, 1 (tr.), *accuse* (18, 1 n.)

ācer, ācris, ācre (adj.), *keen*

aci-ēs, -ēī (f.), *line of battle*

ad-dō, -didī, -ditum, 3 (tr.), *add, impart, bestow*

adduct-us, -a, -um (adj.), (p.p. of addūcō), *in a state of tension, with a serious air*

adeō (adv.), *to such an extent*

ad-eō, -iuī or -iī, -itum, -īre (intr. and tr.), *go to, approach*

adfectō (aff-), 1 (tr.), *aspire to, lay claim to, affect* (16, 1 n.)

adfect-us (aff-), -ūs (m.), *condition, feeling, affection*

ad-ferō (aff-), -tulī, -lātum, 3 (tr.), *bring (news)*

ad-ficiō (aff-), -fēcī, -fectum, 3 (tr.), *affect, afflict with*

ad-fingō (aff-), -fīnxī, -fictum, 3 (tr.), *add to, invent in addition, attach falsely to*

ad-fīrmō (aff-), 1, *affirm, assert, confirm*

ad-flīgō (affl-), -flīxī, -flīctum, 3 (tr.), *strike, shatter, cast down*

ad-fluō (affl-), -flūxī, -flūxum, 3 (intr.), *stream towards, flock to*

ad-gnōscō (āgn-), -gnōuī, -gnitum, 3 (tr.), *recognize*

ad-hibeō, -hibuī, -hibitum, 2 (tr.), *apply to, employ* (53, 3 n.)

ad-iciō, -iēcī, -iectum, 3 (tr.), *throw, to, add*

ad-igō, -ēgī, -āctum, 3 (tr.), *drive towards, constrain*

161

ad-ipīscor, -eptus sum, 3 (tr.), *get,
acquire, seize*
adleuō (all-), 1 (tr.), *relieve,
lighten*
ad-luō (all-), -luī, (no. sup.), 3
(intr. and tr.), *flow near, wash
against, wash*
adminicul-um, -ī (n.), *support, staff*
ad-mittō, -mīsī, -missum, 3 (tr.),
*admit, allow one's self to commit,
commit, permit*
admoneō, 2 (tr.), *remind, admonish,
warn* (62, 3 n.)
adnō (ann-), 1 (intr.), *swim to or
beside*
adnotō (ann-), 1 (tr.), *remark on,
notice*
adnumerō (ann-), 1 (tr.), *count
amongst*
ad-nuō (ann-), -nuī, -nūtum, 3,
nod assent, grant
ad-oleō, -olēuī, (no sup.), 2 (tr.),
offer in worship, make to smoke
(30, 2 n.)
ad-orior, -ortus sum, 3 and 4 (tr.),
assail
ad-scīscō (asc-), -scīuī, -scītum, 3
(tr.), *associate with one's self,
adopt*
ad-scrībō (ascr-), -scrīpsī, -scrīp-
tum, 3 (tr.), *enroll*
adsēns-us (ass-), -ūs, (m.), *assent,
agreement*
ad-sentiō (ass-), -sēnsī, -sēnsum,
and ad-sentior, -sēnsus sum,
(intr.), *agree with, give assent*
adseuērō (ass-), 1, *assert, maintain*
ad-signō (ass-), 1 (tr.), *assign,
ascribe, attribute*
ad-sistō, -stitī, (no sup.), 3 (intr.),
stand by, assist
ad-stō (ast-), -stitī (no sup.), 1,
stand by or near
ad-sum, -fuī, -esse, (intr.), *be
present ;* (w. dat.), *assist*
ad-sūmō (ass-), -sūmpsī, -sūmp-
tum, 3 (tr.), *adopt, assume, take
on*
aduentō, 1 (intr.), *approach, advance*
aduersor, 1 (intr.), *be opposed to*

aduers-us, -a, -um (adj.), *adverse
opposed*
aduersus and aduersum (adv. and
prep.), *against, opposite, toward*
ad-uertō, -uertī, -uersum, 3 (tr.),
turn towards; for animaduertō,
notice, take heed of (43, 3 n.)
adūlāti-ō, -ōnis (f.), *flattery*
adulēscenti-a, -ae (f.), *youth*
adūlor, 1 (w. acc. or dat.), *flatter,
fawn upon*
adūsque = ūsque ad (adv.), *right
up to, entirely*
ae-ger, -gra, -grum (adj.), *sick*
aemul-us, -ī (m.), *rival*
aequō, 1 (tr.), *make level, equal,
attain to*
aequ-us, -a, -um (adj.), *equal,
just, fair*
aest-ās, -ātis (f.), *summer*
aestuāri-um, -ī (n.), *estuary*
aest-us, -ūs (m.), *tide, swell, fire,
heat*
aet-ās, -ātis (f.), *age*
ag-er, -rī (m.), *land, field, territory*
agg-er, -eris (m.), *mound, rampart,
mole*
agm-en, -inis (n.), *troop, crowd,
column, train*
agō, ēgī, āctum, 3 (tr.), *drive,
lead, act, behave* (15, 4 n.)
āl-a, -ae (f.), *wing, wing of army,
division of allied cavalry*
aliās (adv.), *at another time, elsewhere*
aliēn-us, -a, -um (adj.), *belonging
to another, another's, foreign*
aliōquīn (adv.), *otherwise*
aliquandō (adv.), *at some time,
sometimes, at length*
alō, aluī, altum, 3 (tr.), *nourish,
rear*
alue-us, -ī (m.), *hull*
ambigu-us, -a, -um (adj.), *doubtful*
ambiti-ō, -ōnis (f.), *canvassing,
intrigue, currying favour, ambition*
(22, 2 n.; 29, 1 n.)
ambit-us, -ūs (m.), *a going round,
illegal canvassing, ambition, cir-
cumference*

amict-us, -ūs (m.), *cloak, clothing*
ā-mittō, -mīsī, -missum, 3 (tr.),
  send away, put aside, lose
amoenit-ās, -ātis (f.), *pleasantness*
  (of view)
ā-mōlior, mōlītus sum, 4 (tr.), *re-*
  move
amputō, 1 (tr.), *cut off*
an (conj.), *whether, or* (59, 1 *n*.)
an-ceps, -cipitis (adj.), *doubtful,*
  fluctuating, dangerous
ancill-a, -ae (f.), *female slave, lady's*
  maid
angu-is, -is (m. and f.), *snake*
angusti-ae, -ārum (f. pl.), *defile,*
  straits, distress, narrowness
annu-us, -a, -um (adj.), *annual*
an-quīrō, -quīsīuī, -quīsītum, 3
  (tr. and intr.), *search after,*
  inquire
anteā (adv.), *before, formerly*
antecellō (no. pf. or sup.), 3 (tr.),
  surpass (55, 4, *n*.)
ante-eō, -īuī or iī (no sup.), -īre
  (intr.), *go in front, outstrip*
antīquit-ās, -ātis (f.), *antiquity,*
  ancient character
ānxi-us, -a, -um (adj.), *uneasy,*
  anxious, worried
aper-iō, -uī, -tum, 4 (tr.), *uncover,*
  open, reveal
apīscor, aptus sum, 3 (tr.), *get,*
  acquire
appellō (adp-), 1 (tr.), *call name,*
  address, appeal to
ār-a, -ae (f.), *altar*
arbitri-um, -ī (n.), *decision of*
  arbitrator, free choice, control
ārd-or, -ōris (m.), *passion, heat,*
  eagerness
ardu-us, -a, -um (adj.), *steep,*
  difficult
arēn-a, -ae (f.), *sand, arena (of*
  amphitheatre)
argūment-um, -ī (n.), *proof, evi-*
  dence, argument
arguō, arguī (no sup.), 3 (tr.),
  show up, accuse, censure
armātūr-a, -ae (f.), *equipment,*
  armed troops
armō, 1 (tr.), *arm*

ars, artis (f.), *art, skill, device* (15,
  3 *n*.)
art-us, -a, -um (adj.), *narrow, close,*
  tight
art-ūs, -uum (m. pl.), *limbs*
arx, arcis (f.), *citadel*
aspect-us, -ūs (m.), *sight, appear-*
  ance
āspernor, 1 (tr.), *regard with*
  aversion, disdain
a-spiciō (ads-), -spēxī, -spectum, 3
  (tr. and intr.), *look at, look,*
  behold (62, 2, *n*.)
ast-us, -ūs (m.), *adroitness, cunning*
at (conj.), *but* (44, 3 *n*.)
atr-ōx, -ōcis (adj.), *cruel, bad,*
  gloomy
at-tineō (adt-), -tinuī, -tentum, 2
  (tr.), *hold fast, detain;* (intr. +
  ad), *belong somewhere, concern*
auārīti-ă, -ae (f.), *greed, avarice*
auct-or, -ōris (m.), *author, sponsor*
auctōrit-ās, -ātis (f.), *influence, ad-*
  vice, authority
audāci-a, -ae (f.), *boldness, effron-*
  tery
aud-āx, -ācis (adj.), *bold*
audeō, ausus sum, 2, *dare*
audiō, 4 (tr.), *hear, hear of*
āuersor, 1 (intr. and tr.), *turn*
  aside, scorn
auferō, abstulī, ablātum, -ferre
  (tr.), *take away*
augeō, auxī, auctum, 2 (tr.),
  increase
auid-us, -a, -um (adj.), *greedy*
auīt-us, -a, -um (adj.), *belonging*
  to a grandfather, ancestral
āui-us, -a, -um (adj.), *lonely,*
  remote
aure-us, -a, -um (adj.), *golden*
aur-is, -is (abl. -ī or -e) (f.), *ear*
au-us, -ī (m.), *grandfather, ancestor*
auxiliār-is, -is (m.), *an auxiliary*
auxili-um, -ī (n.), *help;* (pl.),
  auxiliaries

balne-um, -ī (n.), *bath, bathroom*
bellō, 1 (intr.), *wage war*
benīgnit-ās, -ātis (f.), *kindness*
bīdu-um, -ī (n.), *space of two days*

caed-ēs, -is (f.), *slaughter, murder*

cael-um, -ī (n.), *sky*

caerimōni-a, -ae (f.), *religious sanctity, sacredness, rite*

caest-us, -ūs (m.), *boxing-glove* (20, 4, *n.*)

calumni-a, -ae (f.), *false accusation* (41, 1 *n.*)

canō, cecinī (no. sup.), 3 (intr.), *sing, play, sound (trumpet), prophesy;* (tr.), *sing of*

cant-us, -ūs (m.), *melody, song, singing*

cap-āx, -ācis (adj.), *capacious, capable of, susceptible*

capess-ō, -īuī (no sup.), 3 (tr.), *catch at eagerly, undertake with zeal*

cārit-ās, -ātis (f.), *fondness, dearness* (44, 2 *n.*)

carni-fex, -ficis (m.), *executioner*

cărō, carnis (f.), *flesh, meat*

castell-um, -ī (n.), *fortress*

cast-us, -a, -um (adj.), *pure, chaste, devout*

cās-us, -ūs (m.), *chance, mischance*

cateru-a, -ae (f.), *band, crowd, troop*

caueō, căuī, cautum, 2 (intr.), *beware* (57, 2 *n.*)

caupōn-a, -ae (f.), *tavern, shop, booth*

caus-a, -ae (f.), *cause, reason, lawsuit*

cēdō, cessī, cessum, 3 (intr. and tr.), *give way, yield, concede* (31, 2 *n.*)

cele-ber, -bris, -bre (adj.), *much frequented, renowned, celebrated*

celebrō, 1 (tr.), *celebrate, frequent*

celerit-ās, -ātis (f.), *speed*

cēnāt-us, -a, -um (adj.), *having dined*

cēnseō, cēnsuī, cēnsum, 2 (tr. and intr.), *estimate; be of opinion, give an opinion, vote for, move resolution*

cēns-us, -ūs (m.), *census, assessment*, (46, 2, *n.*)

certām-en, -inis (n.), *contest, strife, rivalry*

certō, 1 (intr.), *contend, strive, vie*

cert-us, -a, -um (adj.), *sure, fixed, resolved* (36, 3, *n.*)

cēterum (conj.), *however, but* (58, 2, *n.*)

cēter-us, -a, -um (adj., usu. pl.), *remainder, rest*

cieō, cīuī, citum, 2 (tr.), *rouse, excite, summon;* (p.p. as adj.), *quick, swift*

cin-is, -eris (m., frequ. pl.), *ashes*

circum-dō, -dedī, -datum, 1 (tr.), *set around, surround* (53, 4, *n.*)

circum-iciō, -iēcī, -iectum, 3 (tr.), *throw or place around*

circum-sistō, -stetī (no sup.), 3 (tr. and intr.), *stand round, surround*

circum-spiciō, -spēxī, -spectum, 3 (intr.), *look round;* (tr.), *look round at, inspect, consider*

circum-ueniō, -uēnī, -uentum, 4 (tr.), *surround, circumvent*

cithar-a, -ae (f.), *a stringed instrument, cithara*

citus, see cieō

clād-ēs, -is (f.), *disaster, defeat*

clāritūd-ō, -inis (f.), *fame, distinction*

classiāri-us, -ī (m.), *belonging to the fleet, marine, sailor*

class-is, -is (f.), *fleet*

claudō, clausī, clausum, 3 (tr.), *shut, close*

clēmenti-a, -ae (f.), *moderation, forbearance*

clientēl-a, -ae (f.), *clientship, patronage, body of dependants*

cŏ-alēscō, -aluī, -alitum, 3 (intr.), *grow together, take root* (1, 1, *n.*)

cōdicill-ī, -ōrum (m. pl.), *codicil*

coepiō, coepī, coeptum, 3 (tr. and intr.), *begin* (mostly in pf. t.)

cŏerc-eō, -uī, -itum, 2 (tr.), *restrain*

coet-us, -ūs (m.), *gathering, assembly*

cognōment-um, -ī (n.), *name*

co-gnōscō, -gnōuī, -gnitum, 3 (tr.), *get to know*

cōgō, cŏēgī, cŏāctum, 3 (tr.), *drive together, compel, force*

collēgi-um (conl.), -ī (n.), club,
society (17, 2, n.)
col-ligō (conl-), -lēgī, -lēctum, 3
(tr.), collect, assemble
coll-is, -is (m.), hill
colō, coluī, cultum, 3 (tr.), cultivate, cherish, practise, inhabit
colōn-us, -ī (m.), settler, colonist,
farmer
comēt-ēs, -ae (m.), comet
cōmiter (adv.), courteously
comiti-a, -ōrum (n. pl.), elections
(28, 1, n.)
cōmitor, 1 (intr. and tr.), accompany
commeāt-us, -ūs (m.), convoy,
provisions, supplies
commerci-um, -ī (n.), trade, traffic
cōmō, cōmpsī, cōmptum, 3 (tr.),
make neat, comb, adorn
com-pleō, -plēuī, -plētum, 2 (tr.),
fill
com-pōnō, -posuī, -positum, 3
(tr.), put together, compose, arrange,
assuage
con-cēdō, -cessī, -cessum, 3 (intr.
and tr.), yield, retire, grant
concertāt-or, -ōris (m.), rival (29,
2, n.)
con-cidō, -cidī (no sup.), 3 (intr.),
fall to the ground, collapse
con-ciō or -cieō, -cīuī, -citum, 2
and 4 (tr.), excite, arouse, summon
concubit-us, -ūs (m.), a lying
together
con-cupīscō, -cupīuī or -cupiī,
-cupītum, 3 (tr.), covet, conceive
desire for
concurs-us, ūs (m.), a running
together, a gathering
con-cutiō, -cussī, -cussum, 3 (tr.),
shatter, shake
con-dūcō, -dūxī, -ductum, 3 (tr.),
bring together, hire; (intr. impers.), it is profitable, expedient
cō-nectō (conn-), -nexuī, -nexum,
3 (tr.), join together, connect
cōnfect-or, -ōris (m.), a finisher,
conqueror
cōn-ferciō, -fersī, -fertum, 4 (tr.),
cram together, pack tight
cōnfessi-ō, -ōnis (f.), confession

cōn-ficiō, -fēcī, -fectum, 3 (tr.),
overcome, finish, kill
cōn-fīdō, -fīsus sum, 3 (intr.),
believe, be confident; (w. dat. pers.
or thing, abl. of thing), have
confidence in
cōn-fingō, -fīnxī, -fictum, 3 (tr.),
pretend, fabricate
cōnflīctō, 1 (intens. of cōnflīgō)
(tr.), afflict, ruin
cōn-fugiō, -fūgī (no. sup.) (intr.),
fly for refuge
con-gerō, -gessī, -gestum, 3 (tr.),
heap together, build, erect
congiāri-um, -ī (n.), largess (11, 1,
n.)
conglobō, 1 (tr.), bunch together
congress-us, -ūs (m.), a meeting,
encounter
coniectō, 1 (intens. of coniciō)
(tr.), conjecture, guess
coniugi-um, -ī (n.), wedlock, marriage
con-iungō, -iūnxī, -iūnctum, 3
(tr.), join
coniūrāti-ō, -ōnis (f.), conspiracy
conlocō (coll-), 1 (tr.), set, place
conluui-ēs (coll-), -em, -ē (f.),
scum, offscourings, rabble
con-quīrō, -quīsīuī, -quīsītum, 3
(tr.), search out, collect
cōnscienti-a, -ae (f.), consciousness,
conscience, bad conscience
cōnsci-us, -a, -um (adj.), knowing,
privy to
cōn-scrībō, -scrīpsī, -scrīptum, 3
(tr.), enlist, enroll, write
cōnsēns-us, -ūs (m.), agreement
cōn-sīdō, -sēdī, -sessum, 3 (intr.),
sit down together, settle down
cōnsili-um, -ī (n.), plan, consulta-
tion, assembly, council (50, 2, n.;
62, 4, n.)
cōnsociō, 1 (tr.), share with one,
communicate
cōn-sonō, -sonuī (no sup.), 1
(intr.), resound
cōnsorti-um, -ī (n.), partnership,
participation (11, 1, n.)
cōnspicu-us, -a, -um (adj.), striking,
outstanding

cōnstanti-a, -ae (f.), *firmness, courage*

cōn-stituō, -stituī, -stitūtum, 3 (tr.), *set up, fix, resolve*

cōn-stō, -stitī, (fut. p. -stātūrus), 1 (intr.), *stand, be established, consist of;* impers. cōnstat, *it is agreed*

cōnsulār-is, -e (adj.), *belonging to a 'consul, of consular rank*

cōn-sulō, -suluī, -sultum, 3 (intr. and tr.), w. dat., *take counsel for, consult interests of;* w. acc., *ask advice of, consult*

cōnsultō, 1 (intr.), *reflect, take counsel, deliberate*

cōnsult-um, -ī (n.), *decree (of senate)*

cōn-sūmō, -sūmpsī, -sūmptum, 3 (tr.), *consume*

cōn-surgō, -surrēxī, -surrēctum, 3 (intr.), *rise*

con-temnō, -tempsī, -temptum, 3 (tr.), *hold in contempt, despise*

continuō, 1 (tr.), *unite, connect, continue*

contrā (adv. and prep.), *in the opposite direction, against, opposite, on the other hand*

contrādicti-ō, -ōnis (f.), *a speaking in opposition*

con-trahō, -trāxī, -tractum, 3 (tr.), *draw together, gather, concentrate*

contrectō, 1 (tr.), *handle, deal with, man-handle*

contumēli-a, -ae (f.), *insult, affront*

cont-us, -ī (m.), *a pole*

conuenticul-um, -ī (n.), *assembly-room, rendezvous*

con-uertō, -uertī, -uersum, 3 (tr.), *turn around, reverse, change*

conuīct-us, -ūs (m.), *social intercourse, entertainment, banquet*

con-uincō, -uīcī, -uictum, 3 (tr.), *convict, show up, bring home*

conuīuāl-is, -e (adj.), *pertaining to guests or banquets, festal*

conuīui-um, -ī (n.), *dinner-party*

cōram (adv.), *face to face, personally;* (prep. w. abl.), *in presence of*

corn-ū, -ūs (n.), *wing of army*

cor-rumpō, -rūpī, -ruptum, 3 (tr.), *injure, spoil, corrupt, bribe*

crē-ber, -bra, -brum (adj.), *frequent, numerous, crowded*

crēdibil-is, -e (adj.), *credible*

crē-dō, -didī, -ditum, 3 (tr.), *entrust, lend;* (w. dat. of pers. alone), *trust, believe;* (abs.), *believe, think*

crēdulit-ās, -ātis (f.), *readiness to believe, credulity*

cremō, 1 (tr.), *burn, cremate*

crīm-en, -inis (n.), *charge, accusation*

crīmināti-ō, -ōnis (f.), *accusation, complaint*

crīminor, 1 (tr.), *accuse, impeach, charge with* (57, 1, n.)

crīn-is, -is (m.), *hair*

cru-or, -ōris (m.), *blood*

crux, crucis, (f), *cross*

cubicul-um, -ī (n.), *bedroom*

cubitō, 1 (intr.), *lie down*

cult-us, -ūs (m.), *cultivation, elegance, splendid attire, dress*

cum (conj.), *when, since, although* (64, 1, n.)

cumulō, 1 (tr.), *heap up*

cumul-us, -ī (m.), *heap, pile*

cūnctāti-ō, -ōnis (f.), *delay*

cūnctor, 1 (intr.), *linger, hesitate, delay*

cūnct-us, -a, -um (adj.) (more freq. pl. cūnctī), *all together, all, the whole*

cune-us, -ī (m.), *wedge, wedge formation*

cupīd-ō, -inis (f. and m.), *desire, passion, greed*

cupīd-us, -a, -um (adj.), *desirous, eager, fond*

cup-iō, -īuī or -iī, -ītum, 3 (tr.), *desire*

cūr-a, -ae (f.), *care, attention, anxiety, management*

cūrātius (comp. adv.), *with greater attention*

cūri-a, -ae (f.), *the senate-house* (32, 1, n.)

curricul-um, -i (n.), *a course, race, race-chariot*

cūstōdi-a, -ae (f.), *guard, protection ;*
(pl.), *guards, sentinels*

damn-um, -ī (n.), *damage, loss*
dap-s, -is (f.), *solemn feast ;* (pl.),
banquet
dē-cēdō, -cessī, -cessum, 3 (intr.),
withdraw, depart from
dē-cernō, -crēuī, -crētum, 3 (tr.
and intr.), *decide, resolve*
dēclīnō, 1 (tr. and intr.), *turn
aside, parry, go awry*
dēcrēt-um, -ī (n., p.p. of dēcernō),
decree
decuri-a, -ae (f.), *company, division,
jury-panel* (20, 4, *n.*)
dē-currō, -cucurrī or -currī, -cur-
sum, 3 (intr.), *run down, come
down to, have recourse to*
dec-us, -ŏris (n.), *honour, ornament,
glory*
dēdec-us, -ŏris (n.), *disgrace*
dēdĭcō, 1 (tr.), *dedicate*
dēdĭgnor, 1 (tr.), *disdain*
dē-dūcō, -dūxī, -ductum, 3 (tr.),
*lead away, conduct to a place,
escort, introduce*
dēfecti-ō, -ōnis (f.), *rebellion, revolt*
dē-fendō, -fendī, -fēnsum, 3 (tr.),
keep off, defend
dē-ferō, -tŭlī, -lātum, 3 (tr.), *bring
away, report, inform, offer*
dē-fīgō, -fīxī, -fīxum, 3 (tr.), *fix
down, render immovable ;* (pass.)
stand motionless
dē-fleō, -flēuī, -flētum, 2 (tr.),
bewail, lament over
dēfŏrm-is, -e (adj.), *ugly, unseemly,
disgraceful*
dēfūnct-us, -a, -um p.p. of
defungor), *deceased, defunct*
dēgenerō, 1 (intr.), *degenerate*
dĕhinc (adv.), *hence, henceforth, next*
dĕhonestāment-um, -ī (n.), *dishonour, disgrace*
dĕhonestō (no perf. or sup.), 1
(tr.), *degrade, disgrace*
dē-iciō, -iēcī, -iectum, 3 (tr.), *cast
down*
dēleō, dēlēuī, dēlētum, 2 (tr.),
destroy

dēlīberō, 1 (tr.), *weigh (in mind)*
(intr.), *deliberate*
dē-ligō, -lēgī, -lēctum, 3 (tr.),
choose out
dē-linquō, -līquī, -lictum, 3 (intr.),
commit a fault, fall short ; dēlic-
tum, -ī (n.), *a wrong committed*
dē-mētō, -messuī, -messum, 3
(tr.), *mow, reap*
dē-mittō, -mīsī, -missum, 3 (tr.),
send down, lower, humble
dē-moueō, -mōuī, -mōtum, 2 (tr.),
remove
dēmum (adv.), *at last, only then*
dē-pellō, -pŭlī, -pulsum, 3 (tr.),
drive down or away
dē-prehendō, -prehendī, -prehēn-
sum, 3 (tr.), *catch, detect, seize*
dē-scendō, -scendī, -scēnsum, 3
(intr.), *descend, sink*
dē-serō, -seruī, -sertum, 3 (tr.),
desert, leave in the lurch
dēsīderi-um, -ī (n.), *desire, grief,
yearning for*
dēsignāt-us, -a, -um (adj., p.p. of
dēsignō), *nominated, elect*
dēstinō, 1 (tr.), *mark out, choose,
destine*
dē-stringō, -strīnxī, -strictum, 3
(tr.), *unsheathe, draw off covering*
dē-struō, -strūxī, -structum, 3
(tr.), *pull down, destroy*
dē-sum, -fuī, -esse, *be wanting, fail*
dēter-ior, -ius (comp. adj.), *worse,
meaner*
dēterrimus, -a, -um (sup. adj.),
worst, meanest
dē-tineō, -tinuī, -tentum, 2 (tr.),
keep back, keep from, retain
(65, 1, *n.*)
dē-trăhō, -trāxī, -tractum, 3 (tr.),
draw off, take away, detract from
dētrecto, 1 (tr.), *decline, shirk, detract from, disparage*
dē-trūdō, -trūsī, -trūsum, 3 (tr.),
thrust forth, drive away
dictĭtō, 1, *say repeatedly, maintain*
diffāmō, 1 (tr.), *spread (an evil)
report, defame* (22, 3, *n.*)
diffĕrō, distŭlī, dīlātum, 3 (tr.),
defer, put off, disperse

dīgnit-ās, -ātis (f.), *high rank, prestige*

dī-gredior, -gressus sum (intr.), *separate, depart*

dī-lābor, -lāpsus sum, 3 (intr.), *slip away, scatter*

dīlēct-us, -ūs (m.), *military levy, recruiting*

dī-rae, -ārum (f. pl.), *evil portents, curses*

dī-ripiō, -ripuī, -reptum, 3 (tr.), *tear asunder, plunder*

disceptāt-or, -ōris (m.), *arbitrator*

discessi-ō, -ōnis (f.), *recording of votes, division* (49, 1, *n.*)

discidi-um, -ī (n.), *separation, divorce*

discordi-a, -ae (f.), *quarrel, strife, discord*

dis-cors, -cordis (adj.), *discordant, at variance*

discrīm-en, -inis (n.), *dangerous crisis, peril*

dis-cumbo, -cubuī, -cubitum, 3 (intr.), *lie down, take places at table*

dis-iciō, -iēcī, -iectum, 3 (tr.), *dash to pieces, scatter, thwart*

dis-pār, -păris (adj.), *unequal, dissimilar*

di-spergō, -spersī, -spersum, 3 (tr.), *scatter about, spread*

dis-pōnō, -posuī, -positum, 3 (tr.), *arrange, dispose*

dis-serō, -seruī, -sertum, 3 (tr. and intr.), *argue about, discuss, speak, say*

dis-soluō, -soluī, -solūtum, 3 (tr.), *dissolve, loosen, break up*

dissolūti-ō, -ōnis (f.), *a breaking-up*

disson-us, -a, -um (adj.), *discordant, different*

dis-suādeō, -suāsī, -suāsum, 2 (intr. and tr. w. acc. of thing), *advise against, dissuade*

dis-tineō, -tinuī, -tentum, 2 (tr.), *hold apart, distract, delay*

dīt-ior, -ius (comp. of dīues)

diū (adv.), *for a long time*

dīuers-us, -a, -um (adj.), *different, diverse, opposite* (10, 2, *n.*)

diūtīn-us, -a, -um (adj.), *of long duration*

doceō, docuī, doctum, 2 (tr.), *teach, tell, explain*

doct-or, -ōris (m.), *teacher*

document-um, -ī (n.), *proof, example, lesson*

dol-us, -ī (m.), *craft, deceit, plot*

domestic-ī, -ōrum (m. pl.), *domestic servants*

domināti-ō, -ōnis (f.), *domination, rule, reign*

domō, domuī, domitum, 1 (tr.), *tame, subdue*

dōnātīu-um, -ī (n.), *present, largess* (11, 1, *n.*)

Druid-ae, -ārum (m.), *the Druids*

dubitō, 1 (intr. and tr.), *doubt, be in doubt, doubt of, hesitate*

duct-us, -ūs (m.), *leadership, command*

dulcēd-ō, -inis (f.), *sweetness, charm*

dum (conj.), *while, until*

dūrō, 1 (tr. and intr.), *render hard, become hard, steel one's self* (1, 3, *n.*)

dux, ducis (m.), *leader, general*

ēdict-um, -ī (n.), *edict, decree*

ēdit-us, -a, -um (p.p. of ē-dō), *elevated, lofty*

ē-dō, -didī, -ditum, 3 (tr.), *give out, publish, produce*

ēducāt-or, -ōris (m.), *tutor*

ēdūcō, 1 (tr.), *rear, educate*

ef-ficiō, -fēcī, -fectum, 3 (tr.), *effect, bring about, manage*

effigi-ēs, -ēī (f.), *likeness, effigy*

efflāgitō, 1 (tr.), *demand urgently, clamour for*

effugi-um, -ī (n.), *escape*

ef-fulgeō, -fulsī (no sup.), 2 (intr.), *shine out*

ef-fundō, -fūdī, -fūsum, 3 (tr.), *pour out, throw out;* (se), *give one's self up to*

egeō, eguī (no sup.), 2 (intr. w. abl. or gen.), *am needy, in need of*

egest-ās, -ātis (f.), *poverty, want*

ēgregi-us, -a, -um (adj.), *distinguished, outstanding*

ēleganti-a, -ae (f.), *good taste, refinement*

ē-liciō, -licuī, -licitum, 3 (tr.), *lure forth*

ēloquenti-a, -ae (f.), *eloquence*

ē-lūdō, -lūsī, -lūsum, 3 (tr.), *elude, baffle*

ēmin-eō, -uī (no sup.), 2 (intr.), *stand out, project*

ē-mittō, -mīsī, -missum, 3 (tr.), *send out, hurl*

ēmptitō (intens. of emō), 1 (tr.), *buy*

enimuērō (conj.), *of a truth* (14, 1, *n.*)

ē-niteō, -nituī (no sup.), 2 (intr.), *shine out*

ē-nītor, -nīsus or -nīxus sum, 3 (intr. and tr.), *struggle out or up, make an effort; bring forth, bear*

epul-ae, -ārum (f. pl.), *banquet*

epulor, 1 (intr.), *dine, feast*

ē-rubēscō, -rubuī (no sup.), 3 (intr.), *blush, be ashamed*

etiam (adv.), *even, also*

ē-uādō, -uāsī, -uāsum, 3 (intr. and tr.), *get away, escape, evade, turn out*

ē-ualēscō, -ualuī (no sup.), 3 (intr.), *grow strong* (58, 3, *n.*)

ē-uehor, -uectus sum, 3 (intr. and tr.), *ride out, pass* (52, 1, *n.*)

ē-ueniō, -uēnī, -uentum, 4 (intr.), *happen, turn out*

ē-uertō, -uertī, -uersum, 3 (tr.), *overturn, overthrow*

exanim-is, -e; or -us, -a, -um (adj.), *dead, lifeless, fainting*

exanimō, 1 (tr.), *deprive of life, kill*

ex-ārdēscō, -ārsī (fut. p. -ārsūrus), 3 (intr.), *take fire, blaze up, break out*

ex-cidō, -cidī (no sup.), 3 (intr.), *fall out, be let slip*

ex-cīdō, -cīdī, -cīsum, 3 (tr.), *cut out, lay waste, destroy*

ex-cindō (exsc.), -cīdī, -cissum, 3 (tr.), *tear out, destroy*

ex-cipiō, -cēpī, -ceptum, 3 (tr.), *receive, take over, take out, except*

excubi-ae, -ārum (f. pl.), *a keeping watch, guard*

excurs-us, -ūs (m.), *attack, raid*

exempl-um, -ī (n.), *example*

ex-eō, -īuī or -iī, -itum, -īre (intr.), *go out*

exequi-ae (exs-), -ārum (f. pl.), *funeral rites, obsequies*

exerc-eō, -uī, -itum, 2 (tr.), *exercise, work on, practise*

ex-hauriō, -hausī, -haustum, 4 (tr.), *drain, exhaust*

ex-igō, -ēgī, -āctum, 3 (tr.), *drive out, demand, exact*

exili-um (exs-), -ī (n.), *exile*

exim, exinde (adv.), *thence, then, thereupon*

ex-imō, -ēmī, -ēmptum, 3 (tr.), *take out, remove, exempt*

exīstimō, 1 (tr.), *reckon, consider, esteem*

ex-istō (exs-), -titī, -titum, 3 (intr.), *come forth, emerge, exist*

exiti-um, -ī (n.), *destruction, ruin, death*

exit-us, -ūs (m.), *way out, conclusion, result*

ex-olēscō, -olēuī, -olētum, 3 (intr.), *pass out of use*

exolēt-us, -ī (m.), (p.p. of exolēscō), *abandoned youth of mature age*

ex-oluō (exs-), -oluī, -olūtum, 3 (tr.), *release from, discharge, pay*

expectō (exs-), 1 (tr.), *await, expect*

expediō, 4 (tr), *disentangle, make ready, arrange*

ex-pendō, -pendī, -pēnsum, 3 (tr.), *weigh, consider, pay out*

exper-ior, -tus sum, 4 (tr.), *make trial of, test, prove, experience*

ex-pleō, -plēuī, -plētum, 2 (tr.), *fill up, complete, fulfil*

ex-poscō, -poposcī (no sup.), 3 (tr.), *ask, implore*

exprobrō, 1 (tr.), (aliquid alicui), *reproach with*

expūgnō, 1 (tr.), *take by storm*

ex-surgō, -surrēxī, -surrēctum, 3 (intr.), *rise up*

extern-us, -a, -um (adj.), *external, foreign*

exterrit-us, -a, -um (terreō), (adj.), *terrified, frightened* ex-tinguŏ (exs-), -tīnxī, -tīnctum, 3 (tr.), *put out, quench, kill*

extollŏ (no pf. or sup.), 3 (tr.), *raise, exalt*

extr-uo (exs-), -uxī, -uctum, 3 (tr.), *rear, build, erect*

exturbŏ, 1 (tr.), *drive out, thrust forth*

exūberŏ, 1 (intr.), *overflow, abound*

exultŏ (exs-), 1 (intr.), *jump about, exult*

ex-uŏ, -uī, -ūtum, 3 (tr.), *cast off, deprive of*

ex-ūrŏ, -ussī, -ūstum, 3 (tr.), *burn up, consume*

fabricor, 1 (tr.), *construct*

facēti-ae, -ārum (f. pl.), *witticisms, pleasantry*

faci-ēs, -ēī (f.), *face, appearance*

facil-is, -e (adj.), *easy, ready, good-natured*

facilit-ās, -ātis (f.), *easiness, good nature, liberality* (47, 2, n.; 62, 4, n.)

facin-us, -ŏris (n.), *crime, exploit*

factitŏ, 1 (tr.), (frequ. of faciŏ), *do, make, compose repeatedly*

facult-ās, -ātis (f.), *facility, opportunity, ability*

faen-us (fēn-), -ŏris (n.), *interest, investment* (53, 4, n.)

fall-āx, -ācis (adj.), *deceitful*

făm-ēs, -is (m.), *hunger*

famili-a, -ae (f.), *household* (42, 1, n.)

familiār-is, -e (adj.), *belonging to a household, familiar, friendly ;* (res f.), *family property*

familiārit-ās, -ātis (f.), *familiarity, intimacy*

fānātic-us, -a, -um (adj.), *mad, fanatical* (30, 2, n.)

fās (n.), *what is right, lawful*

fastīgi-um, -ī (n.), *summit, high rank* (54, 3, n.)

fatīscŏ (no pf. or sup.), 3 (intr.), *crack, grow weak* (24, 1, n.)

fauc-ēs, -ium (f. pl.), *throat, defile, gorge*

fēcundit-ās, -ātis (f.), *fertility*

fēcund-us, -a, -um (adj.), *fertile, prolific of, abounding in*

fēlicit-ās, -ātis (f.), *happiness, good fortune, prosperity*

fērāl-is, -e (adj.), *belonging to the dead, funereal*

feriŏ (no pf. or sup.), 4 (tr.), *strike*

fermē (adv.), *generally, usually, about*

ferŏ, tŭlī, lātum, ferre (tr.), *bear, relate*

fer-ŏx, -ōcis (adj.), *fierce, spirited, haughty*

ferr-um, -ī (n.), *steel, the sword*

fer-us, -a, -um (adj.), *fierce, wild, cruel*

feruid-us, -a, -um (adj.), *burning, hot*

fess-us, -a, -um (adj.), *tired, worn out*

festīnŏ, 1 (intr.), *hasten, hurry ;* (tr.), *do quickly* (33, 2, n.)

fēst-us, -a, -um (adj.), *festal, holiday-*

fībr-a, -ae (f.), *fibre ;* (pl.), *entrails*

fīniŏ, 4 (tr.), *terminate, end*

fīn-is, -is (m.), *boundary, limit ;* (pl.), *territory*

fīnitim-us, -a, -um (adj.), *neighbouring, adjoining*

fīrmitūd-ō, -inis (f.), *strength, firmness*

fīrmŏ, 1 (tr.), *strengthen, confirm, encourage*

flāgiti-um, -ī (n.), *disgraceful act, disgrace, crime*

flagr-āns, -antis (flagrŏ), (adj.), *glowing with passion* (39, 2, n.)

flecto, flēxī, flēxum, 3 (tr. and intr.), *bend, turn, wind ;* flēxum mare, *winding sea, inlet of coast*

flēt-us, -ūs (m.), *weeping*

flōs, flōris (m.), *flower*

flūct-us, -ūs (m.), *wave*

fluŏ, flūxī, flūxum, 3 (intr.), *flow*

foedŏ, 1 (tr.), *befoul, disfigure, disgrace*

foed-us, -a, -um (adj.), *foul, disgraceful*

foed-us, -eris (n.), *treaty, compact*

fōment-um, -ī (n.), *poultice*

fōns, fontis (m.), *spring, fountain, source*

for-is, -is (f.), *door (one leaf)* ; (pl.), *door of a room (folding doors)*
fōrm-a, -ae (f.), *beauty, shape*
fors (abl. forte) (f.), *chance, luck*
fortuĭt-us, -a, -um (adj.), *fortuitous, accidental*
fŏr-um, -ĭ (n.), *market-place, law-courts, public business*
foss-a, -ae (f.), *ditch*
foueō, fōuĭ, fōtum, 2 (tr.), *warm, cherish, encourage*
frangō, frēgī, frāctum, 3 (tr.), *break, crush*
fraudō, 1 (tr.), *cheat of*
fremit-us, -ūs (m.), *roaring, howling, grumbling*
frem-ō, -uĭ, -itum, 3 (intr.), *roar, howl, grumble*
frequento, 1 (tr.), *frequent, celebrate* (4, 1, *n.*)
frēt-us, -a, -um (adj.) (w. abl.), *relying on, depending on*
frŏns, frontis (f.), *front, forehead*
frūg-ēs, -um (f. pl., rarely in sing.), *fruit, produce, crops*
frūmentāri-us, -a, -um (adj.), *connected with corn;* (rēs) *corn supply*
fruor, frūctus or fruitus sum, 3 (w. abl.), *enjoy*
frūstrā (adv.), *in vain;* frūstrā habēre, *baffle*
fulg-or, -ōris (m.), *brightness, glitter*
fulg-ur, -ŭris (n.), *lightning-flash, thunderbolt*
fulm-en, -inis (n.), *thunderbolt*
funditus (adv.), *from the bottom, completely, utterly*
fundō, fūdī, fūsum, 3 (tr.), *pour, rout*
fungor, fūnctus sum, 3 (w. abl.), *perform, discharge (duty, office)*
fūn-us, -eris (n.), *funeral, death*
Furi-ae, -ārum (f. pl.), *the Furies*
fur-or, -ōris (m.), *frenzy*
fūst-is, -is (abl. reg. fūstī) (m.), *cudgel, club*

gaudi-um, -ĭ (n.), *joy*
gēns, gentis (f.), *family, clan, tribe, nation*

gen-ū, -ūs (n.), *knee*
gen-us, -eris (n.), *class, kind, race*
gestām-en, -inis (n.), *means of conveyance*
gestō (intens. of gerō), 1 (tr.), *carry, bear*
gest-us, -ūs (m.), *gesture, motion*
gignō, genuĭ, genitum, 3 (tr.), *create, produce*
gladiātōri-us, -a, -um (adj.), *pertaining to gladiators, gladiatorial*
gladi-us, -ĭ (m.), *sword*
glīscō (no pf. or sup.), 3 (intr.), *swell, spread, increase*
glob-us, -ĭ (m.), *ball, bunch, company*
glōri-a, -ae (f.) *glory, vainglory, boastfulness*
glōrior, 1 (intr.), *boast, vaunt, brag of*
gnār-us, -a, -um (adj.), *acquainted with, expert, knowing*
grad-us, -ūs (m.), *step, pace, stair, tier*
grātēs (only nom., acc., abl.) (f. pl.), *thanks*
grāti-a, -ae (f.), *favour, influence, kindness, gratitude*
grātor, 1 (w. dat. of pers.), *wish joy, congratulate*
grauēscō (no pf. or sup.), 3, *grow worse* (51, 1, *n.*)
grau-is, -e (adj.), *serious, weighty, burdensome*
grauō, 1 (tr.), *burden, make more grievous, aggravate* (12, 3, *n.*)
gregāri-us, -a, -um (adj.), *belonging to the flock;* (mīles), *common soldier*
gubernācul-um, -ĭ (n.), *helm, rudder*
gymnasi-um, -ĭ (n.), *gymnasium*

habit-us, -ūs (m.), *bearing, appearance, attire*
hāctenus (adv.), *thus far, no further than this*
haereō, haesī, haesum, 2 (intr.), *cling, stick, be in difficulties*
heb-es, -ĕtis (adj.), *dull, stupid*
hēr-ēs, -ēdis (m. or f.), *heir, heiress*

hībernācul-a, -ōrum (n. pl.), *winter quarters*

histri-ō, -ōnis (m.), *actor* (21, 1, *n.*)

honest-us, -a, -um (adj.), *honourable*

hon-or, -ōris (m.), *honour, office*

hort-us, -ī (m.), *garden*

hospitāl-is, -e (adj.), *pertaining to guests or hosts, hospitable, friendly*

hŭm-us, -ī (f.), *ground, soil*

iactō, 1 (tr.), *toss about, discuss, boast of*

iact-us, -ūs (m.), *throwing, aiming, throwing overboard*

iānu-a, -ae (f.), *house-door*

īcō, īcī, ictum, (pres. rare), 3 (tr.), *strike*

ict-us, -ūs (m.), *a blow*

īdeō (adv.), *for that reason, on that account*

īdōne-us, -a, -um (adj.), *fit, suitable*

igitur (conj.), *therefore*

īgnār-us, -a, -um (adj.), *ignorant, unaware*

īgnāui-a, -ae (f.), *idleness, cowardice*

īgn-is, -is (m.), *fire*

īgnōmini-a, -ae (f.), *disgrace, dishonour*

īgnōt-us, -a, -um (adj.), *unknown*

illīc (adv.), *there*

imāg-ō, -inis (f.), *image, bust, shadowy likeness*

imbell-is, -e (adj.), *unwarlike*

immānit-ās, -ātis (f.), *monstrosity, enormity*

immēns-us, -a, -um (adj.), *measureless, vast*

immineō (no pf. or sup.), 2 (intr.), *overhang, threaten*

immīt-is, -e (adj.), *harsh, cruel*

im-mittō, -mīsī, -missum, 3 (tr.), *send in, let loose*

imped-iō, -īuī or -iī, -ītum, 4 (tr.), *hinder*

impedīment-um, -ī (n.), *hindrance, baggage*

im-pellō, -pŭlī, -pulsum, 3 (tr.), *drive against, urge on, impel*

impēnsē (adv.), *earnestly*

impert-iō, -īuī or -iī, -ītum, 4 (tr.), *share with, bestow, impart*

impet-us, -ūs (m.), *attack, forcefulness*

im-pōnō, -posuī, -positum, 3 (tr.), *place on, impose, inflict on*

impotenti-a, -ae (f.), *lack of self-control*

imprōuīs-us, -a, -um (adj.), *unforeseen*

imprūdenti-a, -ae (f.), *want of foresight, imprudence*

impudīciti-a, -ae (f.), *shamelessness, unchastity*

impūnit-ās, -ātis (f.), *freedom from punishment*

inān-is, -e (adj.), *empty, meaningless*

in-calēscō, -caluī (no sup.), 3 (intr.), *grow heated*

incaut-us, -a, -um (adj.), *heedless, thoughtless*

in-cēdō, -cessī, -cessum, 3 (intr.), *proceed, advance, walk, stalk* (53, 4, *n.*)

incendi-um, -ī (n.), *fire, conflagration*

in-cendō, -cendī, -cēnsum, 3 (tr.), *set on fire*

incert-us, -a, -um (adj.), *uncertain*

in-cessō, -cessīuī or -cessī (no sup.), 3 (tr.), *assail, attack* (17, 1, *n.*)

incitāment-um, -ī (n.), *incentive*

inclīnō, 1 (tr. and intr.), *incline, bend, tend in a direction*

incol-a, -ae (m. or f.), *inhabitant*

incolum-is, -e (adj.), *unharmed*

incolumit-ās, -ātis (f.), *uninjured state, safety*

in-crepō, -crepuī, -crepitum, 1 (intr. and tr.), *make a noise; rebuke, upbraid*

in-cumbō, -cubuī, -cubitum, 3 (intr.), *bear down upon, pay attention to*

incūriōs-us, -a, -um (adj.), *careless, neglectful* (38, 2, *n.*)

incursō, 1 (intr. and tr.), *fall upon, attack*

incūsō, 1 (tr.), *accuse, find fault with*

indici-um, -ī (n.), *evidence, sign, information*

indig-eō, -uī (no sup.), 2 (intr., w. abl. or gen.), *need, lack*
indubi-us, -a, -um (adj.), *undoubted*
inerm-is, -e (adj.), *unarmed*
īnfāmi-a, -ae (f.), *ill fame, bad repute, disgrace*
īnfaust-us, -a, -um (adj.), *ill-starred*
īnfēns-us, -a, -um (adj.), *hostile, incensed*
īn-ferō, -tŭlī, -lātum, -ferre (tr.), *bring on, to, into; bellum inf., make war on*
īnfēst-us, -a, -um (adj.), *hostile, dangerous*
īnfīd-us, -a, -um (adj.), *treacherous, false, disloyal*
īnfrequenti-a, -ae (f.), *lack of numbers, sparseness of population*
īn-fringō, -frēgī, -frāctum, 3 (tr.), *break down, weaken*
ingeni-um, -ī (n.), *character, ingenuity, ingenious device*
in-gēns, -gentis (adj.), *huge, vast*
in-gerō, -gessī, -gestum, 3 (tr.), *force upon, hurl at, bear against*
in-gredior, -gressus sum, 3 (tr. and intr.), *enter, advance into*
in-gruō, -gruī (no sup.), 3 (intr.), *assail, break in*
in-iciō, iēcī, -iectum, 3 (tr.), *cast upon, cast into, instil, inspire*
inimīciti-a, -ae (f.), *enmity, hostility*
inīqu-us, -a, -um (adj.), *unequal, unfair, unjust*
initi-um, -ī (n.), *a beginning*
iniūri-a, -ae (f.), *wrong-doing, injury*
inlacrimō (ill-), 1 (intr.), *weep over*
inlecebr-a (ill-), -ae (f.), *enticement, allurement, lure*
inlicit-us (ill-), -a, -um (adj.), *unlawful, illicit*
in-linō (ill-), -lēuī, -lītum, 3 (tr.), *smear, smear on*
in-lūdō (ill-), -lūsī, -lūsum, 3 (tr. and intr. w. dat.), *mock*
inlūstr-is (ill-), -e (adj.), *bright, distinguished, illustrious*
innocenti-a, -ae (f.), *innocence*

innoxi-us, -a, -um (adj.), *harmless, innocent*
innumer-us, -a, -um (adj.), *countless, immeasurable*
inopi-a, -ae (f.), *lack of resources, poverty, want*
in-ops, -ŏpis (adj.), *destitute, devoid of*
inrīs-us (irr-), -ūs (m.), *mockery*
inrītāment-um (irr-), -ī (n.), *inducement, stimulant*
inrītō (irr-), 1 (tr.), *excite, provoke, vex*
inrīt-us (irr-), -a, -um (adj.), *void, of no effect, useless*
in-rumpō (irr-), -rūpī, -ruptum, 3 (tr. and intr.), *burst in, break, attack*
īnsectāti-ō, -ōnis (f.), *censure, derision, blame*
in-sīdeō, -sēdī, -sessum, 2 (intr. and tr.), *sit in or on, be fixed in, occupy*
īnsidi-ae, -ārum (f. pl.), *ambush, trap, plot*
īnsidior, 1 (w. dat.), *plot against*
īn-sīdō, -sēdī, -sessum, 3 (intr. and tr.), *settle on, occupy*
īnsīgn-is, -e (adj.), *eminent, distinguished*
īn-sistō, -stitī (no sup.), 3, *set foot on, press hard on, persist, insist*
īn-sōns, -sontis (adj.), *innocent*
īnstīnct-us, -ūs (m.), *impulse, inspiration*
īn-stituō, -stituī, -stitūtum, 3 (tr.), *set up, establish, instruct*
īn-struō, -struxī, -structum, 3 (tr.), *equip, instruct*
inte-ger, -gra, -grum (adj.), *untouched, unimpaired, whole, pure*
intel-legō, -lēxī, -lēctum, 3 (tr.), *understand, perceive*
intemper-āns, -antis (adj.), *intemperate, profligate*
in-tendō, -tendī, -tentum and -tēnsum, 3 (tr.), *bend towards, stretch out, strain, enhance, increase*
intentō, 1 (tr.) (aliquid alicui), *threaten with*
intent-us, -a, -um (adj., p.p. of intendō), *attentive, alert, ready*

inter-cēdō, -cessī, -cessum, 3 (intr.), *intervene, interpose veto*
intercessi-ō, -ōnis (f.), *intervention, veto* (48, 2, *n.*)
inter-cīdō, -cidī (no sup.), 3 (intr.), *fall between, fall through, lapse*
inter-cipiō, -cēpī, -ceptum, 3 (tr.), *intercept, snatch away, kill*
intercursō, 1 (intr.), *dash between, amongst*
inter-dīcō, -dīxī, -dictum, 3 (tr. and intr.) (aliquid alicui; alicui aliqua re), *forbid*
inter-iciō, -iēcī, -iectum, 3 (tr.), *throw or place between;* (pass.), *come between, intervene*
interim (adv.), *meanwhile*
interpretāti-o, -ōnis (f.), *explanation*
interrogō, 1 (tr.), *ask, inquire, cross-examine* (46, 1, *n.*)
inter-sum, -fuī, -esse, *be present, lie between;* (impers.), *it makes a difference*
intim-us, -a, -um (adj.), *most intimate, innermost*
in-torqueō, -torsī, -tortum, 2 (tr.), *hurl*
intrō, 1 (tr. and intr.), *enter*
inturbid-us, -a, -um (adj.), *undisturbed, quiet*
intūt-us, -a, -um (adj.), *unguarded, unsafe*
inuidi-a, -ae (f.), *envy, hatred, unpopularity*
inuidiōs-us, -a, -um (adj.), *envious, enviable, odious*
inuīs-us, -a, -um (adj.), *hateful*
inult-us, -a, -um (adj.), *unavenged, unpunished*
in-uoluō, -uoluī, -uolūtum, 3 (tr.), *wrap up, surround, involve*
īrācundi-a, -ae (f.), *bad temper*
it-er, -ineris (n.), *journey, route, march*
iubeō, iussī, iussum, 2 (tr.), *bid, order*
iūd-ex, -icis (m.), *judge, juryman*
iūdici-um, -ī (n.), *judgment*
iūdicō, 1 (intr.), *pass judgment, pronounce an opinion;* (tr.), *settle, decide a matter*
iūment-um, -ī (n.), *beast of burden*
iūrō, 1 (intr.), *swear, take an oath* (11, 1, *n.*)
iūrgi-um, -ī (n.), *dispute, abuse*
iūs, iūris (n.), *law, right, privilege, justice*
iūstiti-a, -ae (f.), *justice, uprightness*
iūst-us, -a, -um (adj.), *just, proper, regular*
iuuenīl-is, -e (adj.), *youthful*
iuuent-a, -ae (f.), *youth*
iuuent-ūs, -ūtis (f.), *youth, young people*
iuuō, iūuī, iūtum, 1 (tr. and intr. impers.), *aid, help, it delights*
iūxtā (adv. and prep.), *close beside, next to, equally, alike*

lābō, 1 (intr.), *totter, fall, lose influence*
lābor, lāpsus sum, 3 (intr.), *glide, slip, fall*
lacess-ō, -īuī, -ītum, 3 (tr.), *provoke, irritate*
lāc-us, -ūs (m.), *lake, reservoir, cistern*
laque-us, -ī (m.), *noose*
lascīui-a, -ae (f.), *licentiousness, petulance*
latebr-a, -ae (f.) (usu. pl.), *hiding-place*
latrōcini-um, -ī (n.), *robbery, banditry*
laudō, 1 (tr.), *praise*
lāuō, lāuī and lauāuī, lauātum, lautum and lōtum, 1 (tr.), *wash, bathe*
lau-s, -dis (f.), *praise, merit, worth* (52, 2, *n.*)
lēctitō, 1 (frequ. of legō) (tr.), *read assiduously*
lect-us, -ī (m.), *couch, bed*
lēgāti-ō, -ōnis (f.), *embassy*
lēgāt-us, -ī (m.), *envoy, commander of legion*
lēn-is, -e (adj.), *gentle*
lēnit-ās, -ātis (f.), *gentleness, lenience*
lēnuncul-us, -ī (m.), *small sailing-vessel, skiff*

lĕu-is, -e (adj.), *light, not heavy, insignificant*
līber, librī (m.), *book*
līberălit-ās, -ātis (f.), *generosity*
līber-ī, -ōrum (m. pl.), *children*
lībert-ās, -ātis (f.), *freedom, frankness*
lībertīn-us, -ī (m.), *belonging to class of freedmen*
lībert-us, -a, *freedman, freedwoman*
lībet, libuit or libitum est (impers.), *it pleases, is one's whim*
libīd-ō, -inis (f.), *lust, immoderate desire*
licenter (adv.), *without restraint, impudently*
licenti-a, -ae (f.), *lawlessness, licence, a being uncurbed*
līt-us, -ŏris (n.), *shore*
lŏcō, 1 (tr.), *place; let, farm out*
longinqu-us, -a, -um (adj.), *distant*
lūbric-us, -a, -um (adj.), *slippery*
lūctuŏs-us, -a, -um (adj.), *mournful, pitiable*
lūc-us, -ī (m.), *grove, wood*
lūdibri-um, -ī (n.), *mockery*
lūdi-cer, -cra, -crum (adj.), *theatrical;* (n. as subst.), *public show, stage-play*
lūd-us, -ī (m.), *game*
lūm-en, -inis (n.), *light, lantern*
luō, luī, luitum or lūtum, 3 (tr.), *pay off, suffer (penalty)*
lūx, lūcis (f.), *light, daylight*
lūx-us, -ūs (m.), *extravagance, luxury, debauchery*

māchināment-um, -ī (n.), *machine, contrivance, engine*
maereō (no pf. or sup.), 2 (intr.), *grieve*
maest-us, -a, -um (adj.), *sad*
magistrāt-us, -ūs (m.), *magistrate, magistracy*
māgnitūd-ō, -inis (f.), *size, enormity*
māiest-ās, -ātis (f.), *dignity; treason*
māiŏr-ĕs, -um (m. pl.), *ancestors*
mālō, māluī (no sup.), mālle, *prefer*

mancipi-um, -ī (n.), *chattel, slave*
mandāt-um, -ī (n., p.p. of mandō), *a commission, thing enjoined, message*
mandō, 1 (tr.), *confide to, entrust to; enjoin, order*
manifēst-us, -a, -um (adj.), *plain, evident, caught (in the act)*
manipul-us, -ī (m.), *maniple, company of infantry consisting of two centuries = ₃₀th part of legion*
mānsitō, 1 (intr.), *stay, dwell*
man-us, -ūs (f.), *hand, band*
măr-e, -is (n.), *sea*
marīt-us, -ī (m.), *husband*
mātūrō, 1 (tr. and intr.), *ripen, hurry on; grow ripe, hasten*
meăt-us, -ūs (m.), *passage*
medicām-en, -inis (n.), *drug*
meditor, 1, (tr.), *practise, meditate, intend;* (p.p. in pass. sense), *meditated*
membr-um, -ī (n.), *limb, member*
mĕm-ŏr, -ŏris (adj.), *mindful*
memŏrō, 1 (tr.), *mention, relate*
mēns, mentis (f.), *mind, reason, intellect*
mēnsūr-a, -ae (f.), *measure, capacity*
mer-cēs, -cēdis (f.), *wages, reward, recompense*
mereō, meruī, meritum, and mereor, meritus sum, 2 (tr.), *deserve*
metu-ō, -ī (no sup.), 3, *fear*
met-us, -ūs (m.), *fear*
mīliti-a, -ae (f.), *military service*
mīlităr-is, -e (adj.), *military;* (m. as subst.), *military man, soldier*
min-a, -ae (f.), *threat*
min-āx, -ācis (adj.), *threatening*
minis-ter, -trī (m.), *agent, servant*
minitor, 1 (intr. and tr.) (aliquid alicui), *threaten*
minuō, minuī, minūtum, 3 (tr.), *diminish, reduce*
mīror, 1 (tr. and intr.), *wonder at, be astonished* (39, 2, *n.*)
mīr-us, -a, -um (adj.), *wonderful*
misceō, miscuī, mīxtum, 2 (tr.), *mix, mingle*

miserāti-ō, -ōnis (f.), *compassion*

misericordi-a, -ae (f.), *pity, mercy*

miseror, 1 (tr.), *deplore*

miss-us, -ūs (m.), *a sending, despatching*

mītigō, 1 (tr.), *soften, calm down, pacify*

mīt-is, -e (adj.), *mild, soft, gentle*

mittō, mīsī, missum, 3 (tr.), *send*

moderāti-ō, -ōnis (f.), *moderation, control*, (53, 1, n.)

modesti-a, -ae (f.), *moderation, modesty, good behaviour*

modic-us, -a, -um (adj.), *moderate, medium, poor*

mod-us, -ī (m.), *manner, method, limit, rhythm, measure*

moen-ia, -ium (n. pl.), *city wall, rampart*

mōl-ēs, -is (f.), *huge mass, mole, breakwater*

mōlior, mōlītus sum, 4 (tr. and intr.), *set in motion, contrive, make effort*

molliō, 4 (tr.), *soften, mitigate*

mōs, mōris (m.), *custom, manner;* (pl.), *manners, character*

moueō, mōuī, mōtum, 2 (tr.), *move, disturb, remove*

mox (adv.), *presently, soon after*

muliebr-is, -e (adj.), *belonging to a woman, womanly, female*

muli-er, -eris (f.), *woman*

multō (mulctō), 1 (tr.), *fine, punish*

mūnicipi-um, -ī (n.), *township, municipality*

mūnificenti-a, -ae (f.), *bountifulness, generosity*

mūniō, 4 (tr.), *fortify, defend*

mūn-us, -eris (n.), *gift, service, duty, public show*

mūr-us, -ī (m.), *wall*

mūtāti-ō, -ōnis (f.), *change*

mūtō, 1 (tr.), *change, alter*

mūtu-us, -a, -um (adj.), *borrowed or lent, reciprocal, mutual*

nam (conj.), *for* (11, 2, n.; 44, 3, n.)

narrō, 1 (tr.), *narrate, relate*

nāscor, nātus sum (3), *be born*

nātāl-is, -e (adj.), *belonging to one's birth;* (dies n.), *birthday*

nāti-ō, -ōnis (f.), *tribe* (44, 3, n.)

naufragi-um, -ī (n.), *shipwreck*

naufrag-us, -a, -um (adj.), *shipwrecked*

nāuigi-um, -ī (n.), *ship, boat*

necessit-ās, -ātis (f.), *compulsion, necessity, doom*

nefāst-us, -a, -um (adj.), *unholy, inauspicious* (12, 1, n.)

negō, 1 (tr. and intr.), *deny*

negōtiāt-or, -ōris (m.), *wholesale dealer, banker*

negōti-um, -ī (n.), *business*

nem-us, -ŏris (n.), *grove, wood*

nep-ōs, -ōtis (m.), *grandson*

ne-queō, -quīuī or -quiī, -quitum, 4, *cannot, am unable*

nex, nĕcis (f.), *violent death, murder*

nimi-us, -a, -um (adj.); *excessive*

nītor, nīsus or nīxus sum, 3 (intr.), *strive, exert one's self, rely on*

nō, 1 (intr.), *swim*

noc-ēns, -entis (adj.), *guilty*

nōm-en, -inis (n.), *name, reputation, heading, pretext* (15, 1, n.; 59, 4 n.)

nōminatim (adv.), *by name*

nōnān-ī, -ōrum (m. pl.), *men of the 9th legion*

nōt-ēscō, -uī (no sup.), 3 (intr.), *become known*

nouit-ās, -ātis (f.), *newness, strangeness*

noxi-us, -a, -um (adj.), *harmful, guilty*

nūdō, 1 (tr.), *lay bare, strip*

nūd-us, -a, -um (adj.), *naked*

nūm-en, -inis (n.), *deity*

numer-us, -ī (m.), *number, aggregate, cipher* (27, 2, n.)

nūntiō, 1 (tr..), *announce, report*

nūnti-us, -ī (m.), *messenger, message*

nūper (adv.), *lately, recently*

nur-us, -ūs (f.), *daughter-in-law*

nūt-us, -ūs (m.), *nod, command*

ob-iciō,-iēcī, -iectum, 3 (tr.), *throw up against, reproach with* obiect-us, -ūs (m.), *barrier*

oblectāment-um, -ī (n.), *delight, amusement*

oblīqu-us, -a, -um (adj.), *slanting, indirect, covert*

oblīui-ō, -ōnis (f.), *oblivion*

oblīuīscor, oblītus sum, 3, *forget*

ob-nītor, -nīxus sum, 3 (intr.), *strive against, oppose*

obnoxi-us, -a, -um (adj.), *liable to, exposed to*

oboediō, 4 (intr., w. dat.), *give ear to, obey*

obscūrō, 1 (tr.), *render dark, eclipse*

obsequi-um, -ī (n.), *obedience, obsequiousness*

obseruō, 1 (tr.), *observe, notice, watch, have regard for*

ob-ses, -sidis (m. or f.), *hostage*

ob-sideō, -sēdī, -sessum, 2 (tr.), *besiege, blockade*

obsidi-ō, -ōnis (f.), *siege, blockade*

obsīgnō, 1 (tr.), *seal up*

ob-stringō, -strīnxī, -strīctum, 3 (tr.), *bind, attach to, lay under an obligation* (57, 1, n.)

obtemperō, 1 (intr. w. dat.), *conform to, obey*

obtestor, 1, *testify, declare*

ob-tineō, -tinuī, -tentum, 2 (tr.), *hold down, keep, maintain*

obuersor, 1, *lie opposite, occur to, present itself*

obui-us, -a, -um (adj.), *in the way, so as to meet*

occāsi-ō, -ōnis (f.), *opportunity*

oc-cīdō, -cīdī, -cīsum, 3 (tr.), *cut down, kill*

occultō, 1 (tr.), *hide*

occult-us, -a, -um (adj., p.p. of occulō), *hidden, secret*

oc-currō, -currī, -cursum, 3 (intr.), *run up to, meet, oppose*

occurs-us, -ūs (m.), *a meeting, encounter*

ŏdi-um, -ī (n.), *hatred*

offēnsi-ō, -ōnis (f.), *annoyance*

offerō, obtŭlī, oblātum, -ferre (tr.), *offer*

ole-um, -ī (n.), *olive oil*

ŏmittō, -mīsī, -missum, 3 (tr.), *neglect, put aside, omit*

ŏn-us, -eris (n.), *burden, weight*

oper-a, -ae (f.), *pains, attention, service*

ŏp-ēs (ops), -um (f. pl.), *resources, wealth*

opīni-ō, -ōnis (f.), *opinion, belief*

oportet, 2 (impers.), *it behoves*

op-perior, -perītus or -pertus sum, 4 (intr. and tr.), *wait, await*

oppidān-us, -a, -um (adj.), *belonging to a town, provincial*

opulenti-a, -ae (f.), *wealth*

ŏp-us, -eris (n.), *work, need ;* opus est aliqua re, *there is need of something*

ōr-a, -ae (f.), *shore*

ōrāt-or, -ōris (m.), *orator, spokesman, declaimer*

orbit-ās, -ātis (f.), *bereaved state, childlessness*

orb-us, -a, -um (adj.), *bereaved, childless*

ōrd-ō, -inis (m.), *order, row, rank, detailed account*

orīg-ō, -inis (f.), *source, birth, ancestor*

orior, ortus sum (fut. pt., oritūrus), 4 and 3 (intr.), *arise, spring from*

ōrnāt-us, -ūs (m.), *adornment, attire*

ōrnō, 1 (tr.), *adorn, equip*

ōrō, 1 (tr.), *beg, beseech, ask ;* (causam), *plead*

ōs, ōris (n.), *mouth, utterance ;* ore uno, *with uniform style*

ōscul-um, -ī (n.), *kiss*

ostentō, 1 (tr.), *display, show*

ōti-um, -ī (n.), *leisure, retirement, peace*

pael-ex, -icis (f.), *mistress*

paenitenti-a, -ae (f.), *remorse, change of mind, repentance*

pălam (adv.), *openly ;* (prep. w. abl.), *in sight of*

palāt-um, -ī (n.), *palate*

pangō, pānxī, pānctum, and pēgī or pepigī, pāctum, 3 (tr.), *fix, stipulate, compose, write* pantomīm-us, -ī (m.), *ballet-dancer* (21, 4, *n.*)

pār, părīs (adj.), *equal*

parcō, pepercī or parsī (fut. pt. parsūrus), 3 (intr. w. dat.), *spare, show mercy to*

par-ēns, -entis (m. and f.), *parent*

păreō, pāruī (fut. pt. pāritūrus), 2 (intr., w. dat.), *obey*

pari-ēs, -ĕtis (m.), *wall, side*

pariō, peperī, partum, 3 (tr.), *obtain, produce, give birth to*

părō, 1 (tr.), *prepare, provide*

parricīdi-um, -ī (n.), *parricide, murder of a parent*

par-s, -tis (f.), *part*

parsimōni-a, -ae (f.), *thrift*

part-us, -ūs (m.), *birth, offspring*

part-us, -a, -um (p.p. of pariō)

părum (adv.), *too little, not enough*

passim (adv.), *on all sides, at random*

patern-us, -a, -um (adj.), *paternal*

pateō, patuī (no sup.), 2 (intr.), *lie open, be clear*

patibul-um, -ī (n.), *cross, pillory*

patienti-a, -ae (f.), *patience, endurance*

patior, passus sum, 3 (tr.), *suffer, endure*

patri-us, -a, -um (adj.), *belonging to one's father, paternal, native*

patrăt-or, -ōris (m.), *perpetrator* (62, 2, *n.*)

patrō, 1 (tr.), *accomplish, carry out, complete*

patrōn-a, -ae (f.), *patroness, protectress, mistress*

pauēscō (no pf. or sup.), 3 (intr.), *grow frightened;* (tr.), *become alarmed at* (Introd. III, 1, (i))

paulātim (adv.), *gradually*

pau-or, -ōris (m.), *panic*

paupert-ās, -ātis (f.), *poverty*

pecu-s, -dis (f.), *single head of sheep or cattle*

pell-is, -is (f.), *hide, skin, tent*

pellō, pepulī, pulsum, 3 (tr.), *drive, drive out, banish*

penāt-ēs, -ium (m. pl.), *household gods, household, family*

penetrō, 1 (tr. and intr.), *penetrate, sink into the mind*

pēnūri-a, -ae (f.), *want, need*

per-cellō, -cŭlī, -culsum, 3 (tr.), *beat down, discourage, daunt*

percuss-or, -ōris (m.), *assassin*

perditissim-us, -a, -um (adj., sup. of p.p. of perdō), *most abandoned*

perduell-is, -is (m.), *enemy, rebel* (29, 2, *n.*)

peregrīn-us, -a, -um (adj.), *foreign*

per-eō, -iī or -īuī, -itum, īre, *perish*

per-ferō, -tŭlī, -lātum, -ferre (tr.), *carry to destination, bear to the end*

per-ficiō, -fēcī, -fectum, 3 (tr.), *complete, finish, perfect*

per-fringō, -frēgī, -frāctum, 3 (tr.), *break through*

per-fungor, -fūnctus sum, 3 (w. abl.), *execute completely, fulfil, get through with, have done with ;* (uita, fato), *die*

perfug-a, -ae (m.), *deserter*

per-gō, -rēxī, -rēctum, 3 (intr.), *proceed, go on, continue*

perīcul-um, -ī (n.), *danger*

perītē (adv.), *skilfully, with experience*

permeō, 1 (intr.), *go through, make a journey*

per-mittō, -mīsī, -missum, 3 (tr.), *let through, permit, concede*

per-moueō, -mōuī, -mōtum, 2 (tr.), *move thoroughly, upset*

pernici-ēs, -ēī (f.), *ruin, destruction*

per-nōtēscō, -nōtuī (no sup.), 3 (intr.), *become generally known* (8, 1, *n.*)

per-ōdī, -ōsus sum, -ōdisse (tr., mostly in p.p.), *hate greatly*

perpetrō, 1 (tr.), *carry through to completion*

perpetu-us, -a, -um (adj.), *permanent*

perpopulor, 1 (tr.), *ravage thoroughly*

per-sŏnō, -sonuī, -sonitum, 1 (intr. and tr.), *resound, make to resound*

per-stō, -stitī (fut pt. -statūrus), 1 (intr.), *stand firm, hold out, persevere*

per-uădŏ, -uăsĭ, -uăsum, 3 (intr. and tr.), *go through, pervade*
peruulgŏ, 1 (tr.), *noise abroad*
phŏnasc-us, -ī (m.), *singing-master*
pīgn-us, -oris and -eris (n.), *pledge, security*
pīl-um, -ī (n.), *javelin*
plăcābil-is, -e (adj.), *placable, easily appeased*
plăceŏ, 2 (intr., w. dat.), *please*
plăcid-us, -a, -um (adj.), *calm*
plācŏ, 1 (tr.), *placate, appease*
plānct-us, -ūs (m.), *a beating of the breast, lamentation*
plāniti-ēs, -ēī (f.), *plain, level place*
plān-us, -a, -um (adj.), *even, level, plain*
plaus-us, -ūs (m.), *applause*
plērīque (adj. and pron.), *most, very many* (5, 2, *n.*)
plumb-um, -ī (n.), *lead*
plūrēs, plura, (21, 1, *n.*)
poen-a, -ae (f.), *penalty*
pol-luŏ, -luī, -lūtum, 3 (tr.), *defile, dishonour, pollute*
populār-is, -is (m.), *countryman, native* (24, 3, *n.*)
populor, 1 (tr.), *ravage*
por-tendŏ, tendī, -tentum, 3 (tr.), *foretell, prophesy, portend*
poscŏ, poposcī (no sup.), 3 (tr.), *demand, ask for*
possess-or, -ōris (m.), *settler, squatter, possessor*
pos-sideŏ, -sēdī, -sessum, 2 (tr.), *occupy, own, possess*
post (prep. and adv.), *after, afterwards*
poster-us, -a, -um (adj.), *following, next;* posterī, *descendants;* (comp.), posterior; (superl.), postrēmus
post-pōnŏ, -posuī, -positum, 3 (tr.), *place after, esteem less*
postulŏ, 1 (tr.), *demand, request*
potenti-a, -ae (f.), *influence, power*
potest-ās, -ātis (f.), *legal power, authority (of magistrate)*
potior, potītus sum, 4 (w. abl. or gen.), *be master of, control, gain*
potissimum (adv.), *especially*

potissim-us, -a, -um (adj.), *chief, most important* (65, 1, *n.*)
pōt-us, -ūs (m.), *a drinking, drink, draught*
praebeŏ, 2 (tr.), *furnish, supply, show*
praecept-um, -ī (n.), *precept, maxim, teaching*
praecipu-us, -a, -um (adj.), *chief, especial* (31, 1, *n.*; 58, 1, *n.*)
prae-colo (no pf.), -cultum, 3 (tr.), *cultivate beforehand*
praed-a, -ae (f.), *booty*
prae-dūcŏ, -dūxī, -ductum, 3 (tr.), *draw in front*
praefect-us, -ī (m.), *prefect* (p.p. of praeficiŏ)
prae-ferŏ, -tŭlī, -lātum, -ferri (tr.), *carry in front, display, prefer* (53, 4, *n.*)
praefer-ōx, -ōcis (adj.), *very fierce*
praeferuid-us, -a, -um (adj.), *very hot*
prae-ficiŏ, -fēcī, -fectum, 3 (tr.), *put in charge*
praegrau-is, -e (adj.), *very troublesome*
prae-gredior, -gressus sum, 3 (intr.), *go in front, precede, go by*
praemeditor, 1 (tr. and intr.), *practise beforehand, prelude*
prae-mittŏ, -mīsī, -missum, 3 (tr.), *send on in front*
prae-ripiŏ, -ripuī, -reptum, 3 (tr.), *snatch beforehand*
praesāgi-um, -ī (n.), *presentiment, foreboding*
praesci-us, -a, -um (adj.), *foreseeing, prescient, prophetic*
praes-ēns, -entis (adj.), *present;* ad praesens, *for the present*
prae-sideŏ, -sēdī (no sup.) (intr., w. dat.), *preside over, manage, protect*
praesidi-um, -ī (n.), *protection, garrison, fortress*
prae-stringŏ, -strīnxī, -strīctum, 3 (tr.), *tie in front, dazzle, blind*
prae-sūmŏ, -sūmpsī, -sūmptum, 3 (tr.), *take beforehand*
prae-tendŏ, -tendī, -tentum, 3 (tr.), *hold out, allege, put forward as excuse*

praetōriān-us, -ī (m.), *member of praetorian guard*

praetōri-us, -a, -um (adj.), *belonging to a praetor ;* as noun, *ex-praetor*

praetūr-a, -ae (f.), *praetorship*

prae-ualeō, -ualuī (no sup.) (intr.), *be very strong, prevail*

praeuāricor, 1 (intr.), *act in collusion* (41, 1, n.)

prae-ueniō, -uēnī, -uentum, 4 (intr. and tr.), *go before, forestall*

prae-uideō, -uīdī, -uīsum, 2 (tr.), *foresee*

prǣumbr-āns,- antis (adj.), *overshadowing*

prāuit-ās, -ātis (f.), *crookedness, perversity, badness* (38, 3, n.)

prāu-us, -a, -um (adj.), *crooked, perverse, bad*

prec-ēs, -um (f. pl. ; sing., prex, rare), *request, prayer*

premō, pressī, pressum, 3 (tr.), *press, crush*

prēnsō, 1 (frequ. of prehendō) (tr.), *grasp ;* (manum), *shake hands*

preti-um, -ī (n.), *price, reward, bribe*

prīn-ceps, -cipis (adj.), *chief, leading,* (*of the emperor as First Citizen*)

prō (prep. w. abl.), *on behalf of, in accordance with, in proportion to, in front of, instead of, on front part of* (30, 1, n.)

prŏau-us, -i (m.), *great-grandfather, ancestor*

prŏbō, 1 (tr.), *approve of ;* (w. dat. of pers.), *prove to, win approval for something*

probr-um, -ī (n.), *reproach, insult*

prŏb-us, -a, -um (adj.), *honest, upright*

prŏc-āx, -ācis (adj.), *bold, shameless, pert*

prŏc-er, -eris (m.), *chief, noble, leading man*

prō cōnsule, (46, 1, n.), *proconsul*

procul (adv.), *afar, from far ;* (prep. w. abl.), *far from*

prōdigi-um, -ī (n.), *prophetic sign, prodigy*

prŏdit-or, -ōris (m.), *betrayer, traitor*

prō-dō, -didī, -ditum, 3 (tr.), *publish, record, betray*

proeli-um, -ī (n.), *battle*

prŏfān-us, -a, -um (adj.), *unholy, profane* (2, 1, n.)

prŏfecti-ō, -ōnis (f.), *departure*

prō-ferō, -tŭlī, -lātum, -ferre (tr.), *carry forth, carry further, extend*

prŏficīscor, prŏfectus sum, 3 (intr.), *set out*

prō-fiteor, -fessus sum, 2, *declare publicly*

prōflīgō, 1 (tr.), *strike down, all but finish* (battle, war)

prŏfug-us, -a, -um (adj.), *fugitive*

prōgeni-ēs, -ēī (f.), *offspring, descendants*

prŏhibeō, 2 (tr.), *keep off, prevent, forbid*

prō-lābor, -lāpsus sum, 3 (intr.), *slide forward, fall down, collapse*

prō-loquor, -locūtus sum, 3, *speak out, exclaim*

prŏmisc-us (also -uus), -a, -um (adj.), *open to all, promiscuous, public*

prō-mittō, -mīsī, -missum, 3 (tr. and intr.), *promise*

prŏmpt-us, -a, -um (adj., p.p. of prōmō), *ready, quick, prompt*

prōmunturi-um, -ī (n.), *headland, promontory*

prōnūntiō, 1, *announce, report, proclaim*

prope (adv. and prep.), *near*

proper-us, -a, -um (adj.), *hasty, hastening, eager*

propinqu-us, -a, -um (adj.), *near ;* propinquī, *relatives*

propius (comp. adv.), *nearer*

propri-us, -a, -um (adj.), *special, particular, one's own*

prōpulsō, 1 (tr.), *drive back, keep at bay*

prō-ruō, -ruī, -rutum, 3 (intr. and tr.), *rush forth ; hurl down*

prō-sequor, -secūtus sum, 3 (tr.), *escort*

prōspectō, 1 (intr. and tr.), *look out over, furnish a view* prosper-us, -a, -um (adj.), *fortunate, prosperous*

prō-sum, -fuī, -desse (intr., w. dat.), *be of advantage, benefit, profit*

prō-tegō, -tēxī, -tēctum, 3 (tr.), *cover, protect*

prō-tendō, -tendī, -tentum or -tēnsum, 3 (tr.), *stretch out*

prō-uehō, -uēxī, -uectum, 3 (tr.), *carry forward ;* (pass.), *advance*

prō-ueniō, -uēnī, -uentum, 4 (intr.), *come forth, proceed successfully*

prō-uocō, 1 (tr. and intr.), *call out, challenge ; make an appeal* (ad)

prō-uoluō, -uoluī, -uolūtum, 3 (tr.), *roll forward ;* (pass.), *grovel*

pūblicē (adv.), *on behalf of the State* (17, 2, *n.*)

pūblicō, 1 (tr.), *confiscate*

pudīciti-a, -ae (f.), *chastity, modesty*

pud-or, -ōris (m.), *shame*

puellār-is, -e (adj.), *youthful, girlish*

pueriti-a, -ae (f.), *boyhood*

puluīn-ar, -āris (n.), *couch for the gods, shrine* (12, 1, *n.*)

pūniō, 4 (tr.), *punish*

pūpill-us, -ī (m.), *ward, minor*

quadrīg-a, -ae (f.), *team of four horses, four horse chariot*

quaerō, quaesīuī, quaesītum, 3 (tr.), *seek, inquire, acquire*

quaesti-ō, -ōnis (f.), *investigation,* (*judicial*) *inquiry, examination by torture*

quaestōri-us, -a, -um (adj.), *belonging to a quaestor ;* (m.), *ex-quaestor*

quaest-us, -ūs (m.), *gain, profit, trade*

quāliscumque, quālecumque (rel. adj. and indef.), *of whatever sort, of some sort* (13, 2, *n.*)

quamuīs (adv. and conj.), *however much, although*

quandō (interr. adv. and conj.), *when ? since, seeing that* (31, 2, *n.*)

quartadecimān-ī, -ōrum (m.), *men of the 14th legion*

quartum (adv.), *for the fourth time*

quāsī (adv.), *as if, as though* (Introd. III, 6, ii, (e))

queō, quiī or quīuī, quitum, quīre, *can, am able*

quest-us, -ūs (m.), *complaint, lament*

qui-ēs, -ētis (f.), *quietness, rest*

quiēt-us, -a, -um (adj.), *peaceful, quiet*

Quīnquātr-ūs, -uum (f.), *name of a festival* (4, 1, *n.*)

quīnquennāl-is, -e (adj.), *that takes place every fifth year, quinquennial*

quīnquenni-um, -ī (n.), *period of five years*

quippe (adv. and conj.), *to be sure, in fact*

quod (conj.), *the fact that, in that, because*

rāti-ō, -ōnis (f.), *reason, explanation, method*

rebellāti-ō, -ōnis (f.), *rebellion*

rebelli-ō, -ōnis (f.), *rebellion*

rec-ēns, -entis (adj.), *fresh, recent ;* (also adv.), *recently*

receptācul-um, -ī (n.), *place of refuge*

reciperō, 1 (tr.), *recover*

recitō, 1 (tr.), *read aloud*

reclīn-is, -e (adj.), *reclining*

re-clūdō, -clūsī, -clūsum, 3 (tr.), *unlock, open, reveal*

recordāti-ō, -ōnis (f.), *remembrance, recollection*

rēct-or, -ōris (m.), *leader, ruler*

red-dō, -didī, -ditum, 3 (tr.), *give back, pay as due*

referō, rettulī, relātum, -ferre (tr.), *bring back, refer, attribute, relate*

re-foueō, -fōuī, -fōtum, 2 (tr.), *refresh, restore, revive*

re-fringō, -frēgī, -frāctum, 3 (tr.), *break open, break in pieces*

regim-en, -inis (n.), *guidance, government*

regi-ō, -ōnis (f.), *region, district*

rēgi-us, -a, -um (adj.), *belonging to a king, royal ;* rēgia (sc. domus), *palace, court*

re-gredior, -gressus sum, 3 (intr.), *come back, return*

relāti-ō, -ōnis (f.), *report, motion* (49, 1, n.)

relēgō, 1 (tr.), *send away, banish, relegate*

religi-ō, -ōnis (f.), *religion, religious scruple*

reliqu-us, -a, -um (adj.), *rest of, remaining*

r̆emedi-um, -ī (n.), *remedy*

remeō, 1 (intr.), *go back, return*

rēm-ex, -igis (m.), *oarsman, rower*

rēmigi-um, -ī (n.), *rowing ;* (abstr. for concr.), *the oarsmen, crew*

re-mittō, -mīsī, -missum, 3 (tr.), *send back, remit, relax*

rēm-us, -ī (m.), *oar*

reor, rătus sum, 2 *think, calculate*

re-pendō, -pendī, -pēnsum, 3 (tr.), *pay, repay*

rĕp-ēns, -entis (adj.), *sudden, unexpected*

rĕpente (adv.), *suddenly, unexpectedly*

repentīn-us, -a, -um (adj.), *sudden, unexpected*

rēpō, rēpsī (no sup.), 3 (intr.), *creep, crawl*

reperiō, repperī, repertum, 4 (tr.), *find*

re-petō, -petīuī or petiī, -petītum, 3 (tr.), *seek again, go back to, recall*

repetund-ae, -ārum (f. pl., sc. pecūniae) (ger. adj. of repetō), *money extorted that is claimed back, a charge of extortion*

reposcō (no pf. or sup.), 3 (tr.), *demand back*

reputō, 1 (tr.), *think over, reflect upon*

requīrō, -quisīuī, -quīsītum, 3 (tr.), *search for, inquire after, look in vain for, miss*

reseruō, 1 (tr.), *keep, save, preserve*

re-spiciō, -spēxī, -spectum, 3 (tr.), *look round at, observe, respect*

re-spondeō, -spondī, -spōnsum, 2, *answer, reply*

re-sūmō, -sūmpsī, -sūmptum, 3 (tr.), *take up again, seize back, resume*

re-ticeō, -ticuī (no sup.) (intr. and tr.), *fall silent, not answer, be silent about*

re-tineō, -tinuī, -tentum, 2 (tr.), *hold back, retain*

retrō (adv.), *back, backwards*

re-ualēscō, -ualuī (no sup.), 3 (intr.), *get well again, recover*

reuerenti-a, -ae (f.), *reverence, respect*

rĕ-us, -a, *one on trial, defendant, prisoner*

rīmor, 1 (tr.), *turn up (ground), explore, probe*

rīt-us, -ūs (m.), *rite, observance, rule* (44, 3, n.)

rōb-ur, -ŏris (n.), *oak-timber, strength, the best part of anything*

rogitō, 1 (frequ. of rogo), *ask repeatedly*

rog-us, -ī (m.), *funeral pile*

rub-or, -ōris (m.), *shame*

rudīment-um, -ī (n.), *early instruction, first attempt*

rūm-or, -ōris (m.), *rumour, report, reputation*

ruō, ruī, rŭtum, 3 (intr. and tr.), *fall, crash ; cast down*

sa-cer, -cra, -crum (adj.), *sacred*

sacerd-ōs, -ōtis (m.), *priest*

saepenumerō (adv.), *again and again, often*

saepiō, saepsī, saeptum, 4 (tr.), *fence in, enclose*

saeu-us, -a, -um (adj.), *cruel, savage*

saltem (adv.), *at least, at all events*

sal-ūs, -ūtis (f.), *safety*

sānĕ (adv.), *by all means, to be sure, however* (44, 1, n.)

sangu-is, -inis (m.), *blood*

sarment-um, -ī (n., usu. pl.), *brushwood, twigs*

satell-es, -itis (m.), *bodyguard, henchman* (59, 2, n.)

satiet-ās, -ātis (f.), *satiety, surfeit, disgust*

sauci-us, -a, -um (adj.), *wounded*

sax-um, -ī (n.), *rock, stone*

scaen-a (scēna), -ae (f.), *stage, scene*

scandō, scandī, scānsum, 3 (tr. and intr.), *climb, mount, go aboard*

scăph-a, -ae (f.), *boat, skiff*

scel-us, -eris (n.), *crime*

scienti-a, -ae (f.), *skill, knowledge*

scīlicet (adv.), *forsooth, of course*

scīscitor, 1, *inquire, interrogate*

sĕcess-us, -ūs (m.), *retreat, place of retirement*

sĕcrēt-us, -a, -um (adj., p.p. of sĕcernō), *retired, lonely, secret, private*

sĕcūrit-ās, -ātis (f.), *freedom from care*

sĕd-ēs, -is (f.), *seat, abode*

sĕditi-ō, -ōnis (f.), *mutiny, riot, sedition*

sĕg-ĕs, -ĕtis (f.), *cornfield, crop*

sĕgn-is, -e (adj.), *slothful, lazy*

sell-a, -ae (f.), *chair, sedan*

senect-a, -ae (f.), *old age*

seni-or, -ōris (adj., m. and f. only; comp. of senex), *older*

sĕ-pōnō, -posuī, -positum, 3 (tr.), *set aside*

sepulcr-um, -ī (n.), *tomb, sepulchre*

sequor, secūtus sum, 3 (tr.), *follow*

sĕri-us, -a, -um (adj.), *earnest, grave, serious*

serm-ō, -ōnis (m.), *conversation*

seruiō, 4 (intr.), *be a slave;* (w. dat.), *serve, care for*

seruiti-um, -ī (n.), *slavery;* (pl.), *slaves*

seuĕrit-ās, -ātis (f.), *strictness*

seuĕr-us, -a, -um (adj.), *strict, severe, austere*

sex-us, -ūs (m.), *sex*

sīd-us, -eris (n.), *star, constellation*

sīgn-um, -ī (n.), *signal, sign, standard*

silenti-um, -ī (n.), *silence*

sil-eō, -uī (no sup.), 2 (intr. and tr.), *be silent, be silent about*

similitūd-ō, -inis (f.), *likeness, similarity*

simul (adv.), *together, at the same time*

simulācr-um, -ī (n.), *image, statue, phantom*

simulāti-ō, -ōnis (f.), *pretence*

simulō, 1 (tr.), *pretend, feign, assume the appearance of*

simult-ās, -ātis (f.), *jealousy, enmity, quarrel*

singul-ī, -ae, -a (pl. adj.), *taken singly, separate, each one*

sinō, sīuī, situm, 3 (tr.), *allow, let*

sistō, stitī, statum, 3 (tr. and intr.), *bring to a stop, check; place one's self, stand still*

soc-er, -erī (m.), *father-in-law*

societ-ās, -ātis (f.), *alliance, association*

sōl, sōlis (m.), *sun*

soleō, solitus sum, 2, *to be wont, accustomed*

sōlitūd-ō, -inis (f.), *solitude, loneliness*

sollerti-a, -ae (f.), *ingenuity, ingenious plan*

sollicitūd-ō, -inis (f.), *anxiety*

sōlum (adv.), *only, merely*

sōlum (n.), *soil, ground*

soluō, soluī, solūtum, 3 (tr.), *break up, loosen, solve*

sōl-us, -a, -um (adj.), *alone, only*

sonit-us, -ūs (m.), *sound*

son-or, -ōris (m.), *sound, din*

son-us, -ī (m.), *sound*

sortior, 4 (intr. and tr.), *draw lots, appoint by lot, obtain by lot*

spad-ō, -ōnis (m.), *eunuch*

spargō, sparsī, sparsum, 3 (tr.), *scatter, sprinkle, strew*

spati-um, -ī (n.), *space*

speci-ēs, -ēī (f.), *appearance, shape*

spectācul-um, -ī (n.), *show, spectacle, theatre*

spectō, 1 (tr.), *look at;* (intr.), *look on, be a spectator;* (w. ad), *aim at;* (of places), *face, lie*

spec-us, -ūs (m.), *cave*

spēlunc-a, -ae (f.), *cave*

spērō, 1 (intr. and tr.), *hope, hope for*

spernō, sprēuī, sprētum, 3 (tr.), *scorn, reject, spurn*

spīrit-us, -ūs (m.), *breath*
sponte (abl. f.), *spontaneously, of one's own accord*
stăgn-um, -ī (n.), *pool, lake*
stati-ō, -ōnis (f.), *post, outpost, picket of soldiers*
stat-uō, -uī, -ūtum, 3 (tr.), *set up, fix, decide*
stat-us, -ūs (m.), *posture, condition, state*
steril-is, -e (adj.), *barren*
sternō, strāuī, strātum, 3 (tr.), *stretch out, lay low*
stimulō, 1 (tr.), *goad, stimulate*
stipendi-um, -ī (n.), *pay, service, campaign*
stips, stĭpis (f.), *dole, small payment*
stō, stetī (no sup.) (fut. pt. statūrus), 1 (intr.), *stand*
străg-ēs, -is (f.), *slaughter, butchery, shambles*
strēnu-us, -a, -um (adj.), *quick, active, strenuous*
strepit-us, -ūs (m.), *noise, clamour*
struō, struxī, structum, 3 (tr.), *erect, construct, devise*
studi-um, -ī (n.), *zeal, favour, support, pursuit*
stupr-um, -ī (n.), *rape, defilement*
sub-dō, -didī, -ditum, 3 (tr.), *put under, substitute, forge* (40, 1, *n.*)
subiect-us, -a, -um, (p.p. of subiciō), *lying beneath, subjected, neighbouring*
sub-igō, -ēgī, -āctum, 3 (tr.), *subdue, force, compel*
subitāri-us, -a, -um (adj.), *done suddenly, occasional, temporary*
subit-us, -a, -um (adj.), *sudden*
subleuō, 1 (tr.), *lift up, lighten, assuage*
sub-mergō (summ-), -mersī, -mersum, 3 (tr.), *sink, submerge*
subsidi-um, -ī (n.), *aid, help, relief*
subol-ēs, -is (f.), *progeny, offspring*
sub-trahō, -trāxī, -tractum, 3 (tr.), *withdraw*
sub-ueniō, -uēnī, -uentum, 4 (intr.), *come to one's aid, assist, succour* (w. dat.)

suc-cēdō, -cessī, -cessum, 3 (intr.), *draw near, relieve, succeed*
success-or, -ōris (m.), *successor*
suēscō, suēuī, suētum, 3, *become accustomed ;* p.p. as adj., *accustomed to, usual*
suf-ficiō, -fēcī, -fectum, 3 (intr.), *suffice*
suffugi-um, -ī (n.), *escape, refuge*
sug-gredior, -gressus sum, 3 (intr. and tr.), *come up, approach*
summ-a, -ae (f.), *chief point, completion, sum total*
sūmō, sūmpsī, sūmptum, 3 (tr.), *take up, choose, appropriate*
sūmpt-us, -ūs (m.), *expense, cost*
sŭper (adv., and prep. w. acc. or abl.), *beyond, above ;* (w. abl.), *about, concerning*
super-gredior, -gressus sum, 3 (tr.), *surpass*
superstiti-ō, -ōnis (f.), *superstition, superstitious rite*
super-sum, -fuī, -esse (intr.), *be left over, survive, abound*
sup-petō, -petīuī or -petiī, -petītum, 3 (intr.), *be at hand, suffice, last*
sup-pleō, -plēuī, -plētum, 2 (tr.), *fill up, supplement*
suppl-ex, -icis (adj.), *suppliant*
supplicāti-ō, -ōnis (f.), *a thanksgiving* (12, 1, *n.*)
supplici-um, -ī (n.), *penance, punishment, penalty*
sus-cipiō, -cēpī, -ceptum, 3 (tr.), *take up, undertake*
su-spiciō, -spēxī, -spectum, 3 (intr. and tr.), *look up, look up at, look up to, admire ;* (pt. only), *look askance at, suspect*
suspīci-ō, -ōnis (f.), *suspicion*

tabul-a, -ae (f.), *board, tablet, document*
taedi-um, -ī (n.), *weariness*
tardē (adv.), *slowly*
tamquam (adv.), *as if, to the effect that, on ground that* (Introd. III, 6, ii, (e))
tangō, tetigī, tāctum, 3 (tr.), *touch, strike (of lightning)*

tantum (adv.), *only, merely*

tardō, 1 (tr.), *retard, delay, hinder*

tēct-um, -ī (n.), *roof*

tēl-um, -ī (n.), *weapon, implement*

temerit-ās, -ātis (f.), *rashness*

temperō, 1 (intr., w. dat.), *act with restraint towards, spare, moderate ;* (w. abl. and ab), *refrain from ;* (tr.), *regulate*

temptō, 1 (tr.), *try, test, try to corrupt*

temulent-us, -a, -um (adj.), *drunk*

tenebr-ae, -ārum (f. pl.), *darkness, gloom*

tentōri-um, -ī (n.), *tent*

terg-um, -ī (n.), *back*

terrestr-is, -e (adj.), *belonging to the land, land-, terrestrial*

testāment-um, -ī (n.), *will*

testificor, 1 (intr. and tr.), *give evidence, show, make known*

testimōni-um, -ī (n.), *evidence*

test-is, -is, (m. or f.), *witness*

testor, 1 (tr.), *bear witness to, demonstrate*

theātrāl-is, -e (adj.), *theatrical*

theātr-um, -ī (n.), *theatre*

thēsaur-us, -ī (m.), *treasure, treasury*

tībīc-en, -inis (m.), *flute-player*

tībi-ae, -ārum (f. pl.), *flute*

tolerō, 1 (tr.), *endure, sustain*

torment-um, -ī (n.), *rack, torture, catapult*

tractō, 1 (tr.), *handle, manage*

trā-dō, -didī, -ditum, 3 (tr.), *hand over, transmit, record*

trāho, trāxī, tractum, 3 (tr.), *draw, draw out, prolong, interpret* (32, 1, n.)

trāns-eō, -iī, -itum, 4 (intr. and tr.), *pass over, cross, pass by*

trāns-ferō, -tulī, -lātum, -ferre (tr.), *transfer*

trāns-gredior, -gressus sum, 3 (intr.), *go across, pass over to ;* (tr.), *cross, pass*

trāns-igō, -ēgī, -āctum, 3 (tr.), *pierce through, transfix, transact*

trāns-mittō (trām-), -mīsī, -missum, 3 (tr.), *send over, allow to go through, pass over, omit*

trem-or, -ōris (m.), *trembling, earthquake*

tribūnīci-us, -a, -um (adj.), *belonging to a tribune, tribunicial*

trib-us, -ūs (f.), *division of Roman people, tribe* (13, 2, n.)

triērarch-us, -ī (m.), *trierarch, captain of trireme* (8, 3, n.)

trirēm-is, -is (f.), *vessel with three banks of oars, trireme*

triumphāl-is, -e (adj.), *pertaining to a triumph, that has had the honour of a triumph*

trucīdō, 1 (tr.), *butcher, kill*

trunc-us, -a, -um (adj.), *maimed, mutilated*

tūb-a, -ae (f.), *trumpet*

tueor, tuitus sum, 2 (tr.), *watch, protect, defend*

tumēscō, tumuī (no sup.), 3 (intr.), *swell up*

tumul-us, -ī (m.), *mound, tomb*

turbō, 1 (tr.), *throw into confusion*

turm-a, -ae (f.), *cavalry squadron, crowd*

turp-is, -e (adj.), *ugly, foul, disgraceful*

tūtēl-a, -ae (f.), *protection*

tūt-us, -a, -um (adj.), *safe*

uacu-us, -a, -um (adj.), *empty, vacant*

uādō, uāsī (no sup.), 3 (intr.), *go, advance, wade*

uăd-um, -ī (n.), *ford*

ualētūd-ō (ualītūdō), -inis (f.), *health (good or bad)*

ualid-us, -a, -um (adj.), *strong*

uall-is (or -ēs), -is (f.), *valley*

uānit-ās, -ātis (f.), *emptiness, falsity, vanity*

uari-us, -a, -um (adj.), *varied, various*

uăt-ēs, -is (m.), *poet*

uāstō, 1 (tr.), *lay waste, ravage*

ūb-er, -eris (adj.), *rich, fruitful*

ūberrim-us, -a, -um, superl. of *ūber*

ubicumque (adv. and sub. conj.), *wherever*

uēcordi-a (uae-), -ae (f.), *madness*

uehicul-um, -ī (n.), *vehicle, cart*

uĕhō, uĕxī, uectum, 3 (tr.), *carry, convey*

uelut, uelutī (adv.), *even as, just as*

uĕn-a, -ae (f.), *vein*

uĕnāl-is, -e (adj.), *for sale, venal, corrupt*

uĕndĭtō, 1 (tr., frequ. of uĕndō), *sell*

uĕn-dō, -didī, -ditum, 3 (tr.), sell

uenēn-um, -ī (n.), *poison*

uenerāti-ō, -ōnis (f.), *veneration, reverence*

ueni-a, -ae (f.), *kindness, indulgence, pardon*

uen-ter, -tris (m.), *stomach, womb*

uent-us, -ī (m.), *wind*

uĕnum (acc.), uĕno (dat.) (no nom.) (m.), *sale*

uĕnun-dō, -dedī, -datum, 1 (tr.) = uĕndō, 3

ucrber-a, -um (n. pl.), *blows*

uers-us, -ūs (m.), *line of verse*

uĕrum (adv. and conj.), *but in truth, however*

uest-is, -is (f.), *clothing*

ueterān-us, -a, -um (adj.), *veteran*

uet-us, -eris (adj.), *old, of long standing*

uetust-ās, -ātis (f.), *long duration, old age*

uexillāri-us, -a, -um, (see 34, 1, *n.*)

uīcēsimān-ī, -ōrum (m.), *men of the 20th legion*

uicis (gen.), (f.), *an alternation ; in uicem, by turns, mutually*

uictim-a, -ae (f.), *sacrificial victim*

uīc-us, -ī (m.), *farm, village, street*

uideor, *I seem ;* uidētur, *it seems, seems good ;* (mihi) *I decide*

uigeō, uiguī (no sup.), 2 (intr.), *be vigorous, flourish*

uīl-is, -e (adj.), *cheap, mean*

uincl-um (uinculum), -ī (n.), *cord, fetter*

uindict-a, -ae (f.), *vengeance, punishment*

uiolō, 1 (tr.), *violate, plunder*

uirginit-ās, -ātis (f.), *maidenhood*

uirgult-a, -ōrum (n. pl.), *bush, thicket, brushwood*

uirīl-is, -e (adj.), *manly, male*

uīs, pl. uīr-ēs, -ium (f.), *force, strength*

uīsō, uīsī, uīsum, 3 (tr. and intr.), *pay a visit, visit, view*

uiti-um, -ī (n.), *vice, fault*

uītō, 1 (tr.), *avoid*

ulcīscor, ultus sum, 3 (tr.), *take vengeance on, avenge, punish* (35, 1, *n.*)

ulti-ō, -ōnis (f.), *vengeance, punishment*

ultrā (adv. and prep.), *further, beyond*

ultrō (adv.), *of one's own accord, gratuitously* (7, 1, *n.*)

ululāt-us, -ūs (m.), *howl, shriek*

umb-ō, -ōnis (m.), *boss of shield, shield*

umer-us, -ī (m.), *shoulder*

ūniuers-us, -a, -um (adj.), *whole, entire ;* (pl.), *all (in a body)*

uocābul-um, -ī (n.), *name, designation, term*

uolupt-ās, -ātis (f.), *pleasure*

uōt-um, -ī (n., p.p. of uoueō), *vow, prayer*

usquam (adv.), *anywhere, on any occasion*

uōx, uōcis (f.), *voice, utterance*

ūsurpō, 1 (tr.), *make use of, usurp* (18, 2, *n.*)

ūs-us, -ūs (m.), *experience, usage, use*

uter-us, -ī (m.), *womb, stomach*

ūtilit-ās, -ātis (f.), *usefulness, expediency, advantage*

ūtor, ūsus sum, 3 (w. abl.), *use, employ, avail one's self of* (23, 1, *n.*)

uulgō, 1 (tr.), *noise abroad, spread (a rumour)*

uulg-us, -ī (n.), *the multitude, common people*

uulnerō, 1 (tr.), *wound*

uuln-us, -eris (n.), *a wound*

uult-us, -ūs (m.), *face, countenance*

ux-or, -ōris (f.), *wife*

Printed in the USA
CPSIA information can be obtained
at www.ICGtesting.com
LVHW021757240823
756138LV00002B/127